Muirhead Library of Philosophy

STUDIES IN THE METAPHYSICS OF BRADLEY

MUIRHEAD

Muirhead Library of Philosophy

METAPHYSICS
In 17 Volumes

I	Time and Free Will	*Bergson*
II	Reason and Analysis	*Blanshard*
III	Appearance and Reality	*Bradley*
IV	In Defence of Free Will	*Campbell*
V	Person and Object	*Chisholm*
VI	Non-Linguistic Philosophy	*Ewing*
VII	The Foundations of Metaphysics in Science	*Harris*
VIII	The Concept of Meaning	*Hill*
IX	Philosophy and Illusion	*Lazerowitz*
X	The Relevance of Whitehead	*Leclerc*
XI	Dialogues on Metaphysics	*Malebranche*
XII	The Philosophy of Whitehead	*Mays*
XIII	Studies in the Metaphysics of Bradley	*Saxena*
XIV	The Intelligible World	*Urban*
XV	Language and Reality	*Urban*
XVI	Valuation	*Urban*
XVII	Philosophy of Space and Time	*Whiteman*

STUDIES IN THE METAPHYSICS OF BRADLEY

SUSHIL KUMAR SAXENA

LONDON AND NEW YORK

First published 1967 by
George Allen & Unwin Ltd.

Published 2013 by Routledge
2 Park Square, Milton Park, Abingdon, Oxfordshire OX14 4RN
711 Third Avenue, New York, NY 10017

First issued in paperback 2014

*Routledge is an imprint of the Taylor and Francis Group,
an informa business*

© 1967 George Allen & Unwin Ltd

All rights reserved. No part of this book may be reprinted or reproduced or utilized in any form or by any electronic, mechanical, or other means, now known or hereafter invented, including photocopying and recording, or in any information storage or retrieval system, without permission in writing from the publishers.

The publishers have made every effort to contact authors/copyright holders of the works reprinted in the *Muirhead Library of Philosophy*. This has not been possible in every case, however, and we would welcome correspondence from those individuals/companies we have been unable to trace.

These reprints are taken from original copies of each book. In many cases the condition of these originals is not perfect. The publisher has gone to great lengths to ensure the quality of these reprints, but wishes to point out that certain characteristics of the original copies will, of necessity, be apparent in reprints thereof.

British Library Cataloguing in Publication Data
A CIP catalogue record for this book
is available from the British Library

Studies in the Metaphysics of Bradley
ISBN 978-0-415-29601-4 (hbk)
ISBN 978-1-138-88422-9 (pbk)
Metaphysics: 17 Volumes
ISBN 978-0-415-29532-1
Muirhead Library of Philosophy: 95 Volumes
ISBN 978-0-415-27897-3

MUIRHEAD LIBRARY OF PHILOSOPHY

An admirable statement of the aims of the Library of Philosophy was provided by the first editor, the late Professor J. H. Muirhead, in his description of the original programme printed in Erdmann's *History of Philosophy* under the date 1890. This was slightly modified in subsequent volumes to take the form of the following statement:

'The Muirhead Library of Philosophy was designed as a contribution to the History of Modern Philosophy under the heads: first of Different Schools of Thought—Sensationalist, Realist, Idealist, Intuitivist; secondly of different Subjects—Psychology, Ethics, Political Philosophy, Theology. While much had been done in England in tracing the course of evolution in nature, history, economics, morals and religion, little had been done in tracing the development of thought on these subjects. Yet "the evolution of opinion is part of the whole evolution".

'By the co-operation of different writers in carrying out this plan it was hoped that a thoroughness and completeness of treatment, otherwise unattainable, might be secured. It was believed also that from writers mainly British and American fuller consideration of English Philosophy than it had hitherto received might be looked for. In the earlier series of books containing, among others, Bosanquet's *History of Aesthetic*, Pfleiderer's *Rational Theology since Kant*, Albee's *History of English Utilitarianism*, Bonar's *Philosophy and Political Economy*, Brett's *History of Psychology*, Ritchie's *Natural Rights*, these objects were to a large extent effected.

'In the meantime original work of a high order was being produced both in England and America by such writers as Bradley, Stout, Bertrand Russell, Baldwin, Urban, Montague, and others, and a new interest in foreign works, German, French and Italian, which had either become classical or were attracting public attention, had developed. The scope of the Library thus became extended into something more international, and it is entering on the fifth decade of its existence in the hope that it may contribute to that mutual understanding between countries which is so pressing a need of the present time.'

The need which Professor Muirhead stressed is no less pressing today, and few will deny that philosophy has much to do with enabling us to meet it, although no one, least of all Muirhead himself, would regard that as the sole, or even the main, object of philosophy. As

MUIRHEAD LIBRARY OF PHILOSOPHY

Professor Muirhead continues to lend the distinction of his name to the Library of Philosophy it seemed not inappropriate to allow him to recall us to these aims in his own words. The emphasis on the history of thought also seemed to me very timely; and the number of important works promised for the Library in the very near future augur well for the continued fulfilment, in this and other ways, of the expectations of the original editor.

H. D. LEWIS

STUDIES IN THE METAPHYSICS OF BRADLEY

BY

SUSHIL KUMAR SAXENA
University of Delhi

'In various manners we find something higher, which both supports and humbles, both chastens and transports us. And, with certain persons, the intellectual effort to understand the universe is a principal way of thus experiencing the Deity.'

F. H. BRADLEY

LONDON : GEORGE ALLEN & UNWIN LTD
NEW YORK : HUMANITIES PRESS INC

FIRST PUBLISHED IN 1967

This book is copyright under the Berne Convention. Apart from any fair dealing for the purpose of private study, research, criticism or review, as permitted under the Copyright Act, 1956, no portion may be reproduced by any process without written permission. Enquiries should be addressed to the publisher.

© *George Allen & Unwin Ltd* 1967

Library of Congress Catalog Card No. 66-23900

PRINTED IN GREAT BRITAIN
in 11 *on* 12 *pt. Imprint type*
BY C. TINLING AND COMPANY LTD
LIVERPOOL, LONDON AND PRESCOT

*To the Memory
of
My Mother*

The following abbreviations have been used for F. H. Bradley's books throughout this work:

AR stands for *Appearance and Reality*, A Metaphysical Essay, Oxford, Clarendon Press, 2nd Edition, 1897, 9th Impression (corrected) 1930. (Reprinted lithographically 1946, 1951 from sheets of the ninth impression.)

ETR   *Essays on Truth and Reality*, Oxford, Clarendon Press, 1914.

PL   *The Principles of Logic*, Second Edition, 1922, Corrected impression of 1928, Oxford University Press (The pagination is continuous.)

ES   *Ethical Studies*, Oxford, Clarendon Press, Second Edition, 1927, Reprinted 1935.

CE   *Collected Essays*, Oxford, Clarendon Press, 1935 (Two Vols. The pagination is continuous.)

PREFACE

Bradley has for long been a victim of unfair criticism. The pages that follow should explain why I say so.

It has not been easy for me to differ with great names in philosophy. At times, the thought that I had to defend a metaphysician discouraged me. But, I have found ample sustenance in the vitality of Bradley's own writings. It is my implicit belief that close and patient attention to his dialectic is of great help in meeting most of the accepted objections to his metaphysics. To get at its essence, however, one must learn also to respond to the philosophic insight which in general informs, and occasionally relieves the argument—in accents of literary beauty.

Though its formal function is to open a book, a preface, for the author, is the end of a venture. Here he can relax and look back, and survey in peace the course of creation. As I do so, I think gratefully of all those who have contributed variously to the ultimate production of the book. Some of them, I know, would not like to be thanked; but I cannot help mentioning them. There is, for instance, my little niece, Ujwala, who cooked food for me as I wrestled out, in the solitudes of Simla, my answer to Cook Wilson's protests. And I recall, with pleasure, the delicate help provided by Dr Rajat Arora. My companion on long walks across the hills, he would, by his close yet unobtrusive attention, often enable my thought to objectify itself without ceasing to be self-critical. Mr Sham Lal's assistance has been no less significant. He has typed an illegible manuscript neatly; and has, over years of chequered work, shared my hopes and fears in relation to the outcome. Above all, my wife and children have not only watched my struggles with deep and loving anxiety, but have gladly put up with long spells of indifference just to let me work undisturbed.

Appropriate conditions for writing this book have, in various ways, been provided by: Mr Kuldip Kumar, my old student, whose help has always been ready and ungrudging; Mr Prem Chand, my first philosophy teacher, to me unforgettable; Professor N. V. Banerjee, whose own dedication to philosophy has continually inspired me; and my friend, Dr S. S. Barlingay, Head of the Department of Philosophy during my tenure as a Reader at the University. I am deeply indebted to them all.

To detect mistakes in typing, and in references to other works, I had

PREFACE

to take the help of quite a few other students, friends and relatives. What prevents me from thanking them individually is just their number, not lack of gratitude. I have worked all along in an atmosphere of amity, and my little achievement is due as much to love as to labour.

However mistaken, the views expressed in the book are dear to me, and I am naturally grateful to Messrs. George Allen and Unwin Ltd. for agreeing to publish it.

S. K. SAXENA
Delhi: May, 1966

CONTENTS

PREFACE	*page* 11

I. BRADLEY ON METAPHYSICS
1. The Intuitive and the Rational	15
2. What is Metaphysics? Preparatory Considerations	18
3. Metaphysics as a Sceptical Study of First Principles	22
4. Bradley's Assumption and Conclusions	28
5. The Metaphysical Criterion	33
6. Metaphysics as an Attempt to Know Reality as against Appearance	36
7. Conclusion	50

II. REALITY AND APPEARANCE — 52
1. Reality	54
2. Appearance	66
3. Reality *and* Appearance	67

III. IMMEDIATE EXPERIENCE — 82
1. Is Bradley's 'Feeling' Actual?	84
2. 'Feeling' and Thought	86
3. Feeling and Metaphysics	91
4. Meeting Criticisms	94

IV. THE RELATIONAL FORM — 112
1. Dialectic of Qualities and Relations	115
2. The 'Unreality' of Relations	121
3. Relations as 'Internal'	151
4. Conclusion	168

V. THOUGHT AND REALITY — 171
1. Thought and Reality: the Viewpoint of Science	172
2. Logic and Reality	175
3. Fact and the 'a priori'	182
4. 'Ontologizing' in Bradley	184
5. The Verification Theory	187
6. The Doctrine of 'Degrees'	197

7. Thought's Native Inadequacy	203
8. Meeting Difficulties	206

VI. THE ABSOLUTE AND ITS APPEARANCES 209

1. The Protest from Asymmetrical Relations	211
2. Reality as Experience	217
3. The Absolute and its Appearances	232
4. Meeting Criticisms	241
5. Bradley's Metaphysical Formula	247
6. Conclusion	251

VII. CONCLUDING REMARKS

1. Bradley and Metaphysics Today	254
2. Conclusion: Some Protests considered	262

I

BRADLEY ON METAPHYSICS

1. THE INTUITIVE AND THE RATIONAL

'But to be in earnest with metaphysics is not the affair of perhaps one or two years, nor did any one ever do anything with such a subject without giving himself up to it,'[1] says Bradley. This is as intense, though not as eloquent, a recognition of the rigour of discipline demanded by metaphysics as the one that we find in ETR:

> 'The shades nowhere speak without blood, and the ghosts of Metaphysic accept no substitute. They reveal themselves only to that victim whose life they have drained, and, to converse with shadows, he himself must become a shade.'[2]

The emphasis, here, is on the supreme duty of the metaphysician to think ever more deeply.

Yet it would be wrong to ignore the basic intuition which informs and unifies Bradley's major works. The suggestion that his thought is primarily critical in inspiration, or that it is *based on* a series of rejections and denials,[3] does not quite convey the whole truth about Bradley's works. It is belied by the sameness of purpose which holds his logic, ethics and metaphysics unmistakably together. Nor is it warranted by his own explicit conception of rational doubting. Bradley agrees to regard AR as 'negative, so long as that word implies an attitude of active questioning'.[4] But, if philosophical questioning is, as we shall see in our discussion of Bradley's conception of scepticism, always in part positive, the book cannot be said to be negative merely or even primarily. It is true that he arrives at his monism 'by a devious ... or critical route'.[5] But, why the goal is yet in the end realized is due—at

---
[1] AR 400.
[2] ETR 14, footnote.
[3] R. Wollheim, ed. A. J. Ayer, *F. H. Bradley*, Harmondsworth, Pelican Books, 1959, 17.
[4] AR viii.
[5] Wollheim, *F. H. Bradley*, 47.

least in part—to the continual, if implicit, determination of the details of thinking by the central vision.

Moreover, it appears to us that some obscure passages in his writings, as also some of the more intricate aspects of his metaphysical doctrine, are perhaps easier to unravel in the light of the hypothesis that he is guided continually—at places, even confessedly—by a positive and (could we say?) intuited vision of Reality[1] as working itself out through the differentiated character of the given:

> 'The whole reality is so immanent and so active in every partial element, that you have only to make an object of anything short of the whole, in order to see that object pass beyond itself.'[2]

According to Bradley, a little thinking suffices to show that reality tends everywhere to go beyond the constricted character of objects. In the light of this basic faith of his, it becomes easy to understand, if not to defend, the more important ideas of his metaphysics: the transferability of experienced content from the 'subjective' to the 'objective' and vice versa; the ideality of the given finite; the self-diremption of feeling into the relational form; the essential internality of relations or the 'proprio motu' movement of thought; and finally, what is of surpassing significance, the rise and sustenance of the dialectical process,[3] culminating in the idea of the Absolute.

The intuitive nature of this central insight seems clear enough. Bradley perhaps never subjects it to direct critical inquiry, though he takes great pains to vindicate it indirectly, seeking to redeem it from the region of hypothesis, and to present it as final truth. Moreover, if, as Bergson suggests, intuition is the sympathy by means of which we project ourselves into an object, an identification with what in theory must ever remain incompletely expressed, it seems proper to believe that Bradley's 'immanent' reality is in essence intuited. What confirms our view further is the fact that, though the *criterion* of metaphysical validity is for him intellectual,[4]

---

[1] Even today, the central importance of a 'vision' in 'any philosophy worth the name' is by some thinkers openly admitted. See, for instance, Waismann's article: 'How I see Philosophy', in *Logical Positivism*, ed. A. J. Ayer, The Free Press, 1960, 374; London, Allen and Unwin 1959.
[2] ETR 223.
[3] Cf. PL 410.
[4] AR 133.

Bradley is fully aware that the shift from appearance to reality is not always a consequence of thinking: '*In various manners* we find something higher, which both supports and humbles, both chastens and transports us.'[1] And, though frankly intellectual, Bradley's own way is perhaps not, in inspiration, *merely* so: 'With certain persons, the intellectual effort to understand the universe is a principal way of *thus experiencing the Deity*.'[2] On the other hand, we repeat, in Bradley's works there is no dearth of *argument* in support of his original vision. Chief of them is his appeal to the fact that we seek individuality in all our activities. His own aim throughout is at interpretative wholeness. The Absolute is affirmed as the answer to thought's demand for individuality. In PL Bradley speaks of 'the identity of analysis and synthesis' as 'our soul's ideal';[3] and in ES it is by employing the criterion of individuality that the fallacies of one-sided ethical theories, such as hedonism and rationalism, are thrown into bolder relief. Therefore, though we would like to insist that the intuited vision is throughout an implicit determinant of his thought, it is not our purpose at all to underrate the rational element in Bradley's metaphysics.

His basic assumption, that the true and the real must satisfy the intellect, cannot rationally be questioned. It is therefore hardly a matter of mere faith.[4] Nor is it acting on faith when deductions are made on the basis of a principle, such as that of contradiction, which is theoretically irresistible; for, the sequence is here readily clear to the intellect. If it be argued that Bradley does not apply his metaphysical criterion to *every* aspect of reality, and that therefore he accepts many matters of detail uncritically or merely on faith, his ready answer would be that an unverifiable assumption as to detail is not faith if it is made (as by him) in the interest of theoretical consistency—that is, if 'a principle demands it'.[5]

To conclude: we cannot realize the full and essential significance of Bradley's metaphysics unless we remain continually alive to its two distinct idioms, the intuitive and the rational. His major work, AR, may be said to be in part mystical, that is, in so far as it is

---

[1] *Ibid* 5. Our italics.
[2] *Ibid* 'Thus' here stands for 'supports and humbles' etc. Our italics.
[3] PL 490.
[4] Faith being 'the non-logical overcoming' of doubt. ETR 20.
[5] *Ibid* 24, 20–25.

determined by 'an intuition of the oneness of all things'.[1] Again, it seems safe to say of AR that, though the epistemology is sceptical, the ontology is mystical.[2] For, does not Bradley's conclusion confirm 'the irresistible impression that all is beyond us?'[3] Nor can we brush aside Ward's suggestion that the way in which Bradley speaks of the self—and of our different attitudes and values as merging themselves into the Absolute—smacks of mysticism.[4] Bradley himself agrees that philosophy may be described as a satisfaction of 'the mystical side of our nature', in so far as—if only for some select individuals—the rigorous exercise of critical thought is a way of experiencing the Deity.

But if it be directly asked: 'Is Bradley a mystic on the whole?' no ready answer can be given—not at least till we feel sure that for him the vision counts more than the dialectic. Nor is the intellect in any way slighted if, as in his metaphysics, the intuitive truth accepted squares perfectly with thought's own findings. As a metaphysician, Bradley in fact emphasizes the claims of the intellect. This is borne out clearly by his conception of the nature and method of metaphysics.

2. WHAT IS METAPHYSICS? PREPARATORY CONSIDERATIONS

To the question: 'What is Metaphysics?' a wide variety of answers is, as we know, available. But, for the sake of brevity, we may consider only some such views as are likely to help us in understanding Bradley—either as a foil or as a parallel. Marcel, for instance, is clearly opposed to Bradley's view. Bradley's aim is at understanding all that is, and discursively. His thought traverses diversities intelligently—'with a ground and reason'.[5] To Marcel, on the other hand, metaphysics is not an intellectual and objective survey of things. It is rather an attempt to 'raise ourselves towards

---

[1] It is generally in terms of such an intuition that mystic experience comes to a person of philosophic interests. W. P. Montague, *The Ways of Knowing or the Methods of Philosophy*, London, George Allen & Unwin, 1928, 54.

[2] This view of Höffding is quoted approvingly by James Ward in his article, 'Bradley's Doctrine of Experience', *Mind*, Vol. XXXIV, No. 133, January 1925, 34.

[3] AR 486.

[4] Ward, Bradley's Doctrine of Experience, *op. cit.* 35; Cf. AR 143.

[5] AR 501.

Reality, and approach it more nearly'.[1] Here, he believes, we seek to realize how we are anchored in Being; our reflection is, in metaphysics, 'trained on mystery'[2]—on truths which are not merely beyond us, but engulf us.

The existentialist challenge to Bradley can indeed be sharp. Is not Man inseparably one with his 'situation'?[3] And again, is not the intellect, upon Bradley's own theory of internal relations, linked up inextricably with the other sides of our being? But if this is so, how is Bradley justified in relying exclusively upon the intellect? Should we not philosophize with our whole being?[4] These are philosophers' questions, with a warrant in commonsense. Can Bradley meet them? We believe he can. But let us see.

There is much common ground between Bradley and the objectors. He admits that our being is a wholeness and that it seeks satisfaction entire.[5] Again, on his own view, metaphysics should take account of all the sides of our being.[6] A truth which does not answer all the main demands of our nature leaves us dissatisfied.[7] This is a fact which cannot be ignored. Bradley, however, hastens to add that in metaphysics, where our business is to understand things generally and self-consistently, 'take account of' can only mean: 'take theoretical notice of'. Surely, nothing can be taken in 'bodily' by thought. Feeling, for instance, is here certainly to be considered; but if, during the process, thinking itself is replaced by feeling, the specificity of the metaphysical enterprise is cancelled, not enriched.[8] If the different aspects of our being keep exchanging their native idioms, there is no gain on any side. And we rebel instinctively against such trespasses: 'A

---

[1] Marcel, *Being and Having*, Eng. Translation by K. Farrer, Westminster, Dacre Press, 1949, 169.

[2] *Ibid* 100. This view is accepted by quite a few present-day metaphysicians. See, for instance, *Prospect for Metaphysics*, Ed. I. Ramsey, London, George Allen & Unwin, 1961, 11.

[3] Bradley, of course, does not posit a *separateness* between man and his world. But it is equally true that he does not positively build upon Man's existential involvement with the world, as is sought to be done by men like Heidegger and Ludwig Binswanger.

[4] Holmes, *Philosophy without Metaphysics*, London, George Allen & Unwin, 1930, 35. Also see *Ibid* 13-14.

[5] ETR 4.

[6] AR 130.

[7] Though, of course, we may be unable to reject it rationally. *Ibid*.

[8] *Ibid* 454, 136.

man, we all know, should not be shamed out of his reason, and he cannot rationally, we also know, be argued out of his feelings.'[1] In metaphysics a conclusion cannot be rejected merely because one does not like it, exactly as a feeling is not cancelled by the *argument* that it is (theoretically) unreal or unacceptable. We should rather maintain that the theoretical and the practical standards are distinct and equally important in their own individual fields. By agreeing to this division of labour, nothing is in the end really lost. For, the aim of both practice and theory is individuality;[2] and if (as in Bradley's case) thought's own autonomous development[3] is seen to be capable of leading us to the idea of the Absolute, or to individuality as perfected, there is hardly any point in insisting that the intellect should subserve the interests of practice directly and all along.

It is, of course, true that thought is determined by its setting in various ways. 'Will and thought everywhere ... are implicated the one with the other.' Self-discipline may put an edge on the will and help concentration. Again, it is common knowledge that man's experiences in diverse fields contribute effectively to the growth of his intellect. But this only means that they provide thought with more data to work upon, not that they cancel its 'special function'. The governing principle, within the realm of intellect, must ever remain thought's own. The distinctness of various experiences and attitudes is, by their interrelationship, in no way undone. To hold that things, or aspects of being, are connected from within is not necessarily to deny that they are yet distinct. An argument can be valid independently of the psychological state in which it is developed. The impulse to think is distinct: it can maintain its own against other impulses, and should not be confused with them.[4] It may be admitted that, at least in some cases, the unconscious determinant of the metaphysician's impulse to seek system is his 'dread' of a disorderly world. But, we ask, if, after the initial excitation, the impulse proceeds strictly according to reason, how is the validity of the resulting system *disproved* merely by pointing to its non-intellectual origin? Cannot anxiety itself make for truer thinking? Is theoretical vigilance no

---

[1] ETR 3.
[2] AR 131.
[3] *Ibid* 3, 4, 136, 454.
[4] Cf. AR 134–36.

safeguard against psychological fatigue and make-believe? And what precisely is the alternative to the supremacy of thought in philosophy? To philosophize with our entire being? But, experiences affecting the different sides of our being—and the ideas which they suggest—cannot all be regarded as being equally valid; and if, as is necessary, judgment is exercised as to the comparative truth-value of these ideas, the intellect again becomes the presiding deity at once.[1]

To conclude: in spite of its extreme insistence on the claims of the intellect, Bradley's metaphysics may not be rejected summarily.

But metaphysics, it is said, has many other features. It tries to give us a comprehensive and unified world-view in terms of a conceptual scheme, with emphasis on the general character of the universe we inhabit rather than on its details. We are here supposed to 'get beyond the limits of ordinary, hypothetical and incomplete human knowledge to something absolutely satisfactory and complete'. Again, we are told, the metaphysician should argue 'for existence-conclusions which either belong to theology or are at least theologically interesting'.[2]

Now, it is important to see the precise measure in which Bradley shares these views; for, failure in this respect has been the cause of many mistaken criticisms of his work:

Let us begin by considering the aspect of agreement. With the idea of consistency as his main conceptual tool, Bradley tries professedly to give us an integrated view of reality as a whole. He shares with Descartes, Leibniz and Kant the faith as to the comprehensive, general and ultimate nature of metaphysics; and, in the manner of Aristotle, he tries to proceed with the help of such general notions as identity and difference, unity and plurality.

But, unlike Hegel and to some extent Leibniz, he is not keen to bring out the encyclopaedic potentialities of the metaphysical argument He even takes pains to point out that the metaphysician's interest in details is but secondary; that his own aim is to discover a general and theoretically tenable view of reality;[3] and that 'a general conclusion is not upset by a failure to explain in detail,

---

[1] ETR 220–21.
[2] *The Nature of Metaphysics*, ed. D. F. Pears, London, Macmillan & Co., 1957, 143–44.
[3] AR 302.

unless that detail can be shown to be a negative instance'.[1] This, however, does not mean that he regards his own conclusions as being wholly satisfactory. Though it is by him held to be theoretically unshakable, his idea of the Absolute is admittedly general and, from the viewpoint of detail, 'miserably incomplete'.[2] Finally, it hardly needs mention that Bradley's conclusions are not 'theologically interesting'.[3]

One specific point may, however, be noted with care. Bradley nowhere tries to deduce the existence or non-existence of things from purely conceptual considerations. That he argues their lack of 'reality' is quite another matter.

Our discussion has so far been preparatory. By meeting some of the most obvious objections to it, if only cursorily, we have taken care to ensure that our approach to Bradley's metaphysics is not from the beginning hostile. Moreover, we have by now some idea as to what to look for in this chapter. We may turn next to his explicit definitions of metaphysics.

3. METAPHYSICS AS A SCEPTICAL STUDY OF FIRST PRINCIPLES

a. *First principles*

Metaphysics is, to Bradley, a sceptical study of first principles.[4] Its main aim is to stimulate doubt and inquiry with regard to all preconceptions. Thus understood, metaphysics is certainly important; for, there is no other way to ensure unbiased thinking in philosophy.[5] Bradley's own aim in AR is to prompt us to think, afresh and critically, over such basic notions as identity, resemblance and relation.[6]

But, what exactly is a 'first principle'? Now, where he accuses

[1] *Ibid* 496.
[2] *Ibid* 3. It cannot, therefore, be said categorically that Bradley gives us a closed system.
[3] This is so specially in view of his contention that even God is an 'appearance'.
[4] AR 524 (footnote).
[5] PL Preface x.
[6] And the book certainly achieved its object. Thus, see Ward's article, 'Bradley's Doctrine of Experience', *op. cit.* 38; W. R. Sorley, *A History of English Philosophy*, Cambridge University Press, 1920, 291; J. H. Muirhead, *The Platonic Tradition in Anglo-Saxon Philosophy*, London, George Allen & Unwin Ltd., 274.

the British empiricists of dogmatism as to first principles, Bradley talks mainly of possibility and fact; potential and actual existence; and of identity, diversity and resemblance.[1] These ideas are 'first' in the sense of being the basic concepts on which all knowledge depends. We are forced to consider them when, in controversy, we try to push thought 'far enough'.[2]

Let us illustrate the point. Bradley holds that in metaphysics we are compelled to affirm the reality of a supra-relational Absolute. The compulsion is, in his view, due mainly to the fact that the relational workings of thought are unable to secure the perfect harmony which, in theory, we yet seek to realize. The (alleged) self-inconsistencies of the relational form are, in turn, said to spring primarily from the assumption that identity is relational, or that quality implies relation. But, is identity in fact relational? The importance of 'identity' is here thus basic: it *is* a 'first principle'.

Unfortunately, in the present work we have not found it possible to attempt a direct discussion of all the first principles mentioned above. But the defect, it is hoped, is at least partly set off by our attention to the following ideas which—if we keep to the precise way or context in which they emerge—can perhaps justly be called 'first principles' in Bradley's view:[3]

the self-evident validity of self-consistent thinking;[4]
individuality as the end of both theory and practice;[5]
and the relational character of identity, or 'internality' of relations.
To speak generally, it seems that—in Bradley's view—a 'first principle' is any attitude or idea which, besides having a warrant in fact, cannot in theory be transcended or refuted.[6] Of all such 'principles', the idea of the Absolute is, according to him, the highest; for, it is, he contends, the only idea which can rightfully claim to be both positive and incontrovertible.

We may dwell upon this point a little longer so as to indicate how this idea is central to metaphysics, and how Bradley identifies

[1] AR 524. Also see footnote.
[2] PL. Preface to the First Edition, XI.
[3] Whether they will be accepted by others as being genuine 'first principles' is, of course, quite another matter.
[4] AR 134.
[5] *Ibid* 131.
[6] Our view of Bradley's conception of a 'first principle' is perhaps justified by the various senses in which he uses the word 'ultimate', say, with 'doubt'.

'first principle' with 'ultimate truth'. To begin with, perhaps his very definition of metaphysics makes it clear that he means to identify the two. He describes metaphysics as 'the study of first principles *or* ultimate truths'.[1] Again, the same conclusion is forced upon us if we try to see in detail what he means by a 'first principle':

First, he interprets it not as a mere assumption, however fundamental, but as that which is an ultimate, self-evident truth by reason of its being theoretically irresistible.[2] To take an example, the assumption is certainly fundamental, because everywhere necessary, that 'anything remains the same except so far as (we) have reason to take it as altered'. But far from being irresistible, it is questionable theoretically. That a thing 'remains' in existence means that it survives different moments in the lapse of time. If that is so, some change or diversity is at once seen to be integral to the object, which thereupon ceases to 'remain' strictly the same, unless, of course, we decide arbitrarily to extrude its temporal relations from the thing's actual existence.[3]

Secondly, so far as metaphysics is concerned, a genuinely 'first' or fundamental principle can only be that which, by virtue of its being all-inclusive and perfectly harmonious, is in fact truly individual;[4] for metaphysics is theoretical, and theory, says Bradley, aims at perfect individuality. Such a principle, he insists, can only be our idea of the Absolute. Now, in so far as the latter is also the highest truth, the identity of 'first principle' and 'ultimate truth', as Bradley understands them, is affirmed once again.

b. *Philosophical scepticism*

Now, to scepticism.

Bradley's considered view is that philosophical scepticism is a deliberate method, constructive in ultimate intent. It consists in doubting all preconceptions with the set purpose of rising up to views which are theoretically (more) tenable.[5]

---

[1] AR 1.
[2] *Ibid* 133.
[3] Cf. ETR 163, also footnote.
[4] AR 104.
[5] This is borne out by Bradley's own manner in AR. Cf. R. Metz, *A Hundred Years of British Philosophy*, London, George Allen & Unwin, 1950, 324.

Psychological doubting is different. It is sheer hesitancy. Alternatives, we admit, may here well be present; but so long as the experience remains merely psychological, they are seldom clearly realized. Nor does the self here make any effort, or have a principle, to deal rationally with them. Even if it be allowed that it may lead to questions, psychological doubting is quite different from its philosophical counterpart. The former is casual and intermittent, depending on whether or not we get and remain curious. But the latter is a method, sustained and deliberate; it takes pains in specifying difficulties and in trying to meet them. Again, unlike many stirrings of mere curiosity, philosophical doubting is never an expression of mere bewilderment. It is doubly intelligent. *What* is being questioned and *why*—this is here known, though but imperfectly.[1] The search is intelligent, and implies 'in a certain sense the knowledge' of what is sought.[2]

In its actual working, philosophical scepticism is relative to a particular object or theory with which the enquirer is already in some measure familiar. But, *in principle*, it is applicable to every theory or attitude.[3] Of course, not every view can be doubted at the same time; but nothing prevents the sceptic from turning his gaze to all our beliefs one by one. It is also important to remember that, as philosophical sceptics, we doubt the first view of things only with the purpose of understanding them better: we do not aim at, or work for a practical cancellation of things and beliefs. Therefore, Polanyi's insistence that the ideal of 'a virgin mind' cannot in fact be attained need not disturb us. Our concern in philosophy is with theoretical vigilance, not with practical safeguards. True, some 'perceptive prejudices'[4] are, in fact, inescapable. But is not a prejudice in some sense weakened the moment it is understood as such?

What distinguishes philosophical scepticism most sharply from mere psychological doubting is, however, the adoption of a notion of truth and reality as the criterion of doubting. Failure to appre-

[1] Cf. AR 498.
[2] ETR 16.
[3] AR viii; CE 47. On the other hand, by theoretical scepticism Bradley does not mean a doctrine about the 'necessary limits' of our knowledge. ETR 445.
[4] Polanyi, *Personal Knowledge*, London, Routledge and Kegan Paul, 1958, 295-96.

ciate this has led to a neglect of the positive aspect of Bradley's metaphysics. We may therefore develop it at some length:

Assuming that we keep to reason, at no time can we merely doubt. *In this sense* there can be no radical doubting. Bradley insists that to doubt, and yet not to feel 'sure as to some main feature of truth or reality', is clearly impossible.[1] 'Every negation must have a ground, and this ground is positive.'[2] This is true of every variety of intelligent doubting. We begin by making an assumption about truth and reality;[3] and, as we proceed, our vindication of this assumption, which in use is a criterion, may gain directly from the incisive spread of doubt. Bradley, we admit, does not explicitly argue against the view that doubt is the only heuristic principle. But, is not his entire dialectical labour inwardly sustained by his unremitting, though not unreasoned, dependence on the law of contradiction? Faith can surely be just as dynamic as doubt. The Absolute of Bradley is, in fact, that victory of faith which is affirmed as the final limit to doubt. His sceptical vigour reflects as intense commitment:

> 'The man whose nature is such that by one path alone his chief desire will reach consummation, will try to find it on that path, whatever it may be, and whatever the world thinks of it; and, if he does not, he is contemptible. Self-sacrifice is too often the 'great' sacrifice of trade, the giving cheap what is worth nothing. To know what one wants, and to scruple at no means that will get it, may be a harder self-surrender.[4]

This should perhaps suffice to cancel the suspicion that his metaphysics is merely negative in character or that it is not grounded in any central vision or criterion of worth.

In all his denials, a basic—yet inclusive—conception of truth and reality is vitally involved: hence, perhaps, the continually open and self-critical quality of his manner. In doubting philosophically we agree to be patient. Nothing is rejected summarily. An immediate denial may be no less dogmatic than ready acquiescence. The philosopher has to strike a balance: without inquiry, he is neither to accept nor to reject anything. There is, in Bradley's

[1] AR 454.
[2] PL 117.
[3] ETR 16.
[4] AR 5.

view, no other way to avoid the two extremes of 'dogmatic individualism' and 'mere polemic'.[1]

It may be contended, as Passmore actually suggests,[2] that what is necessarily involved in all doubting, as in all discourse, is merely an assumption of some *general* difference between truth and falsity, and not any specific criterion of this difference. Bradley would, however, point out that philosophical doubting is a much more pointed activity than common discourse; that to think purposefully is to judge; and, finally, that to judge is to criticize by employing a definite criterion of reality. It would, of course, be here legitimate to wonder as to what this specific criterion is, and as to whether it really is involved in all critical thinking. But, in so far as we are not yet really familiar with the details of Bradley's own thought, a direct discussion of these questions will here not be quite intelligible.

Turning again to Bradley's conception of philosophical scepticism, we may add that he takes pains to mark it off from commonsense scepticism. The latter, according to him, lacks thoroughness and purpose. It may well have the vague feeling that certain facts or ideas do not square with one another. But the precise point of conflict is here not brought out: it does not become a theoretical irritant, and thought is therefore not stimulated to overcome the discord. It is true, though not easy to believe, that for long periods even the theories of science refuse to take notice of discordant facts, treating them as 'mere anomalies', this being 'the handiest assumption in the epicyclical reserve of any theory'.[3] Philosophical scepticism, on the contrary, throws inconsistencies into bolder relief till they appear as 'open and staring'[4] discrepancies, whereupon thought finds it impossible to blink them, and (Bradley would add) the dialectical process ensues as an attempt to overcome these contradictions.

It soon becomes clear, as the dialectic proceeds, that the contradictions with which a thing is beset are due to its being but imperfectly inclusive, and that they cannot be overcome unless its bounds are (ideally) enlarged. Every particular view or truth is

[1] *Ibid* VIII–IX.
[2] Passmore, *Philosophical Reasoning*, London, Gerald Duckworth & Co., 1961, 67–68.
[3] Polanyi, *Personal Knowledge*, 293.
[4] AR 28.

exclusive, because finite; and self-inconsistent, because exclusive.[1] It is only the idea of the Absolute, the inclusive harmony of all appearances, which entirely meets the need of thought for final consistency.[2] This is how, in the hands of Bradley, philosophical scepticism tends ultimately to transcend itself by widening its area and by deepening its probe.[3]

Common-sense either quietly buries one inconvenient doctrine under others dogmatically affirmed, or continues to hang on to particular views which, though pointing to one another because of their very exclusiveness, are not as such reconcilable.[4] Bradley, on the other hand, starts by accepting self-consistency as his governing principle, and ends with the picture of a self-consistent whole: 'An honest and truth-seeking scepticism pushes questions to the end, and knows that the end lies hid in that which is assumed at the beginning.'[5] Here, what is 'assumed' is a criterion of truth and reality, and the 'end' is obviously the idea of the Absolute.

4. BRADLEY'S ASSUMPTION AND CONCLUSIONS

But, it may at once be objected, why should Bradley start with this specific assumption? Does it not take for granted what he professes to establish? Do his conclusions really add anything to his initial assumption?[6]

Now, Bradley would here reply as follows:

No deliberate enquiry can begin in an absolutely fluid frame of mind. Intellectual notice, in particular, involves not merely the finiteness of intake, but the particularity of a criterion to which the content is referred. A specific viewpoint, or a definite attitude as to truth or intelligibility, is here necessarily adopted at the very outset. Or else, the effort will lack direction and end in vain. If,

[1] Cf. ES 90, footnote.
[2] AR 379. This drive towards wholeness is a need of cognition. The intellectual bias of Bradley's metaphysics is unmistakable.
[3] ETR 18. As to how science confirms Bradley's conception of scepticism as doubting ever more fully till we come to the indubitable, see Cohen, *Reason and Nature*, Glencoe, Illinois, The Free Press Publishers, 1959, 85.
[4] Bradley brings this out by referring to the attitude of 'popular philosophy' (AR 374) to the rival ethical theories of self-assertion and self-sacrifice (*Ibid* 374-80).
[5] *Ibid* 379.
[6] Holmes, *Philosophy without Metaphysics*, 10.

in metaphysics, we start entirely without any idea as to what it is to be real, how shall we know Reality when, so to speak, we stumble upon it? What we can justly expect of a philosopher only is that his initial assumption, though it must of necessity be specific, is not avoidably (or unduly) narrow, and that it is warranted by the demands of theory or by the evidence of fact. Now, Bradley would insist that—within the limits of theory, and consistently with its native idiom—his own favoured criterion of reality is maximally broad. The abstractness of a (theoretical) viewpoint is, we have seen, inescapable; and, within theory, working in complete independence of practical interests, the most inclusive ideal can only be that of *considering*, from the viewpoint of their claim to (intelligible) reality, the more important forms of human experience and endeavour. This is precisely the task which Bradley sets to himself. His criterion of reality is self-consistency. It seems irrefutable;[1] for, all effective refutation must itself proceed self-consistently. And where the assumption is unquestionable, conformity with it is a symptom of truth, not of mere stability.[2]

But, is it not better, because more catholic, to start by conceiving of the real as that which is compelling to thought *and* also satisfying or useful in practice? Bradley's answer is that with such a hybrid criterion in hand we just cannot proceed. The experiences of practical life are not, merely as such, satisfying to theory. There is no direct road from 'this satisfies me practically' to 'therefore, it is true'.[3] Should understanding submit to fact merely because, though unintelligible, things are clearly there; and, conversely, will practice accept a fact as cancelled the moment it is shown to be unintelligible? Our extended ideal has here nothing to say. Its allegiance is divided, and will just not work. The fact is that a conglomeration of viewpoints is a big blur, not a way to begin; it is no *point* of view, for it lacks the requisite preciseness.

Bradley's viewpoint is admittedly theoretic, and in this sense, exclusive. His 'truth', for instance, is the compulsive for thought, not an intuitive discovery. But having chosen the viewpoint, he surveys every major region of human experience—morality and

---

[1] Provided we assume, with Bradley, that consistency itself presses for the inclusion of facts. ETR 214.
[2] Cf. Polanyi, *Personal Knowledge*, 294.
[3] AR 135–36.

religion, feeling and thought. His choice, as a metaphysician, is certainly theory; but he does not deny that the practical attitude is legitimate and distinct. And is not the initial abstraction of his approach, forced in part by the inherent specificity of a viewpoint, cancelled completely by the vision of the Absolute which he ultimately works up? Here, at our journey's end, nothing at all is kept out: 'This perfect experience . . . is the complete union not of one side but of every side of our being and experience.'[1] It is instructive to contrast with this the way in which the positivist moves. Relying exclusively on the principle of verification, borrowed from science, he begins by dismissing metaphysics as mere nonsense. But, he soon comes to realize that the rigid form in which the principle is first formulated cannot hold; and his attempt to improve it, by reducing its rigour, serves only to take the sting out of the earlier charge that metaphysics is meaningless. Ayer's protest today is not that metaphysical statements are neither true nor false, still less that they are nonsensical, but only that they do not fall in the same category as 'commonsense descriptions of the "natural" world'.[2] From the viewpoint of Bradley, this entire movement of thought may be regarded as a vindication of his central thesis that what is applicable only to an aspect of reality must, in the end, fail to serve as the whole truth.[3]

He is convinced that even in the realm of practice there is nothing which could fairly be said to demand a cancellation of his basic emphasis on wholeness. In ES he argues that individual ethical theories are all inadequate in so far as they cater for mere aspects of our being; and in ETR he tries to show how a theoretical inconsistency always, in the end, leads to practical dissatisfaction.[4]

Finally, it is important to note that the assumption with which Bradley starts does not determine his subsequent thinking in the rigid manner of a die; for, it is itself vivified under the impact of its findings. What we here assume at the outset only is that the real must satisfy the intellect, or that reality cannot be self-inconsistent.

[1] CE 653.
[2] Ayer's Editorial Introduction to *Logical Positivism*, 15–16.
[3] As to how, under the impact of criticism, positivism has been compelled to modify itself continually and often self-inconsistently, see Blanshard, *Reason and Analysis*, London, George Allen & Unwin, 1962, 249–307.
[4] ETR 7.

These are, at this early stage, merely formal ideas. We are yet to realize that the consistency sought is one of content, and is no bare form. As we proceed to see if the different facets of given reality can satisfy the intellect, we find that they cannot—because they are as such beset with incurable contradictions. What is more, we see clearly that the discord is, in every case, due to the imperfect inclusiveness of things and aspects. This adds a new idea, that of richer extent, to the notion of mere harmony from which we started. The viewpoint is thus enriched by its very use as a criterion. Thought's own native manner—the relational form —is examined, and is seen to be unsatisfactory. The actual togetherness of its terms clashes with their necessary self-existence; and yet neither aspect can be ignored. Besides, a relation claims to be— but can never really be—independent of a wider whole from which its terms seem clearly to abstract. The truth dawns upon us, gradually but compellingly, that the internal harmony of every (finite) object or experience is disrupted by, or because of, the seeming self-completeness of its content, and that in actual fact this content always is—as for thought it must ever be—incorporated within increasingly wider wholes. All this, in Bradley's view, serves amply to suggest the theoretical necessity and possibility of an all-inclusive Absolute which harmonizes everything finally.

That the real is self-consistent—this surely we assume. But, why and in what precise manner things are self-inconsistent; how, to shed off this taint, they have to include more and more of content; and what it is to be thoroughly self-consistent—all this is revealed to us only as we rise up to the idea of the Absolute.[1] Far from being a mere repetition of the initial assumption, our 'conclusion' stands for what the latter ultimately delivers; and the demonstration is painstakingly critical and detailed.[2] It is therefore wrong to contend that the conclusions of Bradley's meta-

[1] Bradley certainly assumes that what satisfies thought is true and real, but he insists that as to what precisely will satisfy thought we have no knowledge in advance, and that the method is to that extent experimental. *Ibid* 311.

[2] Ryle's protest that the intellectualist works through the 'visual achievement' verb 'see' rather than through the 'visual task' verbs such as 'peer' and 'scrutinize' is certainly not applicable to Bradley. *The Concept of Mind*, London, Hutchinson's University Library, 1955, 303.

physics are worth no more than its assumptions. The intelligent demonstration of a principle is surely not the same as its mere assumption; and the idea of the Absolute is affirmed as an answer to what thought in the end demands.

It is true that even on attaining to this crowning idea 'ultimate doubts' persist. What it gives us is only the general character of Reality, and we are therefore left with 'due space for the exercise of doubt and wonder'[1] as to the detailed way in which the Absolute gives rise to, includes, and harmonizes all the appearances. With all its theoretical necessity, the Absolute of Bradley is, from the viewpoint of the detailed disposition of its contents, 'a transcendent mystery; it never became, as it tends to become in the hands of some "idealists" transparent'.[2] Yet, as to its general character, its harmonious inclusion of all content, there can hardly be any doubt, provided, we should add, the initial assumption of Bradley, and the dialectics reared on it, are not found basically questionable. Hence, 'scepticism survives as a mere aspect of constructive metaphysics'.[3]

To us it seems clear that neither the conclusions nor the basic assumption of Bradley can be condemned as dogmatic. The details of his arguments may well be questioned, but he cannot justly be accused of having adopted a criterion uncritically.

But, the objector may persist. To assume that reality is that which satisfies the intellect is to decide to ascertain, not what the Real is in itself, but only what it appears to the intellect. Could it not be that the Real is to be realized by a voluntary suspension of all conceptual framework? The mystic's insistence on 'via negativa' is well-known; and so is the poet's protest against the 'meddling intellect'. They could perhaps be allowed to offer a silent clue to theory, if not to dictate to it. In any case, no obvious absurdity is involved in the idea that a direct vision of the Real is vouchsafed only to those who cultivate unobtrusiveness. On the contrary, it may even seem reasonable to suppose that, if we want to know reality's own nature, we should denude it of all interpretations that we habitually overlay it with. Again, it would be dogmatic to assume that our concern with Reality is confined to metaphysics

[1] AR 486.
[2] A. E. Taylor, 'F. H. Bradley', *Mind*, Vol. XXXIV, No. 133, Jan. 1925, 12.
[3] AR 380.

in general, or to the metaphysics of Bradley. The mystic and the poet share the enterprise; and their way, to be sure, is not discursive.

But, to turn to Bradley again, such protests do nothing to damage his basic position. He admits openly that there are many distinct ways of approaching the Real. But, he would contend, what is the harm if out of these various ways we choose only one without denying or underrating the others? Bradley warns us repeatedly against the tendency of metaphysics to encroach upon the realms of the special sciences, and of morality and religion.[1] But, at the same time, he stoutly defends the autonomy of the metaphysical attitude against encroachment by the authoritative idiom of religious realization. If any intuited truth of religion, say, a Reality transcending thought, claims obeisance from metaphysics, it must first pass the test of reason. In metaphysics we have (in general) to *understand* how understanding can be transcended.[2]

As a result of our discussion of Bradley's conception of scepticism, we should find it easy to see

that his metaphysics is not merely negative;

that in the dialectical subtleties of 'Appearance' a criterion of Reality is being continually affirmed;

that his transition from Appearance to Reality may not be really abrupt, though it would certainly seem to be so if we loosen our hold on the criterion while winding our way through the labyrinth of argument; and, finally,

that, because of the full-blooded quality of his scepticism, Bradley cannot for long stop at anything short of the Absolute.

5. THE METAPHYSICAL CRITERION

Finally, and this is important, scepticism delivers to Bradley his criterion of metaphysical validity. Metaphysics is an intellectual enterprise. The valid for thought is that which it cannot resist, but must accept, when it is working according to its own native idiom, that is, in complete freedom from passion and prejudice. Bradley

---

[1] Cf. *Ibid* 252, 401.
[2] To show how thought presses for its own transcendence in the suprarelational Absolute is a part of Bradley's attempt in Ch. XV of AR.

distinguishes sharply between the theoretically compelling and the practically so. A spell of passion may in practice compel us to behave in a manner which, in our cool judgment, is clearly seen to be wrong.[1] The metaphysically valid is the *theoretically* irresistible. Now, there is only one way to discover principles or truths which elicit immediate allegiance from thought; they must come as ultimate limits to doubting. In Bradley's case, however, the *process* of doubting from which the (indubitable) criterion emerges is held back from us. The criterion appears—but only *appears*—to be merely assumed. And its irresistible quality is demonstrated, not *before* it is applied, but recurringly, throughout the dialectical process, as the absolute inability of thought to run counter to it. In so far as the validity of self-consistency is irresistible to thought, and in so far as metaphysics is 'mere theory', Bradley's professed task in AR is to show how the various aspects of our experience are unreal or appearances—because self-inconsistent—in varying degrees; and how thought's consequent dissatisfaction with them leads it finally to affirm the reality of a supra-relational, all-inclusive Absolute.

But is he really true to his chosen ideal? James Ward contends that Bradley does not appear to have been very consistent in his emphasis on the metaphysical requirement of ultimate consistency.[2] To support his contention Ward first refers to AR where Bradley certainly makes theoretical consistency the supreme criterion, and then to ETR where (as in the 'contents', p. xv) we find the clear remark: 'theoretical consistency must be sacrificed.'

We, however, believe that if the relevant portions of AR[3] and ETR[4] are duly taken into account, the alleged contradiction disappears. Our argument is here as follows:

In AR the theoretical standard is certainly taken to be absolute, but only within theory; that is, only with regard to metaphysics. Now, our experience, we know, is not all metaphysical. Morality and religion have their own positive content, the validity of which does not rest primarily on any appeal to theory. The theoretical standard does not *here* hold. But, from the other side, metaphysics, being an attempt to understand (in general) all that is there, must

---

[1] AR 133.
[2] Ward, Bradley's Doctrine of Experience, *op. cit.* 37.
[3] AR 135.
[4] ETR 437-38.

survey even the facts of moral and religious life. When, however, it does this—by applying to them its own criterion of self-consistency—it finds that they are by no means perfectly harmonious, though they are certainly more so than, say, voluntary action.

Now if, out of 'a blind devotion to consistency', we go by the belief that there *is* no (relative) truth besides the one which is perfectly consistent, or that the latter does not admit of relative self-expression in the various appearances, we are compelled to reject morality and religion as being wholly devoid of truth or reality. But such an attitude is at once seen to be untenable. For, first, it opposes common-sense by its 'belittling of what is individual and personal'; and, secondly, it is an outrage upon the native demand of metaphysics itself—the demand for consistency.

The second consideration must, however, be explained. In so far as it is affirmed as the final answer to thought's demand for harmony, the Absolute or ultimate Reality must be seen to include all that is, even the facts of moral and religious life; or else, it would itself be but finite. Mere inclusion would, however, not in this case be enough. The 'facts' must also be harmonized, or held internally as one. But, as soon as they are thus made good, they at once come to partake of the character of ultimate Reality; and the view that there is no truth other than the ultimate one collapses forthwith.

In other words, theoretical consistency has to be 'sacrificed' in the sense that the perfectly self-consistent cannot be regarded as being the *only* truth, though it is admittedly the highest truth. Appearances must all be allowed to have a measure of reality. Otherwise, we are forced to hold, what is obviously untenable, that the Absolute either excludes them, or that it includes, but does not harmonize them. In either case, its status as the Absolute is damaged beyond repair. Besides absolute truth, which is one and final, we must admit truth which is relative. In *this* sense, our pursuit of consistency has got to be tempered; or else, we commit the worse inconsistency of accepting as thought's ideal an Absolute which is either contentless or a bare boundary encompassing the finite, to be sure, but without redeeming it from its defects.

Even in the chapter to which Ward refers, 'On God and the Absolute', Bradley insists that perfect consistency is the essential mark of 'ultimate truth'; in fact, this is why he refuses to regard a personal God as being ultimately true. And, what is more, he yet concedes to our belief in God a positive, though relative, truth —that is, truth which needs supplementation and correction by other beliefs, and so is not perfectly individual.[1]

That things *exist*; that every aspect of human experience has its own (relative) importance; and that popular notions and scientific concepts serve useful purpose in everyday life and thinking—all this is to Bradley acceptable. But, when anything finite—be it a thing, experience or attitude—lays claim to ultimate reality, he subjects it to a process of ruthless examination; and, laying bare the contradictions which beset it, he sets it down as an appearance having but a measure of reality.[2] Nothing, not even the God of religion, can be taken to be ultimately real or true unless it is found to be theoretically tenable.[3]

6. METAPHYSICS AS AN ATTEMPT TO KNOW REALITY AS AGAINST APPEARANCE

All this should become clearer as we proceed to examine Bradley's more detailed definition of metaphysics:

> 'We may agree, perhaps, to understand by metaphysics an attempt to *know reality as against mere appearance*, or the study of first principles or ultimate truths, or again the effort to comprehend the universe, not simply piecemeal or by fragments, but somehow *as a whole*.'[4]

This definition is, to us, important. It indicates the main directions of Bradley's metaphysical thinking; and it is partly in accordance with these that we have determined not only our own emphases, but the organization of our material in the present work. In the remaining part of this chapter, however, only two aspects of Bradley's view have been dealt with: his attitude to 'knowing' and his emphasis on wholeness.

---

[1] ETR 428–47. The truly individual, according to Bradley, is that which is perfectly self-consistent and self-existent.

[2] That is, of the *character* of reality. This will become clearer when in the following chapter we pass on to distinguish the various senses in which Bradley uses 'reality'.

[3] The assumption here obviously is that truth is, for metaphysics, ideal.

[4] AR 1. Our italics.

Metaphysics, according to him, is primarily an attempt to know, to understand the meaning of ideas or to examine their claim to truth, rather than to trace their psychological growth.[1] Now, this conception of 'knowing' as *intellectual* distinguishes his manner clearly from that of the British empiricists, led by Locke. Bradley stoutly opposes all attempts to turn philosophical questions into genetic ones. According to him, the answer to a philosophical problem is to be found not, as Hume thought, in a purely phenomenological account of the workings of mind, but by examining the theoretic tenability of ideas. In PL a vigorous attempt has been made to refute the psychological interpretation of the idea, to interpret it as logical signification,[2] and to redeem logic from psychologism generally; to expose the error of atomism, and of its natural ally, associationism; to emphasize the operation—in thought and experience—of concrete universals; and, finally, to protest against the 'natural' theory of meaning.[3] Bradley's polemic here contains important clues to his metaphysics. If meaning is not a one—one correspondence between a psychical image and an outer fact; and if, again, it operates necessarily by loosening content from existence, and by referring it, through the use of universals, to a *class* of objects,[4] the way is prepared for Bradley's maturer ideas that truth does not consist in the copying of fact by idea, and that thought is less than given reality in so far as it is not merely a movement away from, but is for ever incapable of (ideally) reconstituting the wholeness of, our actual world.

a. *Bradley's conception of knowing*

Bradley is convinced that to understand is neither to follow the succession of images in the mind, nor even to 'copy' the details of

[1] Cf. *Ibid* 224.

[2] Rather than as a mere existent. Bradley warns us against confusing the two senses. If they are identified, two consequences follow. First, the idea gets shut up within the mere present; and we are forced into atomism, against which Bradley protests. Secondly, if an idea is thus confined to the present, knowledge or memory of the past *as past* becomes impossible.

[3] Wollheim gives us an admirable account of Bradley's attempt in these directions. Hence, our discussion is here deliberately sketchy. See: Wollheim, *F. H. Bradley*, 18–43.

[4] As to how symbolism is, in Bradley's view, doubly universal, see *Ibid* 30–32.

existence in slavish passivity, but to try ideally to reconcile the unity and the diversity of the given. In CE he gives us a full, though condensed, account of what he means by 'understanding':

> 'What is to "understand"? It is to have the real as something before us as an object, so that our mind can pass, as to its diversity, from one of the many differences to another, and from each and all to the One, and from the One to each and all —and do this without thereby altering the real so as to make it to be another one and cease to be the same, in the sense of becoming a fresh one generally, or (more specially) by causing it (as we take it) to show a jar and a break in its continuity . . .'[1]

Now, considering the above along with what he says elsewhere, in AR and in PL, his view of the matter may be outlined thus:

To understand is 'to have the real as something before us as an object', so that where—as in Feeling[2]—the object is not marked off from the subject, there can be no *understanding*.

As between the subject and the object, so within the object itself, distinctions are to be posited or perceived before any 'understanding' can begin. Knowing is a discursive movement of the mind intelligently affirmed.

The last consideration may be treated at some length:

We understand by distinguishing. Merely to receive an undifferentiated complex of impressions is no understanding. It is simply the passivity of blank notice. Understanding begins only when the different features of the object are attended to in their distinctive character, or abstracted ideally from the cohesion of the given. But the process of making distinctions is here neither a mere superimposition upon, nor a wanton deviation from what is actually given. It is rather the recognition of the empirical fact of difference and its legitimate development in conformity with thought's own demands.[3]

Again, in understanding, the mind *traverses* diversities. The given is, so to speak, loosened from within, and there is an experienced sense of passage 'in the sense of a going actually from one term to another'.[4] Taken along with the distinctness of terms

[1] CE 659.
[2] In feeling, as Bradley understands it.
[3] AR 423–25.
[4] CE 647, 670.

and their relation, this transition provides us with the necessary form of our relational experience. Diversities are here held *apart*. They cannot be lumped into the selfsame point, for then they are not distinguished, and understanding disappears. It is a contradiction, and in fact impossible, to distinguish diversities and, in the same breath, to ascribe them to the selfsame point. Displacement, though a spatial schema, is yet warranted by thought's inherent need to understand.

But is the ideal transition dictated by mere caprice? No. Every detail of the given, like the object taken as a whole, is not a mere 'that' but a 'what'. Identity is, in Bradley's view, everywhere relational. Quality implies relation.[1] Every given detail, in so far as it is distinct, is known (also) by its being referred to something else from which it differs: '. . . The fact of a difference, when we realize and express its strict nature implies in its essence both relation and distinction'.[2]

b. *Identity as relational*

In so far as the dialectical process and the internality of relations both depend upon the conception of identity as relational, a brief reference may here be made to some of the more important considerations in which this view is grounded. To begin with, if its identity is not relational, how can a thing be said to change? And yet it is a fact that things come to acquire fresh aspects. It may here be maintained, in the manner of Hume, that change is only succession—the sequence of self-identical units upon one another. But, what does this mean? It is obvious that such units must (at least) have two aspects. First, they are (allegedly) exclusive of one another. Secondly, they are said to follow one another in point of time without undergoing any change themselves. But, if every unit is thus *understood* as being exclusive of others, and as persisting unchanged against the flow of time, its identity is at once seen to involve a reference to what is seemingly outside of it, and is hence clearly relational.[3] Moreover, it appears that the notion of identity as absolute runs counter to the very essence of our meaningful discourse about objects. Every object is, by thought, regarded as

[1] This important thesis of Bradley will be discussed in Ch. IV.
[2] AR 461.
[3] Cf. PL 141.

distinct—as different from others. The identity of things is, therefore, undeniably relational. If, as Bishop Butler contends, 'everything is what it is, and not another thing', does it not clearly follow that being-not-another-thing enters into the very essence of a thing?

But, it may be objected, identity appears relational only when we regard things with reference to one another. Why can't we consider a thing entirely by itself? Here, our ready answer would be that the isolation demanded is, in fact, impossible. A thing exists in a time-place setting. To regard it as being in every way self-existent is to talk of a mere character, not of an actual object. Thought may not be able to *prove* that identity is relational; for, it itself works by assuming the latter. But whereas this assumption is, in the region of thought, inescapable—and therefore, for Bradley, metaphysically valid—the belief that identity is absolute seems inconsistent with both theory and fact. Bradley protests repeatedly that, if a thing can neither exist nor be thought of in complete independence of a setting, it is monstrous to regard its identity as absolute.

The relational character of identity is, in his view, affirmed by the very way in which thought functions. Without any difference, there can be no thinking. 'A bare tautology . . . is not even so much as a poor truth or a thin truth'.[1] The intellect, we have seen, is essentially discursive in character; 'to understand it must go from one point to another'.[2] If it merely keeps itself riveted on to one unyielding point which puts forth no plurality of ideas, no second impression, it is merely a kind of mental tension, no thinking. What is more, the different ideas should be affirmed as having a deeper unity than the one implied in the mere perception of succession, for thinking is surely different from mere association of ideas. 'A is A' is barren tautology. 'A is Y' is a clear self-contradiction, if both A and Y are taken as absolutely self-identical. Nor will it do to change it into 'A has Y', if the illusion of absolute identity is allowed to persist; for 'has', in that case, will only fall between, not unite, A, Y. The only way out is to credit both A and Y with an inner diversity—of two distinct aspects held as one—by virtue of which they come to appear as both distinct *and* related. Their identity, thus enlarged, is clearly relational.

[1] AR 501.
[2] *Ibid* 509.

The foregoing discussion enables us to understand two important ideas in the metaphysics of Bradley. First, in so far as it is distinct and is in fact transferable,[1] content or character can everywhere be said to overflow its 'that', so that the abstraction involved in thought is warranted by an actual feature of the given. Secondly, thought's movement across diversities is here without a jar or break; it is affirmed by, and from within, the nature of the terms—by their very specificity. Or, relations are in essence internal.

c. *Thought's discursive movement—and fact*

The ideal transition referred to above is indeed intelligent or 'proprio motu',[2] first, because it acknowledges, even heightens, the distinctness of the given; and, secondly, because the aim of the entire process is to secure a better understanding of the object.

Analysis and synthesis, according to Bradley, are but complementary aspects of the same movement of understanding. True, analysis heightens discreteness; and synthesis, wholeness and continuity.[3] Yet, the two go together. Where we aim at understanding, analysis is no mere division. Rather, the parts are distinguished so as to make them clearer, each against the rest; and to improve our understanding of the whole. The object, when analysed, appears a fuller and a more richly differentiated totality. It is enlarged, though but ideally. Conversely, when we connect some elements rationally, instead of merely forcing them together, what is realized is not only a new synthesis, but increased knowledge of the parts; they now appear, not merely self-existent, but as conducing to a whole.

What Bradley means by the either-way 'one-many' movement should now be clear. The mutual involvement of analysis and synthesis, stressed in CE, is a truth which Bradley takes pains to emphasize.[4] The charge that he regards thought as merely analytic[5] is therefore mistaken. We have only to guard ourselves against a habitual error: 'In analysis we do not keep sight of the synthesis

[1] Say, from the subjective to the objective side of experience, as when a hated individual may seem unduly ugly.
[2] AR 501.
[3] PL 472–73.
[4] *Ibid* 470–94.
[5] Cf. Haldar, *Neo-Hegelianism*, London, Heath Cranton Ltd., 1927, 253.

and in synthesis we forget the act of analysis.'[1] But all this may seem airy. Does it have any relevance to concrete reality? Yes, it has. Consider an instance. Cold, we may say, is the cause of pneumonia. Let us see if it is really so. To begin with, cold is not itself pneumonia. The two are clearly different, and our problem is to see how the one stands to the other. Is cold the cause wholly by itself? No; for the same cold which inflicts pneumonia on me may not have any effect on a stronger man. We should rather say: 'not mere cold, but the low vitality of the individual'—this whole complex—is the cause of pneumonia. On further reflection, we may have to include fresh elements in this complex, say, the individual's carelessness or his predisposition to catch cold. In other words, when we try to understand how cold is the cause of the disease in question, our idea of the cause goes on expanding, not at random, but through an internal necessity.[2] It comes to have more of content every detail of which is seen to conduce to the whole. Thus, what is understood is of necessity enlarged; and what is included is at once harmonized. Harmony and inclusiveness go together; both are necessary marks of the attempt to understand.

Now, is the above account in any way fantastic? We do not think it is. Every step in the process has been taken with an eye on fact. And yet Bradley's talk of 'one and many', and of 'quality and relation' has about it an air of unreality. Why? And why should he at all talk thus? The answer is simple. The individual details of experience are infinite. Every specific bit of content cannot be considered. So Bradley concerns himself with the general problem of understanding, that is, how to reconcile diversity with togetherness, quality with relation; or, more simply, with the problem of holding differences rationally as one. Perhaps, as is the wont today, he should have taken more 'examples'. But when we consider an instance, do we take in the fact literally?[3] And if not, does it (in metaphysics) matter much if, after noticing the general features of reality, we get on without caring much for detail?

Of course, everything here turns on the possibility of discovering some supremely general features of reality—features without which

[1] PL 472.
[2] A narrow conception of 'cause' is, however, practically convenient. AR 295.
[3] Cf. ETR 13.

the latter could nowhere be. The matter is indeed debatable. Bradley is, however, convinced that some such features are in fact there, and that thought is capable of dealing with them. So he talks continually of unity and diversity, of relations and terms. It is not that he is oblivious of the diversity of life and experience. In fact, even such fashionable problems of today, as 'our knowledge of other minds', engage his attention, if only cursorily. Only, he believes that the basic problem to which all philosophical questions can in the end be reduced is that of understanding how diversity stands to unity;[1] hence, the importance which he attaches to his treatment of Relation and Quality. If this basic faith of his could in some way be refuted, his entire metaphysics will collapse forthwith. But his opponents will have to prove that, somehow and somewhere, reality *can* be a mere 'that' without a 'what', mere existence without character. And this, Bradley believes, is an impossible task.[2]

We have always to remember that Bradley's manner is continually intellectual, and 'intellectual' in *his* sense. Or else, we may miss the earnestness of his dialectic, or even dismiss it as a travesty upon philosophical analysis. True, analysis is 'more like unfolding a head of cabbage than carving it into slices with no regard for its natural folds'.[3] Nor can it ever be pushed back to its final limit and thus made complete. Both Bradley and the empiricists would agree on this point.[4] But if it be asked: what are the legitimate limits and the 'natural folds' of analysis?—the answer would surely vary according to the analyst's point of view. Apart from the viewpoint, no one kind of 'ultimates' can claim intrinsic superiority over others. We cannot tell offhand which units are 'the end results of true analysis'—Descartes' Cogito, Hume's impressions, Russell's sense-data or Reichenbach's tables and horses. Again, assuming that we are analysing visual perception and have reduced hue into its 'primaries', what they precisely are will depend on whether it is pigment or light that we are interested in.

Now, Bradley's viewpoint is that of discursive knowing: he tries to understand things self-consistently. Starting from the

[1] Cf. AR 415-17.
[2] *Ibid* 143.
[3] Alan Pasch, *Experience and the Analytic*, Chicago, The University of Chicago Press, 1958, 96.
[4] See PL 486-87; and Pasch, *Experience and the Analytic*, 114-15.

distinctions commonly made—or present—in given reality, he goes on aggravating and multiplying them in the direction, and to the extent, determined by thought's innate need to understand.[1] To say that most of the distinctions which he makes are not there in given reality would prove nothing against him; for, he does not profess to copy facts. And to prove that they are illegitimate, we have to argue that Bradley's entire conception of the theoretical attitude, of what it is and how it works, is basically mistaken.

d. *Consistency: how ultimate?*

The governing principle of this attitude, and so of metaphysics, is, in Bradley's view, consistency. He takes pains to emphasize the distinctness and self-evident validity of this principle. The theoretically self-consistent is that which can be—or is actually—*thought out* without internal jarring. Here we are aware not only of the distinctness of details or sides, but of their being held together; and the experience is always essentially *relational*. The aesthetically consistent, or concordant, is that which is agreeable to, and has the immediacy of feeling.[2] In our awareness of the theoretically harmonious, the emphasis is more on self-comple*tion* than on self-complete*ness*, on ideal self-consistency rather than on sensible pleasantness. To heighten this distinction, Bradley speaks of 'theoretical rest' and 'theoretically harmonious'; and where he talks of the Absolute or of its contents, both supra-relational, or of any mode of co-existence or self-possession in which thought's relational activity has been transcended, he uses such words as 'harmony', 'merged', 'harmonized' and 'concord'.[3]

Nor is it difficult to mark off our standard from the principles of ethics and the 'ultimates' of psychology. Every ethical imperative is open to the question: why should I act in the way in which I am commanded to? The protest is not *obviously* improper. But the question: 'Why should I think self-consistently?' is immediately self-cancelling. The validity of consistency cannot be questioned: it is self-proven.[4] The theoretical criterion is positive,

---

[1] Cf. 'In order to understand, we are forced to distinguish to the end, and we never get to that which is itself apart from distinction'. AR 157.
[2] 'Though it is not the same as mere feeling. *Ibid* 411.
[3] *Ibid* 123, 137, 404, 409, 432.
[4] Cf. *Ibid* 134–36.

because indubitable. The certainty it commands is based on an assent of the intellect, not of the will; it is by no means that purely subjective feeling of conviction which is not incompatible with error or illusion. It is basic metaphysically. We stand self-condemned if we try to transcend it. But with regard to what is psychologically ultimate, this attempt would be theoretically quite legitimate; only, we cannot in fact make it.[1] Again, the psychological compulsion of the given is as such no proof of its being metaphysically valid. To be thus tenable, it must satisfy thought.[2] And, to speak of *our* standard, we are not merely compelled to accept it, but feel justified in doing so.

e. *Truth as coherence*

The acceptance of non-contradiction as the governing principle of thought naturally leads Bradley to conceive of Truth as coherence.[3] The theory, we realize, is open to many objections, chief of them being the protest that it gives us only a criterion, not a definition, of truth. But against two important ones of them, Bradley seems fairly well armed. To the protest—made by Stout and Russell—that, though its applicability to ideas may be admitted, the coherence theory of truth is not relevant to facts of sensible perception and memory, his answer may be put as follows:

Is there any perceived or remembered fact which is proof against modification by fresh data?[4] If not, and we can hardly say 'yes', can it fairly be denied that the seeming finality of such facts consists essentially in their conformity with our known world-order?[5]

But again, a world of sheer fancy can be very self-consistent. Is *it* real? Bradley's answer is: yes, it is—as real as it is self-consistent. To hold that it is wholly unreal would be clearly improper, unless, of course, we dogmatically identify reality with the sensibly solid.[6] Nor can we lapse into the opposite error of saying that such

---

[1] Cf. *Ibid* 30. Also see footnote.
[2] *Ibid* 53.
[3] This is so (partly) because Bradley regards Truth as ideal.
[4] Moreover, even though it must be admitted that the materials of our knowledge are provided by sensation and feeling, can there be any datum wholly without interpretation? ETR 203–04.
[5] *Ibid* 211–12. The greatest objection to the theory is, however, provided by the facts of evil and error.
[6] Bradley, as we know, is firmly opposed to this equation. AR 334–36.

a world is the whole reality. For, if every breath of fancy relates, however indirectly, to some fragment of fact, how can we regard the world in question as reality entire?

To Bradley, everything short of the whole is a contradiction. It only seems—but is not in truth—independent; for, it is determined through and through by what it appears merely to exclude.[1] As against this, the final reality, Bradley insists, is a perfect system. He contends further that 'the idea of system demands the inclusion of all possible material'.[2] Generally, 'a doctrine must not only hold together, but it must hold the facts together as well'; and an ultimate theory must take in all the facts.[3] If there still be any doubts with regard to the substance—as distinguished from the tenability—of Bradley's attitude to metaphysics, the following should dispel them:

> 'By metaphysics I do not mean the doctrine of any one school, but I include under that term all speculation which is at once resolved to keep its hold upon all sides of fact, and upon the other to push, so far as it can, every question to the end.'[4]

Of course, the crucial question here involved is: does theoretical construction, such as Bradley's, give us any truth about actual fact? But, this will be discussed later, as a part of the wider problem, how thought is related to reality; and, for the present, we may only note that the suggestion, that metaphysics is an attempt to understand 'reality as a *whole*', follows naturally from Bradley's conception of the ideal of understanding. There is, in his view, a straight, though difficult, road from 'knowing' (as he regards it) to the idea of the Absolute:

First, what serves as a standard for thought is absolute in the sense of being rationally unchallengeable. In other words, it is at

---

[1] This is, however, merely to assume that the 'internality' hypothesis is true.

[2] ETR 214.

[3] ES 74.

[4] ETR 444. Bradley is, on the one hand, reluctant to *confine* enquiry to visible fact, and is, on the other, keen to remain alive to the necessary, general features of what is given. Should the positivist contend that 'pushing every question to the end' need not take us beyond the region of fact, Bradley's ready rejoinder would be: 'Is *any* fact considered in truth self-complete?'

once a criterion of *absolute* reality. Thought just cannot accept the self-discrepant as real.

Secondly, thought works through analysis and synthesis, the two enriching each other as they carry out their task of understanding the given. In other words, thought aims at system. The culmination of this movement is our idea of a perfect individuality —the idea of the Absolute.

f. Some critical remarks

But here, to keep balance, attention must at once be drawn to the following:

With all his insistence on the importance of 'understanding', Bradley does not claim that *everything* can be understood.[1] Why does the Absolute appear at all, and in the way it does? How, in detail, are the various appearances resolved into the unity of the Absolute? Problems such as these are, to Bradley, insoluble.[2] They bring to light 'the limits of explanation', fulfilling thereby an important function of philosophy itself. The 'limits', however, are here not merely posited, but rationally affirmed.

Nor is Bradley indifferent to the importance of details.[3] This is borne out not only by his professed doctrine that synthesis goes hand in hand with *analysis*, but by the intricacies of his own dialectical reasoning. He even says explicitly that his intention is not 'to pour scorn on the details and narrowness of devoted specialism', but only to emphasize that a periodical attempt to systematize 'the results of the sciences', and 'to arrange these on what seems a true principle of worth, can hardly be called irrational'.[4]

There is, in Bradley's view, no question of a conflict between the special sciences and metaphysics, provided both keep to their legitimate bounds. The task of metaphysics is to understand reality *as a whole*. It inquires into ultimate truth, which a special science does not. The protest that the concepts of science are also ultimate does nothing to erase this distinction; for, they are in fact applied

[1] Bradley refuses 'to wear the airs of systematic omniscience'. AR 440.
[2] This explains the word 'somehow' in 'somehow as a whole'.
[3] Only, concern with the details of *fact* is not, in his view, primarily important for the metaphysician.
[4] AR 440–41.

only to phenomena. Metaphysics has no right to question the validity of these concepts within their own limited fields of application. The trouble arises—and metaphysics is provoked—only when an idea which in fact applies to but a class of phenomena is stretched surreptitiously to cover reality as a whole.[1] Bradley is convinced that all such attempts wilt readily under the impact of criticism.

But, we ask, is his own conception of 'knowing' tenable? As against the modern emphasis on the operational versatility of the word, is Bradley justified in interpreting 'knowing' merely as 'understanding'? It is common knowledge that, in quite a few cases, 'knowing' consists in behaving rather than in abstract cogitation. Nor is serious thinking a monopoly of metaphysics; and it is by no means an essential function of the intellect to formulate world-views. What, then, is the special importance, or even the usefulness or propriety, of a metaphysics such as Bradley's?

Now, it seems to us that the following defence of Bradley is here possible. It may be admitted that all knowing is not primarily intellectual, and that our practical concern with life can sometimes be genuinely thoughtful. But, this does nothing to prove that it is impossible, or wholly useless, to abstract theory from direct subservience to practical ends, and to think in strict conformity with thought's own essential demands. The possibility of this abstraction seems in fact assured. The critical verification of a scientific statement—as distinguished from the practical demonstration of a scientific law—is clearly not as slavish a subordination of thinking to fact as 'tracing out the intricacies of a tangled skein of wool'[2]; and yet it would be improper to regard the one as being less thoughtful than the other. Moreover, the very existence of a metaphysics such as Bradley's proves that it is possible to think in relative independence of practical considerations as we commonly understand them.[3]

If it here be objected that the truths of Bradley's metaphysics

---

[1] *Ibid* 250–52.
[2] Ryle, *Concept of Mind*, 283.
[3] Ryle's emphasis, we may note, only is that a theory *can* be turned to other than didactic accounts, and that 'a lesson in anything is *also* a lesson in giving and receiving lessons of that sort'. *Ibid* 288. Our italics.

are all quite abstract and have no practical value, attention may be drawn to the following:

It seems to be a mere dogma to believe that the practically useful is intrinsically superior to the theoretically necessary. The necessity of a system is no less compelling than the 'givenness' of a fact. Moreover, when it is realized that metaphysics is concerned not with mere ideas, but with the main forms of given reality—though but ideally—the charge of 'abstractness' loses much of its seriousness. True, as Bradley himself confesses, thought works by abstracting content from given reality. But this is unavoidable. Even the simplest perception does not reflect reality exactly as it is, bodily and entire; and thought is clearly involved in distinguishing veridical from erroneous perception. Every mode of experience is specific, and has its own limitations. Thought, we admit, lacks the feel of sense-experience; but, can the latter judge and decide? Neither can shake off its native defect. But surely, both can work as they should—that is, mindful of their limits, and in maximum accord with their own individual idioms and demands.

Now, to this ideal of working, Bradley's manner is, in the main, assuredly true. That thought is something less than reality or does not make fact, and that, further, it presses for its own transcendence in a supra-relational whole; that our best truth, the idea of the Absolute, is not as such ultimate Reality;[1] that, in so far as thought is but a part of the highest side of our nature, the metaphysician's province is only 'special' and is by no means identical with the whole of human experience and endeavour; and, finally, that philosophy is neither the only nor the best way of experiencing Reality[2]—of all this Bradley is continually aware. But within the limits of his calling, he certainly 'burns' to think intensely, and would brook no half-heartedness. Moreover, he would like to remind us that, though as truth it is necessarily abstract, his crowning idea of the Absolute is no abstraction in so far as it is not only warranted by a consideration of the entire range of human experience, but envisages a Reality which includes and harmonizes all that is.[3] Metaphysics, it is true, can give us

---

[1] AR 140.
[2] Cf. *Ibid* 6.
[3] As to how this final truth is clearly superior to finite truths which are precarious even intellectually, see *Ibid* 475–84.

only a general idea of Reality, not a detailed knowledge of the disposition of content therein. But this idea is positive; and, in so far as it is warranted by theory, and seems also to square with our practical demand for a harmony of existence and idea, Bradley dissents 'emphatically from the conclusion that, because imperfect, it is worthless . . .'[1] Finally, to speak generally, can we deny that a metaphysics such as Bradley's enables us to avoid onesidedness in theory—to avoid, that is, the error of regarding any one kind of experience, any exclusive account of reality, as being finally true? This perhaps is the main reason why metaphysics is necessary. Insisting, as it does in the hands of Bradley, on taking into account reality 'as a whole' and guided as it throughout is by the desire to understand, it serves as a protection against 'dogmatic superstition' and 'orthodox theology'; and against unqualified materialism, transcendence and pantheism.

7. CONCLUSION

It is here impossible for us to speak on behalf of every variety of metaphysics. But, if metaphysics be understood—with Bradley—as an attempt to push questions as far as we possibly can, it is difficult to see how it can for long be avoided. On the other hand, it seems tenable to say that the attempt to think deeply has often led even determined anti-metaphysicians into some kind of metaphysics.[2] Again, a survey of the present-day philosophical situation bears out Bradley's insistence that, in so far as changing problems demand continual re-thinking, no age can really afford to dispense with metaphysics. Thus, in our own day, the thought of Marcel and Heidegger—with its emphasis on Self and Being—is in part determined by their desire to fix the ultimate limits of the verification theory, which is, in the main, a modern hypothesis.

Nor is common-sense immediately repelled by Bradley's basic thesis. The fact, on the other hand, is that we tend naturally to prefer the self-consistent and the inclusive to what jars internally and is of poor content. Again, an Experience which is in every way perfect is perhaps the dimly felt ideal of common-sense itself. Nor does it seem to us unnatural to hold that the deeper our analysis

[1] *Ibid* 3.
[2] See, for instance, Blanshard's *Reason and Analysis*, 171–72; 169–75.

of an object, the richer does it grow; and that theory and practice are but relative aspects. It is true that in practice we are often compelled to employ half-truths, and to take our stand on what are but portions. Again, the conclusions of metaphysics may well seem queer to men of mere common-sense. But, on the other hand, enlightened common-sense may itself tend to prefer wholeness.[1] And it seems reasonable to say that, if he were somehow to understand them, the average man would probably be reluctant, and not merely unable to shake off the conclusions of metaphysics.[2]

At the same time, there is much in Bradley's metaphysics which seems obviously unacceptable to common-sense. Such is, for instance, his suggestion that things are 'unreal'. What precisely he means by 'reality' is indeed one of our more difficult tasks in these essays, and we are shortly to set about it. But, it needs no great effort to see how this question may find a place even in the present-day analysis of knowing:

It may justly be said that 'wondering how' means trying to know not only how a task is performed, but how anything is real or could be true. 'Wondering whether' may be said to stand for such questions as whether a man is, or has come here; or again, for the philosophical query, whether a thing is true and real or not. Now, the second senses of 'how' and 'whether' are here clearly allied to each other. To wonder whether a thing is real or true is at once to wonder as to how it is real, unless, of course, wonder is taken in the merely psychological sense of a passive uncertainty which expresses blankness rather than strives to know. It is precisely with this alliance of 'knowing-meanings', this 'how-whether', that Bradley's attempt to understand is concerned. His basic task is to see whether things which claim to be real are really so, and if yes, how and in what measure.

---

[1] CE 640.
[2] AR 485.

II

REALITY AND APPEARANCE

From Bradley's conception of what it is 'to know' we now pass on to what (in his view) metaphysics seeks to know—that is, to 'Reality'. We propose to show that it is not merely possible, but necessary to distinguish the various senses in which the word has been used by him; for, if we fail to do so, quite a few important aspects of his metaphysics are likely to be misconstrued. That Bradley himself has nowhere made a deliberate attempt to specify and to interconnect these different senses may well be true. Yet, on the other hand, it is no less clear that he uses the word differently in varying context, and that he is conscious of the fact that his real view may be missed unless the different 'senses' are duly kept in mind.[1] In PL he sometimes chooses to take 'reality' in 'the sense of a being that exists within the series of phenomena',[2] so that what is true 'in reality' is to be regarded as being 'valid of fact';[3] but elsewhere he tends clearly to move away from this common-sense conception of reality towards a metaphysical one, though the notion of Reality as what is affirmed by thought's own self-consistent workings is developed fully only in AR.[4]

Again, the distinction which Bradley draws between 'immediate reality' and 'ultimate reality', between feeling and 'the total universe' is, in our view, unmistakable.[5] And he would like the reader to distinguish, in particular, between 'common-sense' reality and what is real 'metaphysically'—between 'a thing exists' and 'it is theoretically tenable'.

Yet it is by ignoring *this* distinction that a familiar criticism of

---

[1] Cf. PL 640, AR 496. Also see: 'It is idle to reply that those bodies and their arrangements are unreal, unless we are sure of the sense which we give to reality.' AR 253.

[2] PL 585.

[3] *Ibid* 579.

[4] Cf. *Ibid* 591–92. Here, Bradley warns the reader that he does not accept the common sense view of reality.

[5] AR 466.

Bradley becomes striking. Morris Lazerowitz complains that, in the same breath, Bradley first claims to have proved that time is a self-contradictory appearance and then assumes its reality in saying: 'I will, in the *next* chapter, reinforce and repeat this conclusion by some remarks upon change.'[1] But, we reply, what Bradley here disallows to time, as a result of the query if it is self-consistently intelligible, is (ultimate) metaphysical reality; and what is granted to it is actual existence. Where is the contradiction? He admits openly that 'appearances', such as space-time and cause-effect, have got to be 'used'. His point only is that their 'use' in practice should be throughout subject to the clear realization that they are, none of them, ultimately true.

It is, in our view, easy to argue that Bradley uses the word 'reality' in different senses. Consider, for instance the following pairs of statements:

(i) 'Ultimate reality is such that it does not contradict itself.'[2]
(ii) '... The given reality is never consistent.'[3]
(iii) 'The Absolute, considered as such, has of course no degrees.'[4]
(iv) 'I am endeavouring ... to get a sound general view of Reality ... But, for this, it is essential to explain and to justify the predicates of higher and lower.'[5]

Now, as contrasted with 'given reality', 'ultimate Reality' is the Absolute—the perfectly self-consistent. And, again, in so far as it itself has no 'degrees', Reality as Absolute is to be distinguished from that 'Reality' to understand which it is necessary 'to explain and to justify' the notion of 'degrees'. We are not suggesting, at this early stage, that the distinctions are tenable. We only insist that Bradley makes them; that it is possible to regard them as being, in some sense, interconnected; and that, finally, specially because he does not generally specify its precise sense when he uses the word 'reality', it is essential that we remain continually watchful

---

[1] Lazerowitz, *The Structure of Metaphysics*, London, Routledge & Kegan Paul, 1955, 17. Bradley's words cited here are from AR 36. Our italics.
[2] AR 120.
[3] *Ibid* 145.
[4] *Ibid* 318.
[5] *Ibid*.

in this respect. Or else, we may be tempted to dismiss Bradley's entire treatment of the matter not as merely untenable, but as wholly meaningless.

1. REALITY

a. *The basic assumption*

Turning now to the theoretical basis of Bradley's metaphysics, we are struck at once by his initial assumption as to the nature of 'reality':

> 'The actual starting-point and basis of this work is an assumption about truth and reality. I have assumed that the object of metaphysics is to find a general view which will satisfy the intellect, and I have assumed that whatever succeeds in doing this is real and true, and that whatever fails is neither.'[1]

Now, a little reflection on the extract cited above brings out the following with respect to Bradley's attitude to 'reality':

What satisfies the intellect, because it is demanded by the latter, is self-consistency. So the real is (to Bradley) individual or harmonious. Reality, as contrasted with Appearance, is the character of being free from contradiction. The greater the internal harmony of an object, the 'higher' is its degree of metaphysical reality. But, in so far as neither feeling nor relational experience is, in Bradley's view, truly self-consistent, ultimate Reality is different from both: it is the Absolute. Though affirmed by thought, this perfect reality is not 'intellectual'.[2] Bradley is convinced that the intellect is no exception to the general necessity because of which nothing finite is able to retain its special character when it is consummated.[3]

b. *Reality as a character*

Now, to proceed further, it would be (in our view) quite true to Bradley's own purpose if we distinguish Reality as Absolute from reality as the character of the Absolute *in so far as it is*

---

[1] *Ibid* 491.
[2] Of this truth, emphasized in AR, Bradley is aware even in PL (594, Note 19).
[3] AR 449, 427.

revealed to thought. He himself says: 'This general character of Reality is not Reality itself.'[1] Theoretically, this distinction is needed to prevent Bradley's doctrine of 'degrees' from appearing *immediately* rejectable. Reality *as Absolute* has no degrees. That which can be said to have 'degrees' is only individuality, or the character of the Absolute in so far as it is manifest in appearances and is made an object of thought.

There is a matter of detail which lends further support to the 'sense' of 'reality' we are seeking to stress. 'Truth', according to Bradley, is ideal. So when we find him speaking of 'degrees of truth *and* reality' it would seem reasonable to suppose that, at least in part, he is (here) using 'reality' too in an ideal sense, that is, as being a character which is revealed to thought.[2] The Absolute, on the other hand, is not as such ideal. Ideality is the looseness of content from being. In the Ultimate, contrarily, the two are held perfectly as one. Again, according to Bradley, what metaphysics reveals to us is not the Absolute as such, but only its general character in so far as it is present in truth and knowledge.[3]

We have indeed a right to wonder if this 'general character' or our idea of the Absolute at all refers to a corresponding fact. But, the difficulty may for the present be ignored; for, it is connected with some bigger issues—say, those concerning the relation of thought, and of appearances in general, to reality—which are yet to be dealt with. What may here be stressed only is that Bradley is not merely aware, but professes it as a doctrine, that the 'reality' of which we, in general, talk is primarily what it appears to us from our (relational) point of view; and that—except in moments when we prefer to keep to thought's ultimate direction—it is not Reality itself considered as that final transcendence of thought's own relational form which is, in Bradley's view, affirmed rationally, if but in the abstract. We seem to be gathering strength to meet, if only in part, two important criticisms of Bradley's metaphysics:

> First, how can Reality have 'degrees'? Our answer would be that what *has* 'degrees' is not Reality as Absolute, but Reality as it appears to us, that is, the *character* of Reality.

[1] *Ibid* 485.
[2] Bradley himself speaks of 'the *character* and type of absolute truth and reality. *Ibid* 321. Our italics.
[3] *Ibid* 484–85.

Secondly, how can Reality be said to work itself out through our experience when activity and time represent, on Bradley's own view, a fall from Reality?

Here, the explanation could be that—as borne out by Bradley's own explicit formulation of the central 'vision'[1]—it is only as considered *'from our human point of view'* that Reality may be said to work itself out in and through differences.

Yet, we hasten to admit, a basic difficulty persists. If, as Bradley in fact insists, thought is necessarily less than ultimate Reality, how can it claim to have any positive knowledge of the latter? The question will engage us in the fifth and sixth chapters.

c. *Reality as that-what togetherness*

Another distinct sense of the word follows from the idea of 'reality' as individual. As Bradley understands it, individuality is the identity of differences. Every object holds qualities as one.[2] Again, it exists necessarily 'in more times or spaces than one'.[3] So, everything is individual. It is a fusion of at least two clear aspects, being and character, or existence and quality. Reality is that-what 'togetherness'. As such, it is concrete, and is therefore different from a mere idea which, if considered as a vehicle of thought, is a necessary disjunction of content from its own private existence.[4] Now, by holding on to this distinct meaning of 'reality', we may be enabled to see the following:

(a) It is reality as existence with character, not Reality as Absolute, which appears to Bradley as wearing the relational form with a view, as it were, to holding differences in peace.[5]

(b) Again, it is reality *thus* understood which he regards as never being (quite) consistent. It hardly needs mention that Bradley cannot ascribe any inconsistency (as such) to the Absolute itself.

(c) Finally, where Bradley describes 'reality' as being infra-relational and relational as well, he is talking not of Reality

[1] *Ibid* 161.
[2] Though but imperfectly.
[3] PL 45, footnote.
[4] AR 165–66.
[5] *Ibid* 18–19.

as Absolute, but of the necessary togetherness of 'that' and 'what'.[1] Where the fusion of these two sides is immediate, but passing, we have feeling. Where they are 'held apart'—and unsatisfactorily, for the intellect—we have the relational form of thought. But, the Absolute is superior to both; here, at last, content and existence are fused perfectly and finally as one.[2]

There is, however, one difficulty which we must here face. How does the conception of reality as a that-what *togetherness*[3] square with Bradley's professed belief that content in experience is everywhere loosened from fact? The difficulty may, in our view, be resolved as follows:

Though a specific 'what' may be easily loosened from *its*[4] 'that', a complete sundering of any 'what' from all 'that' (or vice versa) is impossible. It is not that, in the flux of experience, content first detaches itself *completely* from—and then gets conjoined with—being at some (other) point. Rather, 'thatness' is there all along, as the basal region in and across which content is shuffled. The content only slides along the ground, as it were; and, though loosened from one part of the 'that'—or from its own specific existence—it is always in immediate and necessary union with another region of existence. Ideality is an original feature of what is *on any one occasion* given to us, and what is, therefore, necessarily finite.[5] Yet, reality in general may be regarded as being a necessary fusion of 'that' and 'what' in so far as we can nowhere have 'existence' wholly without 'quality', though a loosening of a specific quality from a specific portion of being is a normal feature of experience.

It is in the context of this (common) truth—the *inseparability* of 'that' and 'what'—that Bradley grants 'reality' to both infra-

[1] Interpreting 'reality' as a character revealed to *thought* would not *in this context* be quite as appropriate; for, we are here talking of feeling as well.

[2] CE 649–50. Also AR 338. In Bradley's view, our main attitudes are all attempts to work out and make good the divergence of existence and idea. *Ibid* 413.

[3] It may be noted, in passing, that this sense of reality—emphasized unmistakably by Bradley in Ch. XV of AR—is completely ignored by Moore in his article, 'The Conception of Reality' in *Philosophical Studies*, London, Routledge and Kegan Paul, 1951, 196–219.

[4] Cf. AR 144, 165.

[5] This is why Bradley speaks of the ideality of the given *finite*.

relational and relational modes of experience. In feeling, differences are in fact held as one. Thought, it is true, disjoins[1] quality from being; this is, in fact, precisely what distinguishes it from feeling. But, first, the disjunction is no complete sundering; for the predicate is, in judgment, also ascribed to the subject. Only, the qualification is here not immediate. Secondly, even now the subject is, in part, a fused togetherness of 'that' and 'what'; for the predicate nowhere explicates the entire content of its subject.[2] Finally, Bradley insists that even the most floating predicate or idea is *felt* as attached to reality in general.[3] Content which is repelled by one region of reality is necessarily held captive in another.

d. *Absolute reality*

This brings us to another specific sense in which Bradley uses 'reality'—Reality as a whole which includes and transcends the 'special' worlds; or, Absolute Reality. It is, in our view, important to ascertain the precise use which Bradley makes of *this* sense of the word; for, it is likely to give us an improved understanding of the links that hold some of his main ideas as one. To facilitate understanding, we may proceed piecemeal:

(a) In ETR the mention of 'the whole universe or the Absolute Reality' occurs during the course of Bradley's protest against the 'false assumption as to the limits of the real world'. The common man's attempt to identify the real with the 'group of series and events (which is) in the end continuous . . . with (his) felt waking body' is here rejected, and emphasis is laid on the fact that, underlying our experience of 'special' worlds, there is the positive—though implicit or felt—experience of a unified whole. In spite of the diversity of its regions, the common man's world is actually felt as one and undivided.[4]

(b) Absolute Reality is reality as it comes to us in feeling—or

---

[1] 'Disjoins', and not merely 'loosens'. Thought, according to Bradley, insists on some measure of irreducible self-existence in the terms which it nevertheless seeks to unite.

[2] AR 149.

[3] ETR 28–36.

[4] *Ibid* 30–32. The word 'felt' is here used in the sense which is distinctive of Bradley, that is, as referring to a non-relational experience of diversity.

as one and indivisible. The word 'absolute' here gains its meaning by a contrast with our 'special' or seemingly self-complete regions of experience. In so far as, because of the unreality of rigid divisions in experience, we cannot—even apart from abstract theorizing—stop at anything short of the all, *absolute* reality may be spoken of as 'one' or 'whole' or 'undivided' reality; or, simply, as the universe. And if, on the other hand, an appeal be made to argument, we fail to find any *principle* to justify the identification of reality with merely sensible existence. It is true that the given objects of sense force themselves upon our consciousness. But then, a burning, unrealized ambition can be just as firm in its hold on attention as a present physical object. Where the presence of a man causes us intense uneasiness, is not the psychological aspect of the situation as positively experienced as the man's being there? 'Thatness' is no monopoly of the merely sensible. And again, is not the compulsive quality of an object determined always, though but in part, by some inner response? Can we disentangle a haunting sound from the inner attitudes which keep it astir? The physical and the subjective—the actual and the imagined—are but aspects of the whole reality.[1] This is perhaps the verdict of common-sense itself. But is it not precisely this which is ignored by any view which *identifies* reality with what is verifiable by sense?

It is, in Bradley's view, a mere dogma to equate reality with what is—or can be—presented to sense. Even existence, he contends, is not *merely* sensible. Take a solid object. It is an experienced conjunction of being and quality. But it maintains itself with the support of impalpable laws, and is subject continually to them. Now, if the content is thus determined by what is other than the visible thing, the that-what fusion here cannot obviously be said to be perfect. Bradley, therefore, regards existence as a temporal series the contents of which are either directly perceived or are perceivable; and which is, to speak more fully, an ideal construction made on the basis of what is actually experienced.[2] The sensible always comes as an element in a whole which is experienced: 'it dictates to my idea as well as submits to my dictation.'[3]

---

[1] *Ibid* 44–45.
[2] AR 280, footnote.
[3] ETR 76. Bradley's emphasis on wholeness is, in fact, unremitting. *Ibid* 51.

To conclude: Bradley's idea of Absolute Reality is a protest against the tendency to confine 'reality' to any special region of experience.

(c) Yet, 'absolute reality' may not, in our view, be equated with the Absolute as such. For, first, whereas there is no Other to the Absolute, reality as it comes to us undivided in feeling is different unmistakably from reality as relational; and, secondly, whereas—as we shall see later—feeling is continually self-transcendent, the Absolute is, in Bradley's view, the final individuality. It is hoped that the distinction we have here suggested will be confirmed by a consideration of Bradley's professed thesis that in every judgment the true subject is reality.

e. *Reality as subject*

Here, our main attempt will be to argue that 'the wider reality' which Bradley regards as being the genuine subject in every judgment is only the absolute or felt (or undivided) reality, *not the Absolute as such*. Once again we may be allowed to explain the matter in terms of individual points:

(a) Bradley maintains that 'in every judgment we have the assertion that "reality is such that S is P"; and that "Reality" is here to be taken as "absolute Reality", and also as a specific togetherness of "that" and "what".'

We turn, first, to reality as specific. 'A judgment is about an object . . . (which) is not the whole of Reality as that at some moment is experienced immediately.' In other words, reality as subject is 'special'. Every judgment depends on a selection. Its subject is a specific togetherness of 'that' and 'what'. Bradley would here like to add, first, that the (special) subject is vitally determined by what it seems merely to leave out, this being the reason why no judgment can be truly self-complete;[1] and, secondly, that when we actually *make* a judgment, or ascribe a quality, it is impossible to deny all 'thatness' to the subject.[2]

(b) But, on the other hand, what, in specifying the subject, 'we have distinguished remains also inseparably in one with our whole universe and qualifies that immediately'.[3] In other words,

[1] PL 623–35.
[2] Cf. AR 149.
[3] PL 629.

when we make a judgment there is always an 'unspecified sense of something beyond',[1] and the entire ideal content is referred, though but implicitly, to a wider reality.[2] This reality is the subject of implicit predication. To put it differently, the 'whole' or undivided reality is the subject in so far as content is referred *implicitly* (that is, non-relationally) or is experienced as 'attached' to a wider undiscriminated whole, though, to speak generally, 'this vital connection is neither recognized nor is its precise character known'.[3] The entire reality can never be the subject of *explicit* predication; for, at least the predicate must (in the main) remain estranged from the subject. Bradley's own words may here be cited with advantage:

> 'On the one side the whole universe or the Absolute Reality is the subject to which in the end every idea is *attached*. On the other side ... the subject in a judgment is never Reality in the fullest sense. It is reality ... understood in a special sense ... If the subject were the entire reality, no place would be left for the existence of the idea.'[4]

(c) The notion of implicit predication becomes clearer in the light of the consideration that ideas can qualify a subject even apart from explicit predication. The relation of ideal content to reality may be 'little more than the immediate inherence of one aspect in a felt whole'.[5] To take an instance, when we make the judgment, 'The rose is red', the entire relational complex is (in Bradley's view) felt as attached to a setting from which, as explicit, it seeks to abstract. The content of our implicit awareness is in this case roughly as follows: 'the rose—out of other subjects or flowers —is red, not to speak of its being qualitied otherwise.'[6]

This is, Bradley would insist, no mere fancy. For, even if we consider reality as understood in terms of connections revealed by

---

[1] ETR 225.
[2] In so far as the entire relational complex is here felt as belonging to a wider reality, this reality itself comes to be regarded as an identity-in-difference which is all that Bradley means by a *whole*. He protests explicitly against the attempt to make this reality a mere abstraction to which content is but externally ascribed. PL 628.
[3] *Ibid* 631.
[4] ETR 32 (also footnote). Our italics.
[5] *Ibid* 32–34.
[6] Cf. PL 630–31; 640.

empirical investigation, the determination of an object by its setting is undeniable; and the seemingly enclosed nature of the subject is, in every case, either a failure to perceive or a compromise forced by practice. The content of experience is, in Bradley's view, continuous; and the 'this' and 'that' are both our abstractions from reality. Nor is the predicate absolutely 'floating'. True, it stands estranged from reality as the particular subject, the rose. But its implicit involvement with reality in general is no less a fact. Thus, in our awareness of 'red' as a predicate, a *felt* reference to the world of qualities or colours is always there.[1]

(d) Bradley insists that the assumption that all judgment is about fact or reality is only natural;[2] and that where such words as 'it', 'this', 'here' and 'now'[3] appear as subjects, the real subject is always a wider, continuous reality. Even in such judgments as: 'A four-cornered circle is an impossibility', the subject is, in Bradley's view, reality. We have only to reformulate the judgment thus: 'The nature of space excludes the connection of square and round'.[4]

(e) Admittedly, it is not in every case easy to show how exactly a judgment points to reality. Yet, a complete dissociation of the two is, according to Bradley, nowhere to be found. Is any judgment truly self-complete? Is not even the most trifling judgment felt as grounded in the facts of diversity, distinctness, number or succession?

To sum up, as the subject in a judgment, Reality, on the one hand, 'slides away from itself into our distinction, so as there to become a predicate', and, on the other hand, 'all the time it retains in itself, as an ultimate subject, every quality which we loosen from and relate to it'.[5]

We may, in the end, specify the more important points in our discussion so far about reality as subject. First, the wider reality

---

[1] In Bradley's view, no idea can be absolutely 'floating', and separation by abstraction is no proof of real separateness AR 24.

[2] PL 41.

[3] In Bradley's view, these are all universals. A fact, on the other hand, is unique. (*Ibid* 49–50). It may be added, in passing, that Bradley distinguishes clearly between the grammatical or the obvious subject, and reality or the genuine subject (*Ibid* 27, 108).

[4] *Ibid* 42.

[5] *Ibid* 629; ETR 333. This dual role of reality is, to Bradley, a fundamental, though inexplicable, fact.

which Bradley regards as being the true subject in every judgment cannot be the Ultimate as such. Whereas the Absolute is supra-relational, the subject, on the other hand, must pass into the judgment and become 'infected with the relational form'.[1]

True, following the way of thought, Bradley himself is sometimes compelled to speak thus: 'The Absolute alone is perfectly individual.' But, such utterances of his should always be considered as being subject to 'understood negations';[2] and his final view emphatically is that 'all predication ... is in the end untrue', and that it is, in the Absolute, completely transcended. We here draw support from the following words of his, which are almost a direct rebuttal of the view which Russell attributes to him—the view that in all judgment 'we are *ascribing* a predicate to Reality as a whole':[3]

> 'In short, far from admitting that Monism requires that all truths can be interpreted as the *predication* of qualities *of the whole*, Monism with me contends that all predication, no matter what, is in the end untrue and in the end unreal, because and so far as it involves always and ignores unexpressed conditions.'[4]

It is true that Bradley occasionally speaks of *ascribing* qualities to reality as a whole, but this seems to be due to mere inadvertence, and is not his considered view. Thus, when in ETR he says that 'all judgment ... predicates its idea of the ultimate Reality' he immediately qualifies it by remarking, in the footnote, that 'at the same time the very form of predication prevents any judgment from being perfectly true'.[5]

Secondly, 'the whole reality' is the 'subject' (only) in the sense that the entire ideal content of a judgment is referred implicitly or as felt, in the manner already indicated, to a wider reality which is (as experienced) an indivisible whole. That is why, in this context, Bradley uses such terms as 'totality'[6] and 'universe'.[7]

In the light of this particular aspect of his theory of judgment,

[1] AR 157.
[2] This is Bradley's own phrase, CE 661.
[3] Russell, *Our Knowledge of the External World*, London, George Allen & Unwin, 1949, 48. Our italics.
[4] CE 672. Also see ETR 239.
[5] *Ibid* 253.
[6] PL 631.
[7] ETR 333.

it is easy to see why Bradley insists that our relational experience does not really 'float', though, as such, it is present neither in Feeling nor in the Absolute, and belongs rather to what we may call the 'intellectual middle space'.[1] The most discursive ideal content is, from the outside, *felt* as fused with the wider setting of reality;[2] and the transition from thought to reality is both natural and necessary. Considered as the fusion of 'that' and 'what', Reality is being continually experienced,[3] even in the midst of thinking where the predicate must be held (in the main) apart from the subject. We neither find nor can make distinctions which could be said to hold content entirely pent up. This is a truth which, in Bradley's view, remains a standing challenge to the hypothesis of merely external relations. What is more, it may be said to warrant the view that when we pass on from a particular object to the wider reality in which it is always, in fact, grounded, we merely follow 'the irresistible lead of our content';[4] and that in proceeding thus, we only come to know the object better, for its very specificity is due to its relatedness to what it appears visibly to exclude.[5]

Bradley's hypotheses of immediate experience and internality of relations are, however, yet to be examined; and what we wish to emphasize in this chapter is only the possibility and the theoretical usefulness of distinguishing the various senses in which he uses the word 'reality'.

f. *Unifying the different senses*

Our next task is to ascertain how they are related to one another, and how they square with Bradley's basic assumption that whatever claims to be real must be acceptable to the intellect.

We may proceed thus. What satisfies the intellect must be harmonious. So, as a character revealed to thought, 'reality' is the quality of being individual. That which answers perfectly to the

---

[1] *Ibid* 269.

[2] Mention may here be made of Bradley's general argument that 'everywhere there must be a whole embracing what is related, or there would be no difference and no relation'. (AR 18).

[3] Cf. 'Immediate contact with Reality can obviously, as a fact, never fail us.' *Ibid* 353.

[4] *Ibid* 224.

[5] Bradley's theory of judgment will, of course, collapse were the universe 'a disconnected conjunction, separable at pleasure'. PL 632.

demands of the intellect—without being accessible to it in detail—is, in Bradley's view, the Absolute. This is Reality in the highest sense. The idea is, however, not available to us at the very outset of our enquiry. We have to begin with a survey of what is actually 'given' and to see if, in any of its forms or regions, it really meets the metaphysical criterion of reality.

Now, given reality is everywhere a togetherness of 'that' and 'what'. Let it not be thought that in agreeing to this use of 'reality' we entirely blink the theoretical criterion. For, not to speak of its being 'satisfied', thought (as judgment) cannot even begin its work unless its object is credited with at least two aspects, being and quality, or a 'that' and a 'what'. So, in regarding reality as being the unity of 'that' and 'what' the intellect is not merely accepting the obvious evidence of fact, but is catering, though in minimal measure, for its own essential demands.

A mere jumble of diversities will, however, not do. Thought abhors contradiction. Differences, therefore, must not be ascribed to the selfsame point; or, they must be held apart or relationally. So, it is theoretically tenable to hold that reality is (also) relational. Here, too, we do not lack support from fact. Differences, when we mark them, are actually seen to belong to the diverse aspects of a thing. We must, however, reflect—because our aim is at the perfectly individual—as to whether differences are in a relation held wholly without contradiction. But, as soon as we undertake this enquiry, we find that unless terms in a relation are credited with an internal diversity, it is a clear contradiction to speak of them as being distinctly themselves and *also* as contributing to the relation. In other words, the fact that (distinct) things are related is made (for the present) intelligible by regarding them as being more inclusive and more richly differentiated than they seem to be. We come to insist on inclusiveness as a necessary condition of harmonious co-existence. It is this insistence which ultimately delivers to thought the idea of Absolute or all-inclusive Reality. Besides being in fact the felt, undivided background of every experienced relation, this Reality is thus, in its general character, rationally affirmed.

Increase of extent is, however, not by itself enough. Contradictions cannot be finally overcome by merely enlarging relational experience. For, so long as the essential character of such experience persists, the necessary (though relative) self-existence of terms must collide, without end, with their actual togetherness. The entire relational form must itself be somehow transcended in a perfect whole of Experience where diversities conduce directly and without reserve to one another and to the whole. This supremely unified reality is, we are told, the Absolute. It holds everything as one—in final harmony, because without the help of relations.

Except as the Absolute, 'reality' does not, in any of its other senses, satisfy thought perfectly; but, in so far as they all do so to some extent, they are all metaphysically tenable in different degrees. Reality as Absolute is the crowning conception attained by thought after a critical meandering through the lesser forms of 'reality', and with its eye set throughout on perfect individuality.

The above account is admittedly inadequate. At quite a few places, it is even ambiguous—largely because of its free employment of some ideas which are yet to be explained. An attempt to make amends will be made during the course of later chapters; and, for the present, we may continue our examination of the two central words in Bradley's definition of metaphysics—'reality' and 'appearance'. Enough has been said about the various meanings of 'reality' as employed by him, and we must now turn to 'appearance'.

2. APPEARANCE

What is 'appearance'? From the viewpoint of common-sense, two answers are possible. We may say that appearance is anything which appears to sense, or that it is a fact or an idea which we somehow suspect to be false. Now, when he speaks of a thing as 'appearance' Bradley too means to say that it is (in the end) not true; but in so far as his attitude as a metaphysician is professedly theoretical, the judgment is passed after comparing the object not with another perception, but with the metaphysical criterion of reality. Any object, experienced perceptually or otherwise, which shows a looseness of content from existence falls short of ultimate Reality, and is therefore but appearance.[1] Bradley's view may be developed further as follows:

[1] Cf. AR 165. In so far as it always shows some looseness of character from being, given reality too is, relatively 'appearance'. This, incidentally, reaffirms the need to mark off given reality from Reality as Absolute.

(i) The metaphysical use of the word 'appearance' is a legitimate extension of its common sense meaning. No perception has a character contained wholly within itself.[1] The content of a thing is, in fact, related necessarily to what it may seem merely to leave out.

(ii) This is, however, realized only when we *reflect* as to whether the thing's claim to self-existence is really true. In practice, on the other hand, an object's self-transcendence may well go unnoticed. In other words, things *become* appearances[2]—that is, when we try to understand them.

(iii) And if reflection is continued, two truths emerge:

First, the specificity of every finite object depends vitally upon its relatedness to others. It claims independence from a setting in which it is none the less grounded. *Thus understood*, things are self-contradictory, and therefore appearances.[3]

Secondly, so far as *we* are concerned, things must always remain so. We can certainly enlarge the bounds of a thing ideally, but, in so far as our vision is incurably finite, we can never take into account all that determines the thing's character and makes it what it is. Or, the 'what' of a thing must always remain jutting out partly beyond its 'that', and its taint of unreality can never by us be expunged.

If its metaphysical sense is thus seen to follow naturally from the way we commonly use the word, 'appearance' may, with Bradley, be described as what appears to us in the temporal series, and what is also (or therefore) self-contradictory.[4] Our elucidatory work in this chapter has now come to an end, and what remains to be done is to see how it is of help to us in meeting some objections to Bradley's conception of:

3. REALITY *AND* APPEARANCE

Our discussion here may proceed as an attempt to examine the tenability of the suggestion—accepted by many, and argued at

[1] *Ibid* 335.
[2] *Ibid* 430.
[3] 'The same may be said to hold of finite beings. *Ibid* 370. This does not mean, however, that Bradley nowhere uses 'appearance' in its common meaning. Thus, see his remark about the unrealized capacities of the soul, and the unseen part of nature: 'we may consider them each to be, as such, incapable of appearance.' (*Ibid* 340).
[4] *Ibid* 335.

length by Morris Lazerowitz[1]—that 'appearance' is, to Bradley, wholly devoid of 'reality', and that he denies both existence and value to the world of our everyday experience.

(i) The main points of the protest made by Lazerowitz are as follows:

(a) Bradley's remark, 'Things are but appearances' only means: 'there only appear to be things'. But this is 'an astonishing factual claim'. How can we accept the view that the world is merely 'an illusion of the senses', and things, 'insubstantial phantoms'? Bradley, we know, does not carry out any 'special, out-of-the ordinary observations and ... experiments'. What right does he then have to try to convey any hidden 'information about things'?[2]

(b) The contention: 'things, as we perceive them, merely appear to be' can be accepted only if we are told what it is for things *really* to be. But this is, it is pointed out, precisely what Bradley does not let us know. 'A philosopher who denies the reality of the physical world finds himself in the strange predicament of being unable to give an account of what it would be like for the physical world to be real.'[3]

(c) It may be said that 'the words "things are but appearances" express a position which is partly "a priori" and partly factual, a position, that is, which consists of a combination of propositions one of which is expressible by the sentence "it is logically impossible for physical things to exist" and the other by the sentence "there exist, as a matter of fact, appearances of there being things" '.[4]

Now, let us consider the (supposedly) 'a priori' proposition: 'it is logically impossible for things to exist.' What does it mean? Lazerowitz suggests that it can only mean 'that the term "physical thing" has a self-contradictory meaning, and hence that the term has no descriptive sense'.[5] But, if this is so, the second proposition: 'there exist, as a matter of fact, appearances of there being things', becomes impossible. To the two propositions taken together, Lazerowitz therefore objects thus: 'What cannot exist, because its existence would imply a contradiction, cannot exist

[1] Lazerowitz, *The Structure of Metaphysics*, 199–230.
[2] *Ibid* 199 (footnote)–201.
[3] *Ibid* 204, 203.
[4] *Ibid* 207.
[5] *Ibid* 219.

as "mere appearance", because the existence of the appearance would also imply a contradiction.'[1] Bradley seems clearly unjustified in believing that the contradictions involved in the term 'thing' disprove only the existence of things and not the existence of their 'appearing-to-exist'.

(d) It appears that Bradley is using the term 'thing' in two senses, but the alteration he thus brings about in the structure of language is, we have seen, untenable. One may, therefore, conclude, with Lazerowitz, that 'the utterance "things are but appearances" covertly and indirectly describes a prosaic alteration of language but produces the illusion of making a colossal claim about reality'.[2]

(ii) Now, in our reply, we propose wholly to ignore the attempt of Lazerowitz to explain Bradley's view as being partly the result of 'unconscious self-aggrandizement', or 'overdetermination' to prove the 'omnipotence of thought'; or as being due to a withdrawal of libido brought about by some 'disappointing experiences'.[3] We have to go strictly by Lazerowitz's interpretation of the text of AR, and to examine its tenability in detail:

(a) The entire criticism of Lazerowitz is based on the *assumption* that in saying: 'things are but appearances' Bradley really means: 'there appear to be things, but in reality there are none' in which statement the expression 'there are none' seems 'to be used to put forward a factual claim'.[4]

But what is there, in the *text* of AR, to warrant this assumption? Let us cite Lazerowitz's own words:

'The ... sentence which I propose to examine here, namely, "things are but appearances" ... occurs in the following context:

"The results, which we have reached, really seem to have destroyed things from without and from within. If the connexions of substantive and adjective, and of quality and relation, have been shown not to be defensible; if the forms of space and of time have turned out to be full of contradictions; if, lastly, causation and activity have succeeded merely in adding in-

[1] *Ibid* 209.
[2] *Ibid* 225.
[3] *Ibid* 228.
[4] *Ibid* 205.

consistency to inconsistency—if, in a word, nothing of all this can, as such, be predicated of reality—what is it that is left? *If things are to exist*, then where and how? But if these two questions are unanswerable, then we seem driven to the conclusion that *things are but appearances*. . . ." [1]

By the above Lazerowitz is led to conclude that, in Bradley's view, things 'do not exist' and that, therefore, whatever Bradley 'expresses by the words "things are but appearances" can also be expressed by "there only appear to be things" '.[2]

(b) But, our protest is ready: Lazerowitz does *not* interpret Bradley correctly. This can be argued as follows:

(1) Lazerowitz confines his attention to the italicized words in the last two sentences of Bradley's passage cited above. But, if we consider them, as we should, in the context of what precedes them, they will easily be found to mean something clearly different from what Lazerowitz thinks they do. The 'results' which, Bradley says, have been 'reached' are briefly these: whether we consider them along with, or apart from each other, things are relational; relations are infected with contradictions,[3] to overcome which we are compelled continually to pass on to ever newer relations; the visible individuality of things is, therefore, *theoretically* dissolved.[4] That the 'destruction' here referred to is theoretical is confirmed by what follows the first sentence of the passage under review and also by the following words which occur earlier in the chapter to which the passage in question belongs: 'It is hard to say *what*, as a matter of fact, *is generally understood* when we use the word "thing". But whatever that may be, *it* now seems undermined and ruined.'[5] The different ways in which we generally regard the world of facts are all self-contradictory. Thus regarded, or 'as such',[6] they cannot be said to belong to, or to represent 'reality' as Bradley understands it, that is, as the ideal of thought. Where do the 'things' exist? And in what way, or as what? We have found

---

[1] *Ibid* 199, also footnote. Italics are by Lazerowitz himself. In interpreting the passage from AR (61) here cited, Lazerowitz depends essentially on its last two sentences.
[2] *Ibid* 199, footnote.
[3] This is yet to be brought out clearly, in Ch. IV of the present work.
[4] Cf. AR 19.
[5] *Ibid* 61. Our italics.
[6] See the passage (AR 61) being discussed.

it impossible to answer either question satisfactorily. Space-time, cause-effect, substance-quality, and activity—these have all been found to be self-contradictory. We can only say: 'things exist, but we cannot *explain how*.' Therefore, if the real be that which satisfies the intellect, 'things are appearances'.

(2) Nowhere, in AR, does Bradley clearly say: 'we should not regard things as existent'. He questions only the 'what' and the 'how', not the 'that' or existence of things. It is, in this connection, important to note that, after reminding us as to the self-contradictory nature of the different ways of regarding the world in the second sentence of the passage in question, he does not immediately conclude: 'therefore things do not exist.' On the other hand, he first poses another question: 'If things are to exist, then where and how?' and only then says that things are appearances, the meaning obviously being that because we cannot (satisfactorily) *understand how* they exist, things are appearances.

(3) Things are 'appearances'. This, certainly, is Bradley's view. But we are convinced that it cannot be reduced to: 'there only appear to be things'. Nor does 'appearance', as *he* uses the word, mean mearly that which appears, or 'the quality of appearing-to-sense'. In the main, it rather stands for that which is, for thought, marked by a clear looseness of content from its existence[1] and which is, therefore, self-contradictory. Throughout the first part of AR, devoted to 'Appearance', Bradley uses the word to mean that which is commonly acknowledged to be there, but is not systematically intelligible.[2] See, for instance:

> 'The arrangement of *given facts* into relations and qualities may be necessary in practice, but it is *theoretically unintelligible. The reality, so characterized, is not true reality, but appearance.*'[3]

Lazerowitz, on his own admission, throughout interprets 'appearance' merely as 'sensible appearance'.[4] But this interpretation is

---

[1] AR 165, 404.
[2] It is only in the second book, devoted to 'Reality', that Bradley argues how the metaphysical meaning of 'appearance' follows naturally from the sense it has in daily talk. *Ibid* 335.
[3] *Ibid* 21. Our italics.
[4] Lazerowitz, *The Structure of Metaphysics*, 208, footnote. Bradley, on the other hand, wants us to avoid the mistake of identifying appearance 'with presentation, as such, to sense'. AR 335.

justified neither by the overall import of the passage under review nor by Bradley's own unambiguous summing up of what has been accomplished in the entire section on 'Appearance':

> 'The result of our First Book has been mainly negative. We have taken up a number of ways of regarding reality, and we have found that they all are vitiated by self-discrepancy. The reality can accept not one of these predicates, at least in the character in which so far they have come. We certainly ended with a reflection which promised something positive. *Whatever is rejected as appearance is, for that very reason, no mere nonentity. It cannot bodily be shelved and merely got rid of*, and, therefore, since it must fall somewhere, it must belong to reality. To take it as existing somehow and somewhere in the unreal, would surely be quite meaningless.'[1]

(4) Misconstruing Bradley's use of 'appearance' as perceptual illusion is a case of confusing the idiom of common talk with that of the 'ancillary language' provided by metaphysics. Lazerowitz misinterprets the sentences on which he bases his entire criticism because he ignores not only what goes earlier in the passage to which they belong, but even the more explicit remarks of Bradley, such as the following:

> 'For nothing is actually removed from existence by being labelled "appearance".'[2]
>
> 'An unintelligible fact may be admitted so far as ... it is a fact.'[3]
>
> '... We may keep a fast hold upon this, that appearances exist. That is absolutely certain, and to deny it is nonsense.'[4]

The passage which serves as the main ground of the protests of Lazerowitz occurs when Bradley is just half way through his section on 'Appearance'. He would not have committed the mistake of interpretation he does, had he cared to take into account the concluding remarks of this section:

> 'Our appearances no doubt may be a beggarly show, and their nature ... as it is, is not true of reality. That is one thing, and *it*

---

[1] AR 119. Our italics.
[2] *Ibid* 12.
[3] *Ibid* 126.
[4] *Ibid* 114.

is quite another to speak as if these facts had no actual existence. ... Appearance ... is that which, taken as it stands, proves inconsistent with itself. ... But to deny its existence or to divorce it from reality is out of the question. For it has a positive character which is indubitable fact.'[1]

We therefore conclude that Bradley does *not* deny the existence of things. It may here be noted, in passing, that in the chapters: 'The General Nature of Reality' and 'Solipsism', Bradley rejects subjective idealism;[2] and that in PL he openly protests against the suggestion that 'existence could be the same as understanding', or that 'the sensuous curtain is a deception and a cheat'.[3] He is definitely opposed to the Hegelian view 'that to be real and to be thought are the same thing'.

(5) Bradley's main purpose, we insist, is not to make any factual claim, but only to assess the metaphysical reality of things. We have thought it necessary to insist upon this simple distinction at some length because indifference to it is perhaps the main reason because of which he is often regarded as being malicious towards the claims of our everyday world.[4]

The distinction in question is, in fact, generally ignored by the critics of Bradley's metaphysics. Consider, for instance, Hartland-Swann's remark that the realization that philosophy as such is able neither to increase our knowledge of the world nor to reveal its ultimate constituents marks 'the transition from Bradleian to modern analytical philosophy'.[5] The (wrong) assumption here obviously is that Bradley tries to tell us something about the sensible details of the world in a wholly 'a priori' way; which is, one might add, both improper and futile.

It would here be relevant to note what precisely is Bradley's attitude to our common world. He does not try to deduce it from some more fundamental principle, and the protest that 'existents appear on the scene, let themselves be met, but can never be deduced' has no relevance to Bradley's view. Nor is he an idealist

[1] *Ibid.* Our italics.
[2] *Ibid* 128, 220.
[3] PL 591.
[4] Santayana's general protest, cited approvingly by Russell, *Our Knowledge of the External World*, 55.
[5] John Hartland-Swann, *An Analysis of Knowing*, London, George Allen & Unwin, 1958, 103.

who could be said to proceed 'merely by fiat' and to refuse 'to recognize existence'.

Whether 'second reflection' on the facts of experience leads us to the unitary Absolute or, as Marcel believes, merely to a plurality of 'mysteries' can be decided only after an examination of the arguments supporting either view. What is here essential to point out, by way of a general safeguard against misinterpretation of Bradley's position, only is that, if it be admitted that metaphysics is a theoretical venture, the assumption: 'reality must satisfy the intellect' is clearly not a 'fiat'; and that what Bradley seeks to establish is only the (ultimate) unintelligibility, not the non-existence of the world.

Quite a few objections, we admit, are possible with regard to Bradley's doctrine of Appearance. It can justly be said to appear forced—certainly so, if it is contrasted with Heidegger's view, borrowed from the Greeks, that Being consists in appearing. And it may even be added that it is Bradley's seemingly 'artificial' conception of reality, as what satisfies the intellect or is self-consistent, which compels him to mark off appearance (from reality) by investing it with the contrasting character of self-contradictoriness. But, this cannot justly be said against Bradley's doctrine of Appearance (or even mere appearance) that it turns the world into a mere illusion.

(6) Again, precisely because (as already indicated) Bradley does not object to the 'reality' of the physical world, if by 'reality' we here mean 'existence', it is meaningless to ask him as to how things exist originally, as distinguished from what they merely appear (visibly) to be. Lazerowitz misinterprets 'appearance' as sensible illusion, and therefore desires to know the experience as compared to which the seeming world is (allegedly) unreal. But if, as by Bradley, appearance is taken to mean experience which is self-contradictory, what we can legitimately demand to know only is: how do contradictions arise, and how can they be finally overcome? And these are questions which Bradley has certainly tried to answer. Whether he succeeds in the attempt or not is quite another matter.

(7) The judgment that things are appearances, because self-contradictory, is not 'a priori'. Bradley arrives at this conclusion after applying the criterion—of reality as the self-consistent—to

things as given and as generally understood. The *criterion* itself is, however, clearly 'a priori' in so far as it is not derived from, and is not refutable by experience.

(8) A word, finally, about the charge that Bradley uses the word 'thing' self-inconsistently. As we have seen, the protest here is that, on the one hand, he regards 'things' in 'things exist' as self-contradictory, and so rejects the existence of things; and that, on the other hand, he regards the same term as meaningful in 'there exist ... appearances of there being things'. But, we reply that, in Bradley's view, things do not *exist* as appearances; they only *become* so when they are made objects of thought and are found unintelligible.[1] And, surely, no contradiction is involved in saying that things which exist become 'appearances', or are found self-discrepant, when they are thought of in a particular way. 'A square circle' contains a prima facie contradiction: it cannot exist. This is how the non-existence of some objects may be argued. But, Bradley's procedure is quite different. He accepts the existence of things and *then* proceeds to examine what we mean when we speak of them. Contradictions are brought out only when this meaning, variously understood, is carefully analysed; and it is only then that things are pronounced to be appearances.

(iii) We turn next to some other subsidiary considerations which seem to lend point to the belief that Bradley denies both existence and value to the physical world. Lazerowitz for one is convinced that this impression forces itself upon us irresistibly if we consider the 'emotively derogatory' connotation of the terms which Bradley freely uses—such as 'unreal', 'mere appearance', illusory' and 'beggarly show'—along with such obvious remarks of his, emphasizing the worthlessness of this world: 'The reality threatens to migrate to another world than ours.'[2] Now, with regard to Bradley's use of the individual terms cited above, our view is that, if they are understood with reference to their context and in the light of his general view, they deny neither existence nor value to the world, but only make it unmistakable, by sharpening the

---

[1] It is true that Bradley sometimes says: '... appearances exist' (see for instance, AR 114), but his real meaning on such occasions is: things which (to thought) become appearances are not, for that reason, mere illusions. It is here necessary to remember Bradley's explicit doctrine that, 'in a sense', contradictions *arise* (*Ibid* 505).

[2] *Ibid* 105.

contrast, that the world as such is not *ultimate* reality as understood in (his) metaphysics. The physical world is 'real' in one sense of the term—that is, as existence with character. But, it is 'unreal' in another sense, that is, if by 'reality' we understand 'reality as metaphysical' or as the ideal of thought, and as perfectly self-consistent. Surely, to regard the world as being not ultimately real is not necessarily to treat it as wholly unreal.

Our contention is fully borne out by an examination of Bradley's actual employment of the terms in question. Take 'mere appearance', to begin with:

> 'We have found, so far, that we have not been able to arrive at reality. The various ways, in which things have been taken up, have all failed to give more than *mere appearance*. Whatever we have tried has turned out something which, on investigation, has been proved to contradict itself. But that which does not attain to internal unity, has clearly stopped short of genuine reality.'[1]

Or again:

> ' "That selves *exist* ... is indubitable" [2] ... But the self is so far from supplying such a (metaphysical) principle that it seems, where not hiding itself in obscurity, *a mere bundle of discrepancies*. Our search has conducted us again *not to reality* but *mere appearance*.' [3]

Bradley's meaning here is not that the self is wholly devoid of reality, but only that the difference between its self-inconsistent character and that of the final metaphysical reality is unmistakable. His purpose, when he speaks of 'mere appearance', is only to heighten the contrast, not to suggest a total lack of relation, between appearance and reality: 'The phrase "mere appearance" ... gets its meaning by contrast with the Absolute.'[4] He openly affirms that 'there is no mere appearance or utter chance or absolute error, but all is relative';[5] that 'all appearances for metaphysics

---
[1] *Ibid* 110. Our italics.
[2] *Ibid* 89. Our italics.
[3] *Ibid* 104. Our italics.
[4] *Ibid* 496.
[5] *Ibid* 493.

have degrees of reality';[1] and that 'to arrange them ... in a system of reality and merit' is the task of metaphysics, though he himself has only explained the principle of this arrangement, without trying to apply it to every appearance.[2]

The point simply is that, during the process of examining the theoretic tenability of things that 'appear', or till before the full idea of ultimate Reality emerges, thought is more keenly conscious of the otherness of appearance from reality than of any positive relation between the two. The contrast is, in Bradley's view, inescapable; for, to judge, he insists, is necessarily to mark off the real from the unreal.[3]

And here is an extract which makes it clear beyond doubt that Bradley uses the term 'illusory' for what is 'self-contradictory', not for what is capable of being rubbed out from existence, like a sensible illusion:

> 'All the ways of thinking which introduce a unity into things, into the world or the self—and there clearly is a good deal of such thinking on hand—are of course *illusory*. *But, none the less, they are facts utterly undeniable.*'[4]

Once again, the consideration that we are not able to understand a thing self-consistently is not allowed to militate against its actual existence.

This brings us to reflect how exactly reality, in Bradley's view, 'threatens to migrate to another world than ours'. A careful examination of the passage in which these words occur—and of other relevant remarks throughout AR—effectively dissipates the error of supposing that, according to Bradley, reality is to be found in a region wholly beyond our common world. First, to the passage in question:

> 'Our attempts, so far, to reduce the world's diverse contents to unity have ended in failure. Any sort of group which we could

---

[1] *Ibid* 440.
[2] *Ibid* 433–34. The completeness with which all this has been ignored by Holmes is surprising. See his *Philosophy without Metaphysics*, 33–34.
Bradley, however, confesses that in talking of the relation of appearance to reality he has used 'language which certainly contradicts itself, unless the reader perceives that there is more than one point of view'. AR 496.
[3] *Ibid* 120.
[4] *Ibid* 106. Our italics.

find, whether a thing or a self, proved unable to stand criticism. And, since it seems that what appears must somewhere certainly be one, and since this unity is not to be discovered in phenomena, the reality threatens to migrate to another world than ours. We have been driven near to the separation of appearance and reality; we already perhaps contemplate their localization in two different hemispheres—the one unknown to us and real, and the other known and mere appearance.'[1]

Now, what Bradley here means is this. Our attempt, in metaphysics, is to reduce the entire diversity of world's content to unity; or, as Bradley points out a little earlier, to discover a principle which, 'while wide enough to cover the facts (is) able to be thought without internal jarring'.[2] Such an all-explaining, all-inclusive unity is not provided by anything so far examined, things or selves. But Bradley insists that such a reality must ultimately be there—somewhere else, if not (as such) in the region of our relational experience. The insistence is thought's own. Even generally, to remain contented with what is in principle wholly unintelligible, or merely plural, is for thought wholly impossible.[3] Such an attitude would be, in Bradley's view, opposed to the very conditions of thought's working:

'... To sit down contented is impossible, unless, that is, we are resolved to put up with mere confusion. For to transcend what is given is clearly obligatory, if we are to think at all and have any views whatever.'[4]

As a way out of the difficulty, Bradley suggests that the final Reality, though admittedly an ultimate affirmation of the intellect, is supra-relational. To get it we have to go beyond the form in which the bulk of our experience comes to us. But, what does this mean? Does it mean 'breaking away from', or going 'spatially beyond', or merely 'negating' common experience?

Our answer, following Bradley, is negative. It may be noted that, even in the passage where our proneness to localize appear-

---

[1] *Ibid* 105.
[2] *Ibid* 104. This occurs in the closing section of the Chapter, 'The Reality of Self', a little before the passage under review.
[3] This, of course, is Bradley's view.
[4] AR 110.

ance and reality 'in two different hemispheres' is referred to, Bradley only heightens—to a breaking-point, it is true—the contrast between the two; but the link is not actually made to snap. He certainly says that, by the logic of our prior reasonings, 'we have been driven near to the separation of appearance and reality'. But there is, in the passage under review, nothing to suggest that Bradley accepts, or wants us to accept, an absolute gulf between appearance and reality. In fact, he hastens to refute —in the chapter to which the extract belongs, and in the following one—the twin errors of 'phenomenalism' and 'things-in-themselves'.

Our suggestion that Bradley does not *separate* appearance from reality gains further support from the following unambiguous remarks of his:

> '. . . However much . . . fact may be pronounced appearance, it can have no place in which to live except reality. And reality, set on one side and apart from all appearance, would assuredly be nothing.'[1]

In fact, Bradley insists that what we experience, however imperfectly, is everywhere the Absolute; that Reality must appear; that 'there is no question here of stepping over a line from one world to another';[2] and, finally, that 'behind me the absolute reality works through and in union with myself, and the world which confronts me is at bottom one thing in substance and in power with this reality'.[3] What he really means by saying that 'reality threatens to migrate to another world than ours' may now be put thus. Genuine reality is perfectly self-consistent. In common experience, on the other hand, thought finds nothing that could answer to its cherished ideal. So, refusing to put up with mere confusion, thought rises above finite experience to the idea of the Absolute. But, and this is important, in the transition, our world is not left behind; rather it is included, and, what is more, its contradictions are now fully resolved. Bradley, in fact, explicitly opposes the idea of a separateness between the Absolute and our common world:

[1] *Ibid* 114.
[2] *Ibid* 465.
[3] ETR 218.

'*Within the Absolute* you transcend the lower and the partial forms in which it appears, in order to reach those which are truer. But as for transcending the Absolute to gain my finite centre, or my finite centre to gain the Absolute—everything of such a kind to me is mere nonsense. . . . From the first, if we are to speak of transcendence, my finite centre is transcended. From the first and throughout it is one thing directly with the all-embracing universe . . .'[1]

Two considerations may here be emphasized:

First, it is not in metaphysics alone that we 'migrate' to another world in pursuit of 'reality'. In other fields too, understanding may consist in resolving the discordance of facts in terms of a theoretical scheme which itself is not visibly given. And if the unseen is here welcome, why should it not be so in the case of metaphysics? Of course, everything depends on whether the idea of the Absolute really explains—or is demanded by—facts. But to see if this is or is not so, we have to undertake a careful examination of Bradley's detailed arguments to demonstrate the theoretical necessity of the idea of the Absolute; and this is something which Lazerowitz has just not attempted.

Secondly, when in our attempt to understand facts we go beyond them, their existence as such may remain wholly unquestioned. The theory of Refraction 'reconciles' the bent appearance of a stick immersed in water with its actual straightness. Neither of the two aspects of fact is here 'cancelled' by the theory. It only interprets them, and in so doing, reconciles them; and it is precisely because of this that we welcome the theory as a revealer of 'reality'.[2] We 'transcend' the facts and go to the theory because otherwise we do not understand them. The 'transcendence' and the 'reconciliation' are both here ideal. There is no tampering with facts, and yet the 'migration' involved in understanding is by no means wilful. Could we not say that, like physics and mathematics, metaphysics gives us a theoretical scheme which interprets, but does nothing to cancel the world of our common experience?

Yet, it is not our purpose to suggest that Bradley's conception of the relation between Reality and Appearance is entirely free

[1] *Ibid* 247. Our italics.
[2] Ramsey, *Prospect for Metaphysics*, 156–57.

from difficulties. At the same time, we believe it may be instructive to ascertain with care what precisely these difficulties are, and to what extent it is really legitimate to regard them as genuine objections to a philosophical world view. The task will be attempted in our sixth chapter.

III

IMMEDIATE EXPERIENCE

As we have seen, metaphysics is (in Bradley's view) an attempt to arrive at a tenable idea of ultimate reality, and to see if anything in our experience can justly claim to be finally real. Assuming that the status of ultimate reality can be granted only to that which answers to the full our quest of the consistent, we first turn to examine not the various objects of experience severally, but the two essential forms in which it comes to us—feeling or the non-relational awareness of diversity, and the relational form which works through the mechanism of qualities and relations.

A careful examination of Bradley's conception of feeling is, in our view, doubly important. It may be expected to enable us, first, to expose some gross misinterpretations of his views on the matter; and, secondly, to bring out the central role of 'immediate experience' in his entire metaphysical scheme.

Consider, to begin with, the following criticism of Bradley by Cohen:

> 'The conclusion that everything short of the absolute totality is appearance and not reality is a logical consequence of *an arbitrary view of reality, which identifies it with purely immediate feeling or experience.* But though the *craving of the flesh for strong sensations* and feelings is an important element of life, it is certainly not conclusive even as to the guidance of life.'[1]

Now, this is a complete distortion of Bradley's real views. That he does not wish to *identify* reality with feeling is borne out clearly by the following words of his:

> 'Nothing, I have urged, which is not all-inclusive and complete, can satisfy that want and demand, in which we find our criterion of Reality—a want and demand which to me obviously and plainly cannot be satisfied by mere feeling.'[2]

[1] Cohen, *Reason & Nature*, 164. Our italics.
[2] CE 649, also 663.

'It does not follow, if immediate experience is the beginning, that it is also the end, and is all reality.'[1]

Bradley says unequivocally that, whereas feeling provides us with only 'a low and imperfect example of an immediate whole',[2] thought seeks 'an immediate unity of one and many at a higher remove'.[3] True, he holds that it is only in feeling that reality can be directly encountered.[4] But when he says this, his meaning is not that immediate experience is a *perfect* specimen of individuality, but simply that it is only here that an actual harmony of differences is to be *found*.

Nor is there any warrant for the suggestion that by 'feeling' Bradley means a 'craving of the flesh for strong sensations'. He, in fact, takes pains to keep the two apart:

'Feeling here ... does not mean mere pleasure and pain. ... Feeling is immediate experience without distinction or relation in itself. It is a unity, complex but without relations. ... And a distinction between cognition and other aspects of our nature is not yet developed. Feeling is not one differentiated aspect, but it holds all aspects in one.'[5]

Finally, the contention that 'everything short of the absolute totality' cannot be called 'appearance' loses all force if it is remembered that, as brought out in the last chapter, the word is nowhere used by Bradley to stand for a total lack of reality.

As regards the importance of 'feeling' for his own metaphysical thinking, it is manifest in what he says about his way of working in AR:

'We start from the diversity in unity which is given in feeling, and we develop this internally by the principle of self-completion beyond self, until we reach the idea of an all-inclusive and supra-relational experience.'[6]

In a word, feeling is, first, the starting-point of Bradley's metaphysics; and, secondly, it delivers to him the important idea of

---
[1] ETR Contents IX. Also see AR 406–7, 413; CE 632.
[2] AR 215.
[3] ETR 231.
[4] AR 466.
[5] ETR 194. And, talking of pleasure as a guiding principle of conduct, does not Bradley say: 'Hedonism is bankrupt?' ES 124.
[6] AR 494.

self-completion through self-transcendence, an idea which—when employed in, and confirmed by our survey of the various appearances—leads us finally to the idea of the Absolute.

In view of its central importance for Bradley, the concept of Feeling may therefore be examined at some length. It would perhaps conduce to a better understanding of the matter if our discussion in this chapter is made to proceed as an attempt to answer the following main questions:

(i) What is 'feeling'? Is it, as Bradley understands it, at all an actual feature of our experience?
(ii) How is it related to thought?
(iii) Why should metaphysics take 'feeling' into account?
(iv) Is Bradley's notion of feeling defensible against criticisms?

1. IS BRADLEY'S 'FEELING' ACTUAL?

Now, to begin with, feeling or immediate experience, as Bradley understands it, is the non-relational experience of diversity. It is the experience of diverse content without its being distinguished. Diversities are here felt; they are not held 'apart' with the help of relations. In other words, the differences here are no qualities.[1] Understood in their 'strict' sense, qualities are always the result of distinction.[2] The contrast of feeling with relational experience is, therefore, clear.[3] In feeling, qualification is immediate—a felt inherence of diversities in the psychic whole; but, in the case of thought or judgment, it is relational.[4]

But, do we ever actually have experience which is immediate? Is it at all a fact? Bradley's answer to these basic questions may be outlined as follows:

(a) Our psychic life begins with immediate experience.[5] In

---

[1] 'No qualities', provided we consider 'quality' in what Bradley regards as the 'proper' sense, that is, as a term which is 'distinguished and related'. *Ibid* 513.

[2] This is, of course, Bradley's view. *Ibid* 22.

[3] CE 631–32; ETR 173–74.

[4] Cf. *Ibid* 227.

[5] CE 654. On the whole, however, Bradley seems undecided as to whether feeling really comes first in point of time. Cf. '. . . Everywhere, in the individual as in the race, this stage (viz., feeling) comes first in the development . . .' (*Ibid*) with:

'Feeling is more ultimate; but whether prior in time we have agreed to leave doubtful . . .' (*Ibid* 658).

the beginning, 'there are no relations and no feelings', but only 'differences, that work and . . . are felt, but are not discriminated'.¹ This pre-relational experience of diversity precedes all differentiation of the psychic content, say, into pain and pleasure, or into knowing, willing and feeling as we understand them in psychology.² The external world is here not marked off from the self; and sentience, at this stage, is a fused mass, though not without the shift and stress of experience.³ The total state is 'an immediate feeling; a knowing and being in one . . .'⁴ Thus considered, that is, as the general state of original experience where distinctions and relations have not yet emerged, immediate experience 'is not to be called "subjective", nor is it to be identified with my self';⁵ for, terms such as these derive meaning from a conscious contrast with the not-self. Certainly, the self is here present, as the necessary bearer of experience, and the world too is there, as what is experienced; but in so far as they are not yet distinguished, 'self' and 'not-self', as intellectual constructions, are here absent. The total experience is that of a finite centre which is not the mere 'me'.⁶ Bradley's explicit view is that if the 'self' is understood in its ordinary sense—that is, as that which balances itself self-consciously against the not-self—it is not original, but a later differentiation. At the level of immediate experience what we have is not only that which is subsequently to emerge as the self, but that which is later to be called the not-self; and, on the strength of what is originally given, solipsism has, therefore, no right to take 'self' as the exclusive reality.⁷ To speak generally, not all content comes to us as clearly distinguished, and our experience of undistinguished nebulae, on the sides of both self and not-self, cannot be denied. For example, content is clearly discriminated when one compares two distinct shades of colour; but even here the perception may include a vaguely felt aversion to one of the terms.

(b) What is more, in so far as its felt unity is never quite dis-

¹ ETR 157, footnote.
² Cf. *Ibid* 194. It is here clear that, to Bradley, 'Feeling' does not mean what it commonly does in psychology.
³ *Ibid* 151.
⁴ *Ibid* 159.
⁵ *Ibid* 189.
⁶ Cf. *Ibid* 247; AR 465-66. The experient and the experienced are here one. ETR 194.
⁷ As to Bradley's insistence that the self is essentially relative, see AR 497.

rupted, our experience may be said to remain (in part) non-relational throughout our lives. This leads us to another distinct sense in which Bradley speaks of feeling—that is, not as the general, pre-relational level of experience, but as the wholeness of felt mass at any one time, or 'any particular state so far as internally that has undistinguished unity'.[1]

Here we are on more familiar ground, and can easily cite actual experiences to illustrate Bradley's meaning and to argue its tenability in general. 'The experienced will not all fall under the head of an object for a subject';[2] and in actual cases of emotional experience and volition, we certainly have a diversity which is not joined by relations, not even by the relation of an object as standing against a subject. The analysis of volition into relations falling between complexes of sensations and idea would leave out 'the felt outgoing of myself and from myself'.[3] In spontaneous sympathy, the different accents of our experience—the stir and the vent of emotion—are no mere succession of detached events. Again, desire is characterized by 'an indefiniteness of the felt, to call which an object strikes (us) . . . as even ludicrous'.[4] Purposeful differentiation of the given may be essential for *understanding*; but it is not a necessary mark of all experience.[5] The intensity of a sudden fright may for long be remembered as a mere lump, and the attempt to dwell on its details may just coexist with—rather than cancel—the mass.

There is yet another way to identify the fact of immediate experience. It sometimes serves a distinct criterion of accord and acceptance. Do we not sometimes chuckle with delight on coming across a poetic phrase, or a graphic remark, which expresses perfectly what we had all along been feeling—intensely, maybe—but without the power or occasion to objectify with clearness?[6]

2. 'FEELING' AND THOUGHT

But, though—because of its freedom from distinctions—feeling

---

[1] *Ibid* 405. Bradley insists on distinguishing the two senses. Also see *Ibid* 198.
[2] ETR 159.
[3] *Ibid* 189.
[4] *Ibid* 197.
[5] Cf. *Ibid* 159.
[6] Cf. *Ibid* 185–86.

is quite different from our relational experience, it would be wholly untrue to fact to suppose that the two kinds of experience do not or cannot go together. Thought itself is not fully considered unless we take into account its essential non-relational basis. In Bradley's view, feeling may be said not only to precede the workings of thought, but to encompass and sustain them continually.

First, *before* the theoretic effort commences, content is just quietly owned by us; it may well be felt, so as to cause a tension in the self, but it need not yet appear as opposed to the latter.[1] What, otherwise, is the difference between getting psychologically adjusted to understand and objectifying the content self-consciously during the actual attempt to understand? Of all theorizing, the starting-point, though not the governing principle, is experience as 'this-mine'—say, some content, whether a sensation or an idea, of which the self is directly aware.[2] The 'this-mine' stands for the immediacy of presentation.[3] But, Bradley wants us to remember that the 'this' 'is present just as much in mere internal fancy as in external perception',[4] and that 'it belongs everywhere to that which is immediately experienced'.

Secondly, whatever we know not only arises from, but must (in a way) pass through the 'this'.[5] Thought is at no time discursive breathlessly. Even in our most intense spells of thinking, there are instants of repose—of coming-to-know, or of preparing-to-understand—when, with mediation suspended, the content is merely accepted, if only as a breather for harder thinking ahead; and the felt reality of the self, which is never quite dissipated, and of content fused with it, is heightened anew to give us a feeling of individual reality.

Thirdly, in one sense, feeling is, so to speak, the necessary wrapping of relational experience. What is it to be aware of a relation? According to Bradley, it means the awareness not only of the mutual distinctness of terms and relations, but of their being actually held together. Now, the latter element of the experienced

---

[1] Cf. 'We needs must begin our voyage of reasoning by working on something which is felt and not thought.' PL 480.
[2] Direct experience is 'merely felt or presented'. Indirect experience includes what is constructed from the basis of the 'this-mine'. AR 219.
[3] *Ibid* 198.
[4] PL 659.
[5] Cf. AR 198.

situation, or the singleness with which the psychical complex is presented to the mind, is (in his view) provided by feeling. 'An experienced relation seems to involve an experienced whole, but this whole is at once supplied by feeling.'[1] Further, besides providing to relational perception its experienced *unity*, feeling is here manifest as the *directness* with which the content is, in one sense, presented. As it distinguishes, the mind certainly moves from this to that; but when it thus traverses diversities, what is there between the subject on the one side, and the 'this', the 'that', or the movement between the two, on the other? All are here directly presented, 'and if you remove this direct sense of my momentary contents and being, you bring down the whole of consciousness in one common wreck'.[2] The discursive manner of thought, we may say, involves a lateral, not a frontal displacement; and, though the details are here distinguished *from* one another, the directness with which they are all, as a whole, presented to the self remains unharmed. This partly explains why Feeling is, in Bradley's view, ultimate.

We are now on the verge of realizing how, according to Bradley, immediate experience is more fundamental than relational experience:

Feeling continually sustains—but is itself independent of—analysis and synthesis. The 'givenness' of terms; the fusion of the experienced with the experient; and the directness with which what is *understood* is owned by the self, or with which the entire experienced content is presented to it—these are the various ways in which feeling contributes vitally to the workings of thought. But itself it does not in the same way depend on any activity of thought.[3] Analysis does nothing to explain—it only presupposes—the fact of feeling; for, how can there be any analytical activity of thought at all unless the contents analysed, nay even the entire process of analysing itself, are presented directly to the self?[4] Nor can the cohesion of feeling be captured by any rational synthesis. Without the mutual distinctness of terms and relations, there *is* no thought; and so long as this distinctness persists, the self-existence

---

[1] ETR 195.
[2] *Ibid* 160.
[3] CE 654.
[4] ETR 176.

of the sides clashes with their togetherness. The manner of feeling is different from that of thought. Nor does it *claim* to be intelligible so long as it remains strictly itself.[1]

The importance of feeling should by now be clear. In so far as, besides being the starting-point of all knowledge, it is—in different ways—the recurring manner of relational experience, feeling is by Bradley believed to be 'the ground and foundation of further developments'.[2]

But, a reality which claims to be a foundation in the metaphysical sense must at least have two features. First, it must have a minimal stability of character which permits—and so predetermines, though but in broad outline—the order that is to be reared on it.[3] Secondly, it must throughout contribute vitally to those other realities which are said to be grounded in it. The mere temporal fact that it existed when they were still to emerge would not justify its claim to 'metaphysical' superiority.

Now, feeling may be said to meet both these requirements, if but incompletely. It is a visible specimen of individuality—of differences actually held as one; and, to speak in Bradley's abstract manner, the task of thought is merely to reconstitute this wholeness rationally. Nor is feeling, we have seen, at any time suspended. And, as to its being conducive to mediate developments, there could hardly be any doubt.[4] Feeling is not a solid end-point tagged to its 'mediate' developments, nor a rigid mould which merely contains them. It is experience,[5] fluid and vital; and the myriad influences to which we are always subject, from within and without, continually shuffle its content, heightening sensations, may be, into thinking articulate. The constant togetherness of feeling and relational experience, and the ease with which we oscillate between the two, are in fact our daily experience. As one writes, the organic sensations—providing, till before mention, a background vaguely felt—may easily become objects of clear

---

[1] CE 662.
[2] AR 407.
[3] PL 495, 16th Note.
[4] Feeling bears its further developments by 'a ceaseless lapse from itself'. AR 407.
[5] As such, feeling has all the shift and stress of sentient life (ETR 174). Only, the changes are here felt, not discriminated, as in a state of ennui characterized by continual fickleness of content.

consciousness; and the attempt to explain the point in hand may recede, and become, for the moment, a part of the felt background. Again, on coming to the ruins of what once was great, our experience may be intense, yet blurred. The diverse content of quiet, inward sadness and fancies half-astir is, for the most part, merely felt. But, though generally wan, the feeling occasionally deepens into a twinge; and the crumbling majesty of a wall or the corroded quiet of a dome may ruffle the felt vein of gloom into clear thoughts of grief.

Bradley, in fact, insists that, though it is never entirely cancelled, feeling tends continually to go beyond itself. The 'this-mine' is certainly not the only reality, though whatever is experienced by me must of necessity be (in part) immediate. All that I experience, so far as I experience it, is certainly my state; but it is not hereby proved that this experience is *merely* my state, and has no other status.[1] Feeling always involves a remoter fringe of experience which is at once 'the assertion and negation of *my* this'.[2] It is, in fact, impossible to remain for long in any specific 'this'; for, 'the whole movement of the mind implies disengagement from the mere "this" '.[3] In the very act of asserting that immediate experience is actual we (so far) transcend the region of mere feeling.

The 'this' is essentially self-transcendent. In spite of its apparent self-completeness, it is always in fact the member of a wider whole. Seemingly forlorn, the 'this' is really an accent, not a mere point; it steadies the mind athwart the flow of thought, and defines content against perspective. It is true that with every 'this', 'with each chance mixture of psychical elements, we have the feeling of one particular *datum*. We have the felt existence of a peculiar sensible whole'.[4] But, on the other hand, even dimly to feel the presence of diverse content in the 'this' necessarily implies a reference to what is beyond its visible limits; for, co-existence means existence in one time–place setting as distinguished, however vaguely, from another. The content here gains specificity by seeming to be quite removed from 'that', but 'uniqueness ... means difference, and difference ... a quality',[5] which is, in

[1] Cf. AR 224.
[2] *Ibid* 223.
[3] *Ibid* 221.
[4] *Ibid* 199.
[5] ETR 263.

Bradley's view, never quite independent. And, to turn to 'this' as experienced:

> 'We have not only its movement to expand beyond itself through continuity of content, but we have also the tendency of its internal aspects to become each a "this" against "that", and so to rupture its given unity.'[1]

Even a past 'this' is not wholly self-existent. Do not the past experiences tend continually to steal into, and to modify the self's present content? Finally, were it not in fact referred to—and included by—the wider deposit of experience which is 'myself', how could the 'this' at all appear 'mine'?

Now, it is easy to see how this emphasis on the self-transcendence of the 'this–mine' is relevant to Bradley's ultimate metaphysical purpose. Were immediate experience wholly self-existent, it would resist incorporation in the Absolute, and so cancel the latter's claim to be perfectly inclusive or individual. Bradley's view, on the other hand, is that there is nothing which could successfully decline 'union with a higher system'.[2] Thought seeks irrepressibly to comprehend things 'somehow as a whole'; and the nature of feeling, we have seen, is by no means hostile to assimilation in a more inclusive complex.

'The fact of actual fragmentariness'—or why there should be any 'This–Mines' at all—we are admittedly not able to explain. But, to be inexplicable, and to be incompatible, are not the same thing;[3] and there is, Bradley insists, no warrant at all to maintain that the 'this' is too self-existent to admit of inclusion in the Absolute.

3. FEELING AND METAPHYSICS

A clear realization of its self-transcendent character enables Bradley to adopt towards 'feeling' a carefully balanced attitude. He marks it off, on the one hand, from the *final* individuality that is the goal of metaphysics. But, on the other hand, he sees it clearly that the very self-transcendence of feeling provides visible

---
[1] PL 654.
[2] AR 206. On the other hand, Bradley openly admits that 'the visible internal self-transcendence of *every* object' cannot be verified.
[3] *Ibid* 200.

evidence—as distinguished from theoretical justification—for a principle which is of supreme importance for metaphysics.

This principle, of self-completion through self-transcendence, is to thought irresistible. The point here involved is, in Bradley's view, obvious. Thought must manage to avoid contradictions; but this, in turn, can be done only in one way—that is, by enlarging the subject (ideally) through increased internal differentiation. Consider an instance. We say: A is the cause of B. Now, A's being itself, and its being the cause of B—these are, to be sure, two distinct ideas. And both of them cannot without contradiction be ascribed to the selfsame point. So, in order that our talk about A's being a cause may be theoretically defensible, we are forced ideally to enlarge its being, and to say that it has two distinct aspects, one of which explains its self-existence, and the other, its self-transcendence—its going out of itself, as it were, to produce something else.

Now, to turn to immediate experience, Bradley is convinced that—though no contradictions, because no distinctions, are here *manifest*—we find in such experience features which entirely warrant the suggestion, from the viewpoint of thought, that the self-transcendence of feeling is due to its inherent contradictions; and that, therefore, the starting-point of his metaphysics does not in any way clash with the principle which regulates his subsequent thinking. That the content of feeling is diverse, though not distinguished, has already been brought out. Nor can we deny the actual finitude and the continual fickleness of feeling.[1] Experience is perhaps never *merely* immediate;[2] and, in so far as it differs clearly from the relational manner of a great part of our experience, feeling cannot be said to exhaust the way in which things are presented to us. Again, the mere unreflecting 'this–mine' holds us but for a moment. We either look beyond it, or explore it internally. In either case, the diverse content of feeling grows quickly distinct, and its place is (in great part) taken by the relational manner of thought.

Even generally, it seems reasonable to suggest that, so long as it lasts, feeling suffers internally from a contradiction. The point may be illustrated. Consider, for instance, the felt sense of bodily

[1] CE 658, 662–63.
[2] ETR 175.

welfare and mental ease, consequent upon taking a hot cup of tea after the day's hard work. The mental act of *traversing* diversities may, for some time, be here wholly suspended; and the psychic whole may seem to contain the subject entirely, with no conscious urge on his part to look beyond the experience. Here the 'that' of experience, or the manner of its existence, is obviously immediate; but it is easy to see that the content or the 'what' is vitally determined by—and is in this sense continuous with—a host of environmental factors, say, the situation of there being no work presently on one's hands, the homely character of surroundings, and the preceding awareness of having completed the day's work. The fact that they are not *seen* to enter into the experience, or that they seem to be merely left out by its immediacy, does not mean that they do not in fact determine it.

Bradley is convinced that the 'this-mine' is an eddy *because of* surrounding pressure, and that the wholeness of feeling is in no case absolute. To put it simply, the immediate manner of feeling only seems—but is not really able—to hold its content truly pent up. The 'that' here is not big enough to hold its 'what'; and—in so far as, from the viewpoint of thought, the attempt to ascribe diversities to an inadequately differentiated object is at once to incur contradiction—the self-transcendent character of feeling may be said to be due to its internal contradiction, the collision of its 'what' with its 'that'; unless, of course, exception is taken to our account of the way in which contradictions are (in theory) overcome.

It should now be easy to see what Bradley means by saying that the content of feeling is:

> 'necessarily determined from the outside; its external relations (however negative they may desire to remain) penetrate its essence, and so carry that beyond its being . . . the "what" of all feeling is discordant with its "that", it is appearance, and as such, it cannot be real . . . And, both from within and without, feeling is compelled to pass off into the relational consciousness.'[1]

But, it may be asked, why is it at all necessary to answer the 'why' of feeling's self-transcendence? And is our explanation really tenable?

Now, it is true that so long as we remain confined to mere feeling

[1] AR 407.

there are no contradictions, in so far as diversities are here neither distinguished nor *ascribed* to any one point; and that consequently there is, at this stage, no need of the explanation outlined above. But, the self-completeness of feeling, we have seen, is in every case short-lived; and, it may be of some help to us in our search for a *perfected* individuality if we forearm ourselves with a knowledge of the factors which make the available cases of wholeness imperfect and fickle. Again, in so far as we do not remain confined to feeling for long—and are in fact forced to take to the relational way of thought—we must (in metaphysics) examine the claims of feeling, as of everything else, to be finally real. It is then—that is, 'when we have taken the way of ideas and ask for truth'[1]—that we are compelled to think in the manner indicated above, attributing the self-transcendent character of feeling to the contradiction which infects it internally. As to doubts regarding the correctness of our explanation, the (negative) answer may simply be that it is perhaps difficult to *prove* that it is wrong. What thought wants basically is to avoid contradictions; and, therefore, the self-transcendence which is to it most readily acceptable is that which is said to result from an attempt to overcome contradictions. If it still be contended that feeling is not actually infected with any contradiction, we may appeal to the following insistence of Bradley which seems grounded in fact:

> 'But, passing . . . to Feeling, we can verify there at once the principle of discord and development in its essence. The sides of content and existence already strive to diverge. And hence feeling changes not merely through outer force but through internal defect.'[2]

4. MEETING CRITICISMS

Here, however, we must face a question. Is it at all proper to speak of feeling, *rather than of a conscious subject*, as striving to get rid of a defect through the process of self-transcendence?

The question may be answered by considering the following protest of Ward to Bradley's view that the 'blind uneasiness' of feeling insists 'tacitly on visible satisfaction':[3]

[1] CE 660.
[2] AR 413.
[3] ETR 161.

'How such a blind and blurred whole could "insist" even tacitly on visible satisfaction, it would be hard to say; but that an experient made uneasy by its situation should strive for a satisfactory alteration of it seems plain enough.'[1]

By Bradley, the charge would (in part) be met thus:

Are we to believe that in every 'uneasy' situation the subject *strives* for 'a satisfactory alteration'? The answer is both 'yes' and 'no'; 'yes', if by the 'subject' we here mean a mere bearer of the striving, and 'no', if by it we mean the *self-conscious agent* of the effort. Surely, not all our strivings are self-conscious. There are moments of vague uneasiness when we do not know what to do, and when, far from striving consciously towards an end, we appear merely to serve as channels for an impulse working itself out. In such cases our experience is too amorphous—and the self a bit too fused with what it experiences—to permit the clear realization that *we* are striving for a '*satisfactory* alteration of the situation'. There is no warrant for supposing that in *all* experience the subject and the object stand opposed to each other.

(i) We may now turn to consider, at some length, if Bradley's conception of Feeling is theoretically tenable. Is it really the basic element in our experience? Russell, as we know, would like to answer the question negatively. His view,[2] along with some other important protests, may be formulated as follows:

(a) What is fundamental in our experience—fundamental in the sense of being wholly empirical and beyond our 'thought or opinion about' it—is atomic fact, that is, a thing having a quality, or things having a certain relation, such as is expressed by the proposition: 'This is before that.' Russell insists that atomic fact 'is never simple, but always has two or more constituents'.[3] One kind of 'atomic' or 'ultimate' fact is, in his view, provided by asymmetrical relations.

(b) Bradley is himself aware of a consideration which could be appealed to with a view to arguing that such relations are more

---

[1] Ward's *Mind* article, 'Bradley's Doctrine of Experience,' *op. cit.* 22.
[2] Russell does not explicitly criticize Bradley's view of Feeling, not even 'as an actual error'. (CE 656). But his own view of 'atomic fact' as fundamental is so different from Bradley's conception of Feeling that it may be used as a criticism of the latter.
[3] Russell, *Our Knowledge of the External World*, 60–63.

fundamental than feeling. Upon his own view, feeling is *subject to* change; and, in so far as change is an asymmetrical relation,[1] should not such relations be regarded as being, in the main, more basic than feeling?

(c) Apart from 'atomic facts', there is, in Russell's view, no mental fact which cannot be 'analysed in the sense of being shown to be a relational complex'.[2] The alleged unanalysability of feeling is, therefore, but spurious. Now, Bradley's reply would here run thus:

'Atomic facts' are said to have an inner diversity. But, generally, we cannot speak of a diversity without distinguishing; and actively to distinguish is admittedly an operation of thought. So the 'atomic facts' cannot be said to be 'ultimate' in the sense of being beyond thought. This is specially true of an asymmetrical *relation*. In the perception of a relation, contradiction is avoided by holding diversities 'apart'. That is, they are duly distinguished through the comparative activity of *thought*. If it be said that the diversity of an 'atomic fact', though experienced, is not actively distinguished, we at once come to admit feeling as the non-relational experience of diversity, and, what is more, feeling becomes a condition of, and so superior to 'atomic fact' which, in turn, ceases to be ultimate. Russell, of course, would here dissent emphatically. But, if we agree with him in ignoring the reality of feeling, it becomes impossible to speak of an experienced diversity which is quite beyond thought. This is precisely the point in Bradley's protest against Russell's failure to perceive that that ' "the problem of Inherence"—the question, that is, of a non-relational qualification—arises even with regard to the atoms themselves'.[3]

As to change, its presence in feeling may be readily admitted, but only in a restricted sense. The change experienced in feeling 'is subordinate to the whole felt aspect of oneness';[4] it is but 'a practical collision' and a struggle of felt details, not an alteration distinctly perceived.[5]

Finally, how can we say that, leaving out 'atomic facts', every mental fact can be analysed 'in the sense of being a relational

[1] CE 671.
[2] *Ibid* 656.
[3] Cf. *Ibid* 657.
[4] *Ibid* 671.
[5] *Ibid* 659.

complex'? Take a sensation. It has a tone or strength. But, the 'that' and the 'what' are here held non-relationally. Again, 'extension and colour as they come first are not given as related'.[1] This is at least the evidence of plain fact.

(ii) The most direct and detailed criticism of Bradley's doctrine of Immediate Experience is, however, attempted by Ward, to whom we finally turn:

(1) Ward suspects that the notion of immediate experience is psychologically not quite sound,[2] and that, far from being 'an indubitable fact', it is a speculative conviction which Bradley has merely inherited from Hegel.[3]

Now, there is no doubt as to the borrowing; Bradley himself admits it.[4] But, this in itself is no argument against the soundness of the notion. One may accept a fact pointed out by others, and yet accept it *because* it is really there. Concrete instances of experience as non-relational have already been given in this chapter, but if doubts still linger as to the actuality of such experience, Bradley's own words may be cited for final reassurance:

> 'To take an ordinary sense-perception—say, for instance, that of a green leaf—as a unity which consists in one or more relations is to me to go counter to the plainest fact. And the same result to my mind is obvious when we look at some experience, which is aesthetic or consider again any, no matter what, emotion.'[5]

True, it is difficult *for thought* to see how differences could be merely felt, and not united by relations. But, the evidence in favour of Bradley is here overwhelming. Thus, even a partially successful attempt to recall the memory of emotional experiences reveals the impropriety of saying that diversity is in such cases experienced as (merely) conjoined by relations. Again, the realm of aesthetic creation provides us with visible instances of how distinctions can be deliberately so tempered as to become more

---

[1] *Ibid* 631.
[2] Ward's *Mind* article, 'Bradley's Doctrine of Experience', *op. cit.* 15.
[3] *Ibid* 29.
[4] What, however, is actually borrowed is perhaps not the notion of feeling as such, but the idea 'that this beginning is not the whole of our actual world, and cannot possibly be the end'. ETR 157, footnote.
[5] CE 633.

effective in a felt effect. Notes in music may appear as a mere succession of detached units, or they may be breathed out daintily as a continuity which they directly enrich, yet not severally. Surely, not all differences are equally full-blown; and merely or cleverly to suggest is not the same as fully to mark. A note may be merely suggested, *not marked*, as the fading of a luminous, musical flow.

Finally, immediate experience is not only a fact, but seems demanded by theory. For if we deny that sensations can be experienced directly, are we not forced to accept the untenable alternative that coenesthesia is throughout an object?[1]

(2) Ward's next objection may be put thus: Immediate Experience, we may admit, is given, 'but "given" by what and to what?'[2]

Now, does not the very putting of this question summarily efface the difference, so essential for theory, between the 'given', as the not-yet-acted-upon, and the intellectually 'constructed'? To keep close to the given, so far as it is possible in idea, we have to avoid, rather than resort to theoretical construction. If it be contended, as Ward actually does,[3] that to be 'given' is more than merely to be, and that Bradley should not speak of feeling as 'given' after referring to it as something that merely is,[4] our answer would be that Bradley uses the terms: 'isness' 'being' and 'given' in the same sense—that is, to stand for that original level of experience where distinctions and relations have not yet emerged.[5]

(3) But admitting that immediate experience is a fact, the question arises:[6] can we *say* that it is immediate? Does not the mention at once cancel the immediacy of feeling? Can one at all observe what he feels without destroying its felt character?

Our answer, following Bradley, is here as follows:

When we *speak* of immediate experience, it only ceases to be *merely* immediate,[7] without losing this character altogether. It is

---

[1] ETR 194.
[2] Ward's *Mind* article, 'Bradley's Doctrine of Experience', *op. cit.* 29.
[3] *Ibid* 14, footnote.
[4] *Ibid* 29.
[5] As to this use of 'being', see AR 215.
[6] Here, for some time, we turn away from Ward.
[7] Even generally, we have seen, Bradley is not sure if experience can be merely immediate.

true that in describing an actual emotion we objectify it at once. It is now used as a criterion to see if the description is true. Yet, throughout this process, the experience as felt may also continue—as a general, yet positive awareness of diversity held as one.[1] A simple instance should here serve. The fused character of felt embarrassment may persist even where it is in part self-conscious. Objectification can never cancel—for it always presupposes—the felt background of the self. 'In order to have an object at all, you must have a felt self before which the object comes.'[2] The whole of the felt self can never be turned into an object. Nor is experienced content always in fact objectified. Emotion as experienced is, we have seen, non-relational. And yet awareness is here undoubtedly present; or else, how could we, in the future, judge the success or failure of our attempt to recall this experience?

Here, in passing, a brief mention may be made of another difficulty, closely allied to the one we have just now considered. Bradley himself admits that 'a relation exists only between terms, and those terms, to be known as such, must be objects'.[3] But if this is so, is not, Ward wonders,[4] a contradiction at once committed in speaking of a *relation* between feeling and the relational developments it is said to support?

Now, it seems to us that material for a vindication of Bradley's conception of feeling against this objection is provided by the following remarks of his:

'... Immediate experience taken as the term of a relation, becomes *so far* a *partial* object and ceases so far to keep its nature as a felt totality.'[5]

'The relation (*so to express ourselves*) of immediate experience ... to these contents which transcend it, must be taken simply as a fact.'[6]

Bradley's meaning is here clear:

First, as we have already seen, feeling is never entirely cancelled

[1] Cf. 'What I feel, that surely I may still feel, though I also and at the same time make it into an object before me.' ETR 166.
[2] *Ibid.* Also footnote.
[3] *Ibid* 176.
[4] Ward's *Mind* article, 'Bradley's Doctrine of Experience', *op. cit.* 17–18.
[5] ETR 176–77. Our italics.
[6] *Ibid* 177. Our italics.

by relational experience; and when we speak of its relation to 'mediate developments', it is only 'so far' that it becomes a 'partial object', 'and ceases *so far* to keep its nature as a felt totality'. Secondly, while speaking of a relation between feeling and its mediate developments, we should never forget that the fact referred to (or the relation) is really a felt togetherness; that we are only *expressing* it as a relation; and, finally, that our description is as such untrue to the intended fact.[1]

Finally, we may add, if there is a fact which is necessarily (in part) changed by the very acknowledgement of it, such a minimal inconsistency is for us inescapable; for, in metaphysics where our aim is to consider all the main forms of experience, a mention of feeling—and of its involvement with relational experience—cannot obviously be avoided.

(4) Exception may, however, be taken to the alleged *diversity* of feeling's content, if not to its non-relational manner. Is the content of feeling itself diverse, or is it that diversity is merely attributed to, or projected into feeling when we attend to it?

Bradley's reply to this is that, in so far as attention takes time to be effective, the diversity that is revealed must have been there prior to—and so cannot be said to have been created by—the act of attention. Attention to a finger which has been bitten by an insect certainly makes us conscious of sensations of pain not noticed earlier; and the notice itself is a felt change. But, attention does not *create* the pain; or else, just a look at another (whole) finger should make it tingle similarly: 'My attention always gives me a felt change, but it will not give me these other special feelings, which therefore, I infer, have come to me otherwise.'[2]

(5) But, why can't we begin with consciousness rather than with feeling? How is feeling more fundamental than consciousness?

Now, if but incompletely, Bradley's answer to these questions has already been outlined. According to him, the subject–object distinction is only a later differentiation of immediate experience. Further argument as to the primacy of feeling may, in his view, be attempted thus:

What is consciousness? Does it stand for an object presented to

[1] CE 662–63.
[2] ETR 164.

the subject *thought of*, or for an object (or objects) presented to a *felt* subject? Evidently, the latter; for, the subject as thought of would be an object. Or, without the self as its felt ground, consciousness simply cannot be. Feeling is, therefore, the more basic of the two.

Bradley's other arguments with regard to the possibility of a felt awareness of the self and its superiority to consciousness assume the truth of his general view of terms and relations. The being of a term is not *exhausted* by its participation in a relation.[1] The subject, which is a term in the relation called consciousness, should therefore also be allowed to be (relatively) other than what it is *in* this relation. In other words, we may agree that it can exist non-relationally, or as felt.

Actual consciousness is in fact never a mere correlation of subject and object. The unitary and direct way in which content is here experienced is, we have seen, always the contribution of feeling. But, though the immediacy of feeling is to be distinguished from the distinctly relational character of consciousness, the distinction should not be heightened into an absolute contrast. Feeling is no inmate of the subliminal regions of the self, but is itself positive awareness.[2]

(6) The ultimacy of feeling may, however, be questioned in one other way. Is it tenable to assume that experience must always involve feeling as Bradley understands it? Or, to put it differently, how does immediate experience include all its subsequent developments?

Bradley's answer to these questions is contained in a passage which may be quoted in full, specially because Ward objects to it in detail:

'Immediate experience, however much transcended, both remains and is active. It is not a stage which shows itself at the beginning and then disappears, but it remains at the bottom throughout as fundamental. And, further, remaining it contains within itself every development which *in a sense* transcends it. Nor does it merely contain all developments, but in its own way it acts to some extent as their judge. Its blind uneasiness, we

[1] *Ibid* 193.
[2] *Ibid* 172–73.

may say, insists tacitly on visible satisfaction. We have on the one hand a demand, explicit or otherwise, for an object which is complete. On the other hand the object which fails to include immediate experience in its content, is by the unrest of that experience condemned as defective. We are thus forced to the idea of an object containing the required element, and in this object we find at last theoretical satisfaction and rest.'[1]

(a) Ward's first objection to the above is this. How can immediate experience be said 'to contain within itself every development which *in a sense* transcends it'? 'Surely not: surely the fact is ... that this feeling "so far as it keeps its nature as a felt totality" cannot, strictly speaking, "contain anything which goes beyond itself".'[2]

Bradley's explanation would here run thus:

In one sense, we must admit, feeling may be easily transcended. Thus, to take a simple instance, a chance collision against something on the ground may easily turn a detail of coenesthesia—say, a feeling of soreness in the leg—into an object clearly affirmed. Here, feeling as the non-relational awareness of bodily condition has in part been clearly transcended. But then, the change in experience is itself presented directly to the self, and so feeling in the (other) sense[3] of the directness with which, at any one moment, content is as a whole presented to sentience, has not been transcended, and is very much there.

(b) Again, Ward protests:

'But there is a vital difference between an explicit and a tacit demand. A demand for "an object which is complete" can surely not be attributed to immediate experience, nor "the object which fails to include that experience in its content" be condemned by any unrest of that experience itself. No *idea* of a lacking "element" can be forced on the experient at this level, least of all the idea that the lacking element is its own experience.'[4]

[1] *Ibid* 161. Our Italics.
[2] Ward's *Mind* article, 'Bradley's Doctrine of Experience', *op. cit.* 26.
[3] Ward's objection to Bradley's use of 'in a sense' does not here seem proper; for, as already brought out, Bradley knowingly uses 'Feeling' in more senses than one.
[4] Ward's *Mind* article, 'Bradley's Doctrine of Experience', *op. cit.* 22.

Now, to us this criticism seems questionable as follows:

The 'demand, explicit or otherwise, for an object which is complete' is attributed (by Bradley) not to immediate experience, but to the desire to know. And the simple meaning is: we seek wholeness, explicitly or vaguely, as the ideal of theory. Bradley himself seems to be clearly aware of the difference between an explicit demand and a tacit one. This is precisely why he speaks, as we have seen, of the *blind* uneasiness and *tacit* insistence of immediate experience? To say that he attributes an *explicit* demand to feeling is, therefore, improper.

Our view is borne out further by a close analysis of the passage to which Ward here objects. The point at issue is as to how immediate experience contains all mediate developments and how 'in its own way it acts to some extent as their judge'. Naturally, it would help if some 'mediate development' is mentioned before it is argued how immediate experience could act as a judge with regard to it. Precisely this mention—of the theoretical ideal—is provided by the sentence: 'We have on the one hand a demand, explicit or otherwise, for an object which is complete'.

Finally, our contention is supported by a consideration of Bradley's language in the passage under review. 'On the one hand' and 'on the other hand' envisage a contrast; which is, in our view, not fully brought out unless we regard the 'demand, explicit or otherwise, for an object which is complete' *as a demand of thought*.

We would, therefore, like to interpret (a part of) the passage in question thus. Theoretically, we want a whole of experience which includes everything harmoniously or non-relationally.[1] Immediate experience itself insists on being included—we shall presently see how—in a whole of understanding, and on providing a non-relational consummation to this totality. There is thus complete agreement between the implicit direction of feeling and the explicit ideal of thought. Our desire to find 'theoretical satisfaction and rest' in an object which holds diversities non-relationally as one is, so to speak, approved even by feeling.

We must, however, explain how feeling can 'insist tacitly' 'for an object which is complete', and in which it itself is included;

---

[1] Why a perfect harmony must (in Bradley's view) be non-relational, or rather supra-relational, will be brought out in the chapters that follow.

and how an object which does not contain immediate experience is 'condemned as defective' by the very unrest of this experience.

Consider a common situation. A man sets out to understand something. Now, his ideal contact with the object is, at the outset, an orientation pressing for its own release. It is, in part, merely felt—inarticulate, and *in this sense* vague. But, it presses and is intensely experienced; and, though not (wholly) reducible to any deliberate endeavour, it throughout sustains and impels the subject's explicit effort to understand. When this attempt bears fruit, or when he actually comes to understand, if but incompletely, the attempt to understand is naturally suspended, may be only for a moment; and content is now merely owned directly or non-relationally by the self. Immediate experience, which worked earlier as a felt striving after clear awareness, is now manifest as the 'atonceness' with which the content is appropriated by the self. This moment, experienced as 'I see', is non-relational: it includes or itself is feeling. And unless this is secured—that is, unless the man actually succeeds in 'knowing', however imperfectly —his conscious efforts in the direction are likely to continue, and this because of the uneasy stress of the keenly 'felt' tension.

This is what we regard as Bradley's real meaning when he says: 'The object which fails to include immediate experience in its content, is by the unrest of that experience condemned as defective'. So long as the 'uneasiness' continues, it is as such only a felt symptom, not an explicit affirmation, of the incompleteness of our knowledge. If only 'to some extent', feeling acts as a judge of the mediate developments, not explicitly, but 'in its own way', that is, as a felt protest against what is incomplete. The felt striving—or immediate experience as the fusion of agent and impulsion— continues until, in the whole of understanding which later supervenes, the tension is let go, insight is secured, and immediate experience gets included as the directness of manner with which the content is accepted by the self as its own. True, 'no idea of a lacking "element" can be forced on the experient' at the level of immediate experience, but no such idea is here required; for, the self-transcendence of feeling is no *intellectual* striving. To Bradley, it is rather a symptom of reality's pre-cognitive attempt to shake off the finiteness with which it is, as appearance, everywhere beset.

(7) How feeling provides a clue to the nature of the Absolute is another controversial point in Bradley's doctrine of immediate experience. His meaning here is, however, simple. Being itself a concrete instance of wholeness, feeling lends some point to our speculative affirmation as to the reality of the Absolute as a perfect individuality:[1]

> 'From such an experience of unity below relations we can rise to the idea of a superior unity above them. Thus we can attach a full and positive meaning to the statement that Reality is one.'[2]

Ward's objection to the above is this:

> 'An experience which merely *is* a unity and below relations, is not an experience *of* unity at all, and could not therefore, of itself, give rise to the idea of a *superior* unity. Unity of experience is one thing, experience of unity is quite another. The idea of unity implies thought.'[3]

Does not Bradley himself say: 'This idea of unity (is) itself the result of analysis?'[4]

Now, the criticism can, by Bradley, be met as follows:

Two distinct ideas are here involved. There *is* an experience of unity below relations; and, using it as a clue, '*we* can rise to the idea of a superior unity above them'. Bradley nowhere expresses the view that immediate experience *itself* leads us to the idea of the Absolute,[5] and so Ward's protest that feeling cannot 'of itself give rise to the idea of a superior unity' loses all point. Feeling is certainly taken into account, first, as an actual, though imperfect, specimen of individuality; and, secondly, as a visible illustration of the necessary self-transcendence of whatever is imperfectly inclusive—a fact which is, to thought, a principle in so far as it is

---

[1] AR 470.
[2] *Ibid* 462.
[3] Ward's *Mind* article, 'Bradley's Doctrine of Experience', *op. cit.* 14, also footnote.
[4] AR 461.
[5] It is *we* who start 'from the diversity in unity . . . given in feeling', and again *we* who reach the idea of the Absolute, by employing a principle which is quite acceptable to thought—self-completion through self-transcendence. *Ibid* 494.

the only way in which contradictions can be (ideally) overcome, and, again, in so far as it is borne out everywhere by the different regions of our experience.[1] But that which recognizes the fact of feeling as being the deliverer of a principle and as a visible pointer to the possibility of what we—at least in theory—seek is *thought*. However various be the evidence which is used during the process, in metaphysics it is, in the main, thought which fixes the ideal and regulates our ascent towards it.

Again, Ward is right in saying that feeling is 'not an experience *of* unity' if the phrase is taken to mean an experience of something which is held up distinctly as an object before the mind. But, when we deny that feeling is an experience *of* unity—in the sense just mentioned—we should at the same time remember that it *is unified experience*, 'unified' in the sense of being fused or non-relational; and 'experience', because it *is* a state of awareness, though not relational. A felt cohesion of content is something that we all often experience; and if we at all agree to speak of it, how shall we proceed except by saying that it is 'unity of experience', it being implicit admittedly that it is not, in the questionable sense, an experience *of* unity? The word 'unity', as we commonly understand it, is clearly not appropriate to the (allegedly) non-relational character of feeling. It is perhaps because of a realization of this difficulty that Bradley generally speaks of immediate experience as a 'cohesion' or as 'fused'. But even the word 'unity' can perhaps be used to describe a felt togetherness provided we remember that in this case it is being used differently from the way we use it intellectually. The real point to be noted, however, is that in immediate experience, as Bradley understands it, there is only a felt unity, not an *idea* of unity. The *idea* of unity may imply analysis, but a felt unity does not do so. When we *speak* of such a unity, some analytical activity of thought does necessarily creep in; but it is easy to prevent this activity from distorting our view of the fact, because this fact is always in some form there, and can therefore be readily appealed to.

Finally, in drawing the fine distinction that 'unity of experience' is not an 'experience of unity', why should Ward forget, or fail to emphasize, that a unity of experience is a unity not of anything, but *of experience*? Perhaps the delight of subtlety secured by

[1] This aspect of Bradley's argument will be discussed later.

IMMEDIATE EXPERIENCE

transposing the words in question makes him blink their intrinsic significance. For, if it be remembered that feeling is a unity *of experience*, which everywhere is visibly fluid and self-transcendent, it becomes easy for us to see how it tends to be included in bigger wholes, and to enlarge its own orbit, so that, using feeling as a clue, 'we' *as thinkers* can certainly 'rise to the *idea* of a superior unity'—of an immediate experience which is self-existent, because all-inclusive and all-harmonizing.[1]

(8) Ward complains of another inconsistency in Bradley's doctrine of immediate experience. How can Bradley regard feeling and self as each the fundamental fact upon which his view is based, specially when he dismisses the soul or Ego (metaphysically) as a mere mass of confusion?[2]

Now, it is obvious that the protest is directed against the self in particular. Feeling and self cannot both be regarded as being central to metaphysics; for, whereas the self is, by Bradley, explicitly 'dismissed', feeling is not. Here the following questions have to be met:

(a) What does Bradley really mean by 'dismissing' the self?
(b) In what precise sense, if at all, can metaphysics yet be based on the self?

Now, to turn first to Bradley's (alleged) 'dismissal' of 'self', we have seen already that what it in fact means is the denial not of the very existence of the self, but only of its claim to *ultimate* metaphysical reality.

The second question may be answered thus. Metaphysics is an attempt to *understand* what *is*. It is grounded in both theory and fact. The criterion of understanding is provided by theory. Thought alone can decide as to what *principle* may be used in distinguishing the real from the unreal. But the object of understanding—or what is to be understood[3]—is the entire given reality. Now, we can easily be true to both. There is nothing unnatural or absurd about our attempt to understand what-is systematically. Difficulties arise only when thought begins to affirm the *non-existence* of things merely because of their failure to

---

[1] The fact of feeling is, however, only one of the several considerations which enable Bradley to rise up to the idea of the Absolute.
[2] Ward's *Mind* article, 'Bradley's Doctrine of Experience', *op. cit.* 34.
[3] 'Understood', in Bradley's way.

conform to *ideal* consistency; or when fact is allowed—on the strength of its mere actuality—to suppress the demands of understanding. But, as for Bradley, in maintaining that the self is (in a sense) the basis of metaphysics, he does not commit himself to any one of these extreme alternatives. The self is a 'basis' in so far as, by virtue of being implicit in immediate experience, it is the most persistent of facts;[1] and in so far as, in metaphysics, every fact must (in general) be considered. It is important in the sense of being the point *where* we start. According to Bradley, we have seen, all knowledge begins from some immediate presentation to the self; or, to speak strictly, from the self as *involved in* feeling which is never wholly cancelled. But, a fundamental fact is not, merely as such, a fundamental principle for theory;[2] and if by the 'basis' of metaphysics is meant the criterion of metaphysical worth, it is emphatically not supplied by the self as commonly understood. To start from the self or feeling as a *fact* is not the same as to start with it as in itself an accepted *criterion* of metaphysical worth. The latter is provided by the principle of contradiction.

(9) Here, however, another objection may be raised. What is the warrant for preferring 'feeling' to self-consciousness as the starting-point of our metaphysical enquiry? This indeed is an important protest of Ward:

'... while we keep within our domain, we begin in the middle of it. In other words, we start working continuously from our own self-consciousness, first psychologically backwards, and then, epistemologically or rather speculatively, forwards. We 'depotentiate' our experience in our attempt to reach the lower limit, and we idealise it in straining to conceive the higher. Self-consciousness being our "locus standi" we are led to regard the duality of subject and object as the essential characteristic of experience. It follows then that we cannot recognize either Bradley's immediate experience or his absolute Experience as actual at all,'[3]

[1] As a fact, the self is, in Bradley's view, probably 'the highest thing that we *have*'. AR 497. Our italics.
[2] Cf. 'A foundation used at the beginning does not ... mean something fundamental at the end.' ETR 211.
[3] Ward's, *Mind* article 'Bradley's Doctrine of Experience', *op. cit.* 31.

IMMEDIATE EXPERIENCE

But, our protest is here ready. *All* our experience is not in truth self-conscious. This has already been argued at fair length. And, to turn to another idea in the passage under review, how are we to understand the 'lower' and the 'higher' limits if not as being *below* and above the relational form which characterizes consciousness?

(10) But if, as is by now obvious, Bradley is utterly convinced of the fundamental importance of immediate experience, why should he think it necessary to pass on from feeling to the idea of the Absolute? And can he really make the transition? Does not the 'this' represent a solid datum which refuses to be swamped in the Absolute?

Here, it seems possible to offer the following defence on behalf of Bradley:

First, feeling is only the starting-point, not the goal, of his metaphysical endeavour. Secondly, in arriving at the idea of the Absolute, we do not exclude the 'this'; rather, it is here included and made good. The ultimate Reality as affirmed by thought is, in Bradley's view, an Experience which is perfectly individual, and, what is more, direct and non-relational.[1] Finally, as has already been brought out, feeling, as we find it, tends continually to transcend itself; and to hold that it defies inclusion in a wider whole is to run counter to the testimony of plain fact.

We may end this chapter by indicating how, in a metaphysics such as Bradley's, it is both necessary and helpful to attend to the fact of feeling:

(a) Generalities of manner are, here, our primary concern. Feeling is one important way in which experience comes to us: so metaphysics cannot ignore it. How can a study which seeks to be comprehensive afford to neglect the original manner of the given?

(b) With all his emphasis on the supreme importance of thinking in metaphysics, Bradley wants us to remember that to think is necessarily to abstract some content from given reality, and that an abstraction is never as such the given reality. Now, it becomes easy to see this deficiency of thought if we remember the fact of immediate experience. Visibly, feeling is experience as not yet sundered.[2]

[1] AR 160–61.
[2] Cf. ETR 200.

(c) Again, the aim of metaphysical thinking, according to Bradley, is to realize the perfect identity of existence and character. Individuality may therefore be said to be the essential mark of what is metaphysically real. Now, in feeling, diverse content is in fact held as one, however precariously. Bradley therefore insists that, if a harmony of being and quality be our criterion, feeling should be regarded as a truer revealer of reality than a relational complex which is, as we shall see later, incurably self-discrepant.[1] It may, of course, be contended that in such a complex the different elements are in fact together, and that, if we only keep to this fact, there *is* no clash. But, and this is what Bradley emphasizes, in refusing to notice the distinctness of terms and relations we only abdicate the true manner of thought, which works by distinguishing, and lapse surreptitiously into the manner of mere feeling. In fact, it is attention to feeling which gives us the important metaphysical clue that where individuality is actually found, the manner of experience is not relational.

(d) What is more, in so far as it is self-transcendent, feeling may be said to prescribe to thought its characteristic task, though not against the latter's will. Differences break away continually from immediate experience. Thought must notice them; and—in so far as they are in feeling actually held as one, and, again, in so far as it itself aims at individuality—thought must reflect as to *how* differences could at all be held as one. This is precisely what Bradley seeks to do in his treatment of the relational form.[2]

(e) Lastly, the attempt to answer the 'why' of feeling's self-transcendence brings out some evidence to support what is (to thought) a truth that the movement is due to internal contradictions, which, in turn, are consequent upon imperfect inclusiveness. From this it seems but a step to expect that, as is allegedly the case with the Absolute of Bradley, a final individuality will not only be non-relational, but perfectly inclusive.

But, in the metaphysics of Bradley which is committed to

---

[1] Bradley insists that in immediate experience, diversities are merely felt, and that, instead of being opposed to the unity of experience, they here conduce to it unreservedly.

[2] Cf. The relational form 'is an attempt to unite differences which have broken out of the felt totality. Differences forced together by an underlying identity, and a compromise between the plurality and the unity—this is the essence of relation'. AR 159.

heed the demands of thought, mere expectations are of no great consequence. And we turn to the next chapter with the intention of arguing in his manner how thought's relational form is in essence self-contradictory; how it cannot therefore claim to be finally real; and how, above all, the very dissatisfaction of thought with the way it must work is an implicit, but powerful emphasis on the ideal of a Whole which includes both feeling and relational content in a way that is the ideal of theory—that is, non-relationally and therefore harmoniously.

IV

THE RELATIONAL FORM

The metaphysics of Bradley is an attempt to know reality as against appearance. Why, in spite of its admitted importance, feeling cannot be regarded as being ultimately real has already been brought out; and so, in the present chapter, we direct our attention to the relational form.

Two questions deserve notice at the very outset. What do we mean by the relational form? And, what is its place in Bradley's general scheme? Now, as already hinted in our first essay, when Bradley speaks of the relational *form* he refers not merely to qualities and relations, but to thought's *movement* through them. This is borne out by the consideration that whereas in the chapter on 'Relation and Quality' (in AR) he emphasizes only the unintelligibility of the two—whether taken along with, or apart from each other—in his treatment of the relational form in CE he notices the additional facts that a passage, both ways, is involved in all relations, and that highly reflective thinking is perhaps not possible without the spatial schema of 'between', 'apart' and 'together'.[1]

The general relevance of this chapter to Bradley's metaphysics may be brought out thus. His purpose all along is to *understand*; for, it is only by trying to understand things that we can come to know if they are really intelligible, and so ultimately real. But, what is it to understand? The question is obviously pivotal; and, by way of reinforcing what has already been said about it in the first chapter, the following general remarks may here be made:

(a) In so far as we understand the given only by loosening the felt diversities into clear terms and by positing relations between them, all explanation is, in Bradley's view, mediate; and, in so far as the content is distinguished into terms by thought, and not displaced in actuality, the bond that connects them is also ideally affirmed. The given togetherness of diversities is but a brute fact. It is, we have seen, only by resorting to ideal abstraction and

[1] AR 18–19; CE 644.

synthesis that we begin to understand what is otherwise merely presented.

(b) Again, the entire movement of understanding, though clearly ideal, is no mere imagining. It is from *given* diversities that it takes off. Nor is the ideal *linkage* involved in distinction wholly without its practical warrant. Is it not a fact that qualities never come to us singly?[1] Bradley, of course, does not posit a one–one correspondence between the details of thinking and those of given reality. Understanding is no mere mirroring of the given. A detail of fact does not become *theoretically* compelling merely by being shifted from the region of immediate experience to that of explicit awareness. The given is to become—or to appear—self-consistent before it can be accepted (as valid) by thought. It is to this end that the relational form conduces, however imperfectly. It prevents immediate contradiction—and makes for intelligibility —by holding diversities clearly apart. Yet, we repeat, the entire movement of thought would be clearly untrue to—because unwarranted by—given reality, were not the latter itself an actual togetherness of diversities. In brief, Bradley's view is that understanding neither copies nor merely ignores the character of given reality. It is an attempt to see if what is given is intelligible; and the movement towards—or away from—actuality is here determined not by caprice, but entirely by the demand for self-consistent knowing.

(c) Finally, Bradley is convinced that to understand is never merely to follow a succession of detached events. Thought's passage through diversities is no purposeless flitting. It is governed essentially by the desire to see everyone of them more truly itself as against the others, the relations affirmed between them being internal or implied in their very specificity. The transition is necessitated, and so justified, by the realization that in a given complex, say A–B, A, when we seek to understand it, points naturally to B as its complement. In other words, understanding implies internality of relations, or the mutual necessitation of the parts of a complex which therewith comes to appear as a system.

This necessity, we may add, is no shadowy form superimposed ready-made by thought on facts. It is the finding of an ideal

---

[1] 'What is more natural than for qualities always to have come to us in some conjunction, and never alone?' AR 23.

operation on the concrete nature of things. The ideal of theory, as Bradley regards it, is met neither by a collocation of mere abstractions, nor by any sensible linkage of events, but only by a positive and self-consistent—though general and abstract—understanding of the whole reality. It is, as Blanshard puts it, the concrete necessity of a system. It is the mutual determination of the whole and its parts taken in all their richness and specificity of content—and not any abstract thread running in and through them—which ultimately explains why any two diversities are in fact together. The doctrines of identity in difference and the concrete universal are, for Bradley, therefore essential.

To conclude, the manner of thought is necessarily relational. Its aim, on the other hand, is at perfected individuality. But, does its way of working really conduce to its goal? This is the question which we now seek to answer along the following main lines of enquiry:

(i) The dialectics of qualities and relations.
(ii) The relational form in general: its 'unreality' or its self-transcendent and self-inconsistent character.
(iii) The theory of the essential internality of relations.

Following Bradley, our conclusion will be that, though it is practically necessary and even theoretically an essential step in our ascent to the idea of the Absolute, the relational form is not ultimately real, because it cannot be understood self-consistently.

Notice has, however, to be taken of the powerful criticisms to which Bradley's view has been subjected by various thinkers. Therefore, in this chapter, an attempt has been made to formulate and to examine the following:

(1) Russell's opposition to the doctrine of the 'unreality' of relations.
(2) Cook Wilson's criticism of Bradley's contention that our attempt to understand how a relation stands to its terms forces us into an infinite regress, and that the relational form is therefore unreal—because unintelligible.
(3) The arguments advanced by Schlick to disprove the 'internality' of causation.

This, then, is an outline of our task in this chapter. Before, however, we begin essaying it, it seems essential to sound a note of warning. The doctrine which is the logical—if not the sufficient—pre-condition of Bradley's idea of the Absolute does not say that 'internality' of relations is the final truth, but that all relations, whether internal or external, are self-transcendent, because self-contradictory. Bradley criticizes the entire relational form as such, and not merely relations which are (alleged to be) wholly extrinsic. This is sometimes forgotten in the heat of the controversy as to whether relations are internal or external. Why Bradley yet *prefers* the doctrine of the essential internality of all relations to the view that at least some of them can be merely external will become clear in the course of our present enquiry.

1. DIALECTIC OF QUALITIES AND RELATIONS

We may now turn to Bradley's dialectic of Qualities and Relations. Except in feeling, every object of our experience comes to us as a relatedness of qualities. If this essential form of our experience is itself proved to be self-contradictory, it would be easy to see, with Bradley, that phenomena, though undeniably actual, are none of them ultimately real.[1] This indeed is why he says:

> 'The reader who has followed ... the principle of this chapter ... will have seen that our experience, where relational, is not true; and he will have condemned, almost without a hearing, the great mass of phenomena.'[2]

We propose to argue that the main conclusion of Bradley's dialectic of qualities and relations—that is, the view that the relational form, being self-inconsistent and self-transcendent, is not in the end true—is tenable. This will obviate the necessity of discussing his examination of individual phenomena.[3]

Now, the main argument of Bradley in his treatment of quality and relation is, in general, this. When we try to understand them, each demands the other irrepressibly; and yet, even when considered together, they remain unintelligible. It may therefore be

[1] 'Real', we repeat, in the sense of being finally acceptable to thought.
[2] AR 29.
[3] Bradley's treatment of individual phenomena has therefore not been dealt with by us.

said that 'the very essence of these ideas is infected and contradicts itself'.[1]

Let us begin from the side of quality. What is a quality? In Bradley's view, two answers are possible. First, anything that is somewhat at all may be said to be or to have a quality. Thus understood, 'quality' means an aspect merely felt. Secondly, in what Bradley calls its 'special' or proper meaning, 'quality' may be said to stand for a diversity developed by analysing a whole into terms and relations.

Now, in neither sense can quality be said to exist apart from a whole. A felt aspect is never given in isolation. And, on the relational level, a quality is what it is because it is (also) marked off from others. This leads us to the following considerations:

(a) Quality is *unthinkable* without relation. In support of this thesis, Bradley points (also) to what he regards as the *fact* of immediate experience. In 'mere unbroken feeling' we only have felt aspects, no qualities in the 'proper' sense and so no relations. But, his primary appeal is to the *unthinkability* of quality without relation. A quality is essentially something distinct—from something else. In other words, we perceive it and maintain it as distinct by referring to some other quality, or through comparison, which is a relational activity of thought. That which seems distinct must necessarily be (in part) the result of an act of distinction. It may be contended that this 'distinguishing' is merely our activity,[2] and that, considered in itself as a part of the given reality, the quality remains different even when relations, incidental to the perception of distinction, have been removed. Bradley's answer here would be that the objection takes its stand on an impossibility. To hold that the ideal process involved is merely *our* activity, and that the quality remains different even *apart* from this activity is to make the impossible hypothesis that we can *know* a quality as different *without* distinguishing it. In point of fact, the product in this case cannot be disentangled from the process. We have no way of getting at the individual nature of a quality without distinguishing it; and the burden of proof lies wholly on the man who asserts that a quality can be different even without its being *distinguished* from others. A quality, duly marked off from an aspect merely

[1] AR 21.
[2] *Ibid* 22-23.

felt, is always the result of distinction. True, we may quietly ignore the process while considering the product. But, does not the product itself 'bear internally the character of the process'? A quality, in fact, appears distinct from others. Its very existence is relational. This is why qualities always 'come to us in some conjunction and never alone'. One way of denying the relational character of a quality is to say that the relations in which it may in fact be found do not really touch its inner nature. But then, the distinction of 'inner' and 'outer' is itself a result of the relational activity of thought, and the quality, thus diversified, is clearly relational.

So far we have been considering how a singular quality implies relation. If we now attend to 'qualities', or to the fact of diversity, the same conclusion will be seen to emerge. Diversity without relation seems a mere word without meaning. Consider an instance. As qualities, A and B are different. Now, where does this difference lie? If it lies (in any measure) outside of them, the two become related at once by what lies *between* them. Thus, to take an instance of positional difference lying (in the main) outside of the terms, if one thing is by us placed a foot behind another, they are related at once by the distance which separates them, and also to the onlooker who may be sitting between the two. Separateness (as judged) implies separation, which is a relational process.[1]

Even where the difference falls largely *within* the terms, diversity seems necessarily to involve some relations. This can be argued thus. Suppose, of the two terms that we consider one is a man, and the other, a stone. Adopting the idiom of everyday parlance, we may say that the two differ not merely because they are compared from the outside, but primarily because they are different from inside, or different intrinsically.[2] But, if a thing is distinctive from inside, does it not mean that it not merely is (anything) but is (also) different from other things? It comes to appear as the relatedness of two aspects, its own being and its otherness.

Here one might object that it is improper to *break up* the given thing into two, because the *fact* of a distinctive thing is one and continuous. Bradley's reply to this would be that we are not

---

[1] *Ibid* 23–24.
[2] The difference is, however, not confined wholly to the 'insides' of the terms; or else, they would not differ *from* each other.

breaking up, but only distinguishing the two aspects. And distinguish we must, if we at all care to *understand* the given fact of a distinct thing. Is it possible to ascribe to this fact any simpler meaning than that the thing in question has a nature which at once distinguishes it from the other things? Bradley does not suggest that the thing first is and *then* is different. That would be to postulate a quality without relations, for however brief a time, and so incongruous with his own professed thesis of 'no quality without relation'. Moreover, the question here is not with regard to priority in respect of time. What is sought to be stressed only is that if we *think* that a thing is distinct (even from inside) we are compelled to bring in at least two ideas—the existence of the thing *and* its distinctness from others. 'Being' and 'being different' are not identical ideas, though they may characterize the selfsame object. A quality which is regarded as being internally different from another thus soon comes to appear, when we try to understand its being different, as itself a relatedness of qualities. So, Bradley concludes: 'Have qualities without relation any meaning for thought? For myself, I am sure that they have none.'

(b) But, even if we consider them along with relations, qualities are unintelligible. On the one hand, the distinctness of the two must be maintained: qualities cannot be reduced to relations. After all, there must be some specific things to be related; 'nothings cannot be related, and . . . to turn qualities in relation into mere relations is impossible'. The relational activity involved in an act of distinction only heightens the differences: it does not (entirely) create them.[1]

But, on the other hand, when we consider qualities and relations as a togetherness of distincts, we get lost in an endless process of division in which the mind's transition from one step to another does not add a whit to our understanding. This can be brought out as follows:

If we assert that 'qualities must be, and must *also* be related', a diversity is at once introduced into each quality. Each comes to have a dual character. First, it is itself, and as such supports, rather than is made by, the relation. In this aspect, which we may agree to call (a), the quality A is the difference on which the distinction is based. Secondly, it is made by the relation. In this

[1] AR 25.

aspect, say (a'), it is 'the distinctness that results from connexion'. So 'A' comes to appear (for thought) as the totality of (aa'). This inner differentiation of A is essential. Its two aspects, being-itself and being-different, cannot be ascribed to it 'immediately', that is, to it as a point of mere self-sameness; for, that would be, in Bradley's view, a clear contradiction. But, when we look on A as being the relatedness of (aa') our troubles only increase. The two aspects are not each the other; nor is anyone of them, taken by itself, A. So A has to be taken as the unity of two clearly *distinct terms*, (a) and (a'). But, if these *distinct* terms are held in relation, each one of them itself comes to have two aspects in relation, in the manner already indicated, and so on ad infinitum. At no point can we swamp qualities in relations, or vice versa, and when we regard them as being a connection of the diverse, their seeming solidity is dissipated into a 'fission which conducts us to no end'. So, qualities in a relation are 'as unintelligible as . . . qualities without one'.[1]

(c) We may now turn to relations. It is obvious that relations *without* qualities are unintelligible. Bradley's own words may here be quoted with advantage:

> 'At least, for myself, a relation which somehow precipitates terms which were not there before, or a relation which can get on somehow without terms, and with no differences beyond the mere ends of a line of connexion, is really a phrase without meaning.'[2]

(d) But, relations are unintelligible even if they are taken *along with* qualities. How the relation (r) stands to the qualities A, B is a problem which, as we shall presently see, defies solution. And the problem cannot be blinked. In metaphysics we cannot refrain from trying to understand the given. And we are forced to admit as given the *relatedness* of (r) with A, B. This can be argued. If the relation is nothing to the qualities, they are not related at all. And if they are wholly unrelated, they are no qualities either, because, as we saw earlier, qualities without relations are unthinkable. But

[1] *Ibid* 27, 26–27.
[2] *Ibid* 27. The differences which a relation relates are distinct terms. This is what Bradley means by protesting against the idea that a relation can carry on 'with no differences beyond the mere ends of a line of connexion'.

if there are thus no qualities, the relation itself, which is alleged to have nothing to do with qualities, disappears forthwith. So we have to concede that the relation somehow affects the terms. But how? Bradley answers: through a *'new* connecting relation'.[1]

The necessity of a new relation (r'), we may note, arises when we take theoretical notice of the togetherness of two distincts. That A and (r) are together is here accepted; for, we are considering the intelligibility of relations taken *along with* qualities. And, it is only the distinctness of A and (r) that there needs a word of comment. The mutual distinctness of terms is, of course, obvious; or else, there would be only one term in reality, and so no relation, for a relation cannot be regarded as the mere elongation of any one term. As for the (relative) individuality of the *relation*, Bradley's remarks with regard to it easily bear it out. The relation (r) cannot be the mere adjective of A. Were it that, it would not relate; for 'relating' requires that there be at least two terms. Nor can it be the mere adjective, the common property, of *both* A and B. For, if it represents merely what is common to them, it cannot keep them 'apart' or distinct. To prevent them from coinciding, the relation has to assert itself, as it were, against the terms: it must have its own distinct nature, or be different (not separate) from them.[2]

So, we agree that, as A and (r), two distincts appear to be held together. Now, the fact of their togetherness has got to be explained; it cannot be merely accepted. If, as in feeling, the differences did not at all assert their individuality, each against the other, their co-existence would not demand any explanation, for each would appear directly and wholly conducive to the other, which is precisely what Bradley means by the thoroughgoing qualification of feeling. It would be harmony entire, and no discordance would be felt. But if, as in the instance under review, the two distincts, A and (r) remain (in part) stoutly themselves even when they are together, the question surely arises, how they are yet together.

Now, two answers are possible. To begin with, we may say that A and (r)—though, or rather *because*, distinct—are not simple

[1] *Ibid*: That is, through a relation which not merely prevents the terms from coalescing with each other by holding them 'apart', but connects them positively.
[2] *Ibid*. Also see footnote.

entities, but complex ones, each having two aspects one of which explains its self-existence, and the other, its self-involvement with what is beside it. But, in a manner familiar to us, this would at once force us into positing ever newer terms and relations within both A and (r). And we have seen how we can neither justifiably stop nor dispense with this process of ideal fission; for, at no stage of this process can we deny either the distinctness or the relatedness of the terms.

The other way would be this. The two distincts, A and (r), may each of them be allowed a solid singleness, and the problem of their relatedness may be considered wholly from the outside. This alone is the alternative which Bradley considers here,[1] for the logic of the other has been examined earlier.[2] Now, if the inner dissolution of A and (r) is thus sought to be avoided, and if, as is admittedly the case, we can ignore neither their distinctness nor their togetherness, the only rational way open to us is to say that they are held together—in spite of themselves, as it were—by being included in a new link (r'). But, this (r') itself, if it is to be a positive, cementing force and no mere vacuum between (what are now) the terms, must have its own character, and so its linkage with what it connects, which is equally self-assertive, demands a new relation (r^2).

The difficulty arises and persists because the terms and relations have both their distinct individuality. If they are at all *thought of*, they do not form a continuous, undifferentiated mass, and are not seen to run into each other directly:

> 'The problem is to find how the relation can stand to its qualities; and this problem is insoluble. If you take the connexion as a solid thing, you have got to show, and you cannot show, how the other solids are joined to it. And, if you take it as a kind of medium or unsubstantial atmosphere, it is a connexion no longer.'[3]

2. THE 'UNREALITY' OF RELATIONS

a. *The protest of Russell*

If relations are unintelligible, whether taken without or along

[1] *Ibid* 27–28.
[2] *Ibid* 26.
[3] *Ibid* 28.

with qualities, Bradley cannot regard them as being *ultimately* real. It is clear that if we wish to challenge his view as to the 'unreality'—by which he means the metaphysical untenability—of relations, we have to question either the arguments which he advances to demonstrate their unintelligibility, or the central assumption of his metaphysics that the real is the self-consistent. The protest that relations *exist* just makes no point against Bradley; for, he is himself convinced of their *existence*. As a practical device, the relational form is, in his view, 'most necessary'.[1] Relations, he insists, cannot 'fall somewhere outside of reality'.[2] Unfortunately, to talk first of what he says in *Our Knowledge of the External World*, a part of Russell's criticism of Bradley's attitude to relations seems to ignore all this completely. Cook Wilson's criticism is, on the other hand, relevant; for, he criticizes Bradley's *arguments* to establish the unintelligibility of relations.

Agreeing, for the present, to ignore his remarks in *An Outline of Philosophy*, Russell's criticism, therefore, may be dealt with but briefly. His arguments relating to the point in question may be summed up thus:

Error can creep easily into Bradley's subtle arguments to demonstrate our inability to understand how the relation could stand to its terms. The 'interrelatedness of things in the world' is, on the other hand, 'a patent fact'.[3] That 'certain things have a certain relation is an "atomic fact" '. It is wholly empirical, or objective—that is, independent of our thought or opinion about it. Thought does not construct such facts: they are just there.

If relations are such a distinct feature of given reality, how could Bradley manage to dismiss them as unreal? Russell suggests that Bradley was led into this mistake by his acceptance of the view that all propositions have the subject–predicate form. From the viewpoint of this attitude to propositions, it seems natural to suppose that 'every fact consists in something having some quality'; that we cannot speak of things as *being in relations*; or that relations 'must be reduced to properties of the apparently related terms'. A 'logic which reduces everything to subjects and predi-

---

[1] *Ibid.*
[2] *Ibid* 468.
[3] Cf. Russell, *Our Knowledge of the External World*, 18.

cates is compelled to condemn (relations) as error and mere appearance.'[1]

Propounding his own view, Russell contends that a proposition may easily ascribe a relation to a subject;[2] and that specially when the relation ascribed is an asymmetrical one—say, 'A is greater than B'—the irreducibility of the relation to a mere property of the terms is absolute. Properties, whether similar or different, 'cannot account for the existence of asymmetrical relations'.[3]

Now, to us the general irrelevance of *this* criticism to Bradley's view is obvious. But let us first put the essence of Russell's objection in the form of a simple argument:

Relations cannot be reduced to mere properties of the terms; they are a distinct part of the actual world; *therefore* they are real.

This basic argument—taken along with Russell's general attitude outlined above—can, on Bradley's behalf, be met as follows. Bradley nowhere denies the actual relatedness of things. As already indicated, he in fact insists on it as a positive truth. This will become clearer when, later in this chapter, we turn to see how he talks emphatically of the necessary self-transcendence of a term, and how he holds it as an explicit doctrine that, in metaphysics, the main task of thought is to understand how diversities are in fact held together.

Nor is Bradley oblivious of the distinctness of a relation. To us it appears to be a complete distortion of his real view to suggest that he attempts (or intends) to reduce relations to mere properties of their terms. The fact is that, as we have seen, he is explicitly opposed to any such reduction.[4] In this connexion,[5] Russell's appeal to the fact of asymmetrical relations does not really constitute any objection to Bradley's view; for, Bradley is convinced that *no* relation, whatever be its kind, can be regarded as a mere property of its terms.

Russell's objections built around the subject–predicate form of

[1] *Ibid* 59, 56–63.
[2] Russell believes that 'failure to perceive this ... has been the source of many errors in traditional metaphysics'. *Ibid* 54.
[3] *Ibid* 59.
[4] Thus, see: '... The relation can hardly be the mere adjective of one or both of its terms; or, at least, as such it seems indefensible.' AR 27, also footnote.
[5] The other aspect of the matter—whether or not asymmetrical relations disprove monism—is to be dealt with later, in Ch. VI.

propositions are, in our view, equally ineffective. Does the acceptance of this form actually compel Bradley to believe that it is always a mere quality, never a relation, which can be predicated; or, to suggest that, in so far as the 'thing–quality' manner is the only idiom of fact, relations must somehow be reducible to mere properties of the terms? It does not, and it need not:

(a) First, Bradley openly admits that what is 'predicated' may well be a relational complex. In 'A precedes B' the whole relation A–B is, in his view, the predicate.[1] Talking of such relations as 'A is simultaneous with B' or 'C is to the east of D', he says that 'the ideal complex, asserted or denied ... takes the form of two or more subjects with adjectival relations existing between them'.[2] The point we are seeking to make is hardly cancelled by the reflection—which, in fact, is Bradley's own—that the subject is, in such cases, not merely A or C, but a wider reality. For, even with regard to judgment in general, Bradley's view is that what is asserted of a subject is no mere self-sameness, but 'both diversity in unity and identity in difference—(the) subject being at once the whole or undivided and a special reality'.

(b) Secondly, it is not correct to suggest that, according to Bradley, something having some quality is the only kind of fact. Feeling is, to him, an indisputable fact; but he never speaks of it as 'something having some quality' in the same sense in which a subject has a predicate. The invariable togetherness of qualities is also, in his view, a fact. What is more, far from regarding it as being the only kind of fact, Bradley insists that the subject-predicate arrangement always leaves out a wealth of concrete detail; and that, to speak generally, every ideal arrangement of terms and relations falls short of the given reality.[3]

(c) Thirdly, as we have already seen, Bradley nowhere maintains that relations can be reduced to mere properties of their terms. And, to talk generally, his treatment of relations is, in a way, less guilty of slurring ideal distinctions than Russell's. Thus, whereas Russell seems content with a mere classification of rela-

---

[1] PL 28.
[2] *Ibid* 22. Bradley is, of course, not unaware of the existence of asymmetrical relations.
[3] AR 143–58. See the following, in particular: 'I do not deny that reality *is* an object of thought; I deny that it is barely and *merely* so.' *Ibid* 149.

tions, Bradley finds it necessary to mark off the relational form from the relational situation, on the one hand, and from relational matter,[1] on the other. Russell speaks of 'one inch taller' and 'one year later' as intransitive relations.[2] But, Bradley would insist that these represent a mere character abstracted from the whole fact of a relation which is always a connection *between terms*. A relation without terms is an abstraction, not a fact. It is against the failure to draw such necessary distinctions that metaphysics protests. And the protest is helpful. But for it, we may be easily tempted into the belief that, in so far as a relation is often talked of without referring to the terms, it can (even) in fact be wholly without them.

In fine, Bradley denies neither the actuality nor the distinctness of relations. But, and now we turn to protest against the basic part of Russell's argument, how does the acknowledgement of this mere fact *prove* that relations are real, unless we assume that 'givenness' is as such a *criterion* of reality? Relations, according to Bradley, are, like appearance in general, 'unreal' not in the sense of being non-existent, but only in the sense of being finally unintelligible.

It may here be contended, as Russell actually does, that it is not proper to raise the question of intelligibility with regard to the inter-relatedness of things which is 'an atomic fact' and is quite independent of our thought about it. But, the contention would, in our view, be untenable. As distinguished from a relatedness which is merely felt, a relation, perceived as such, is not a genuine datum, for it is a clear result of some ideal abstraction and construction.[3] Even if we agree to ignore the setting from which an 'atomic fact' is of necessity abstracted, does it not contain within itself features which compel reflection? Consider one of Russell's own instances: 'Napoleon married Josephine.' He holds that this 'fact' has three constituents—the two terms and the relation; and that it is 'objective' in the sense of being 'independent of our

---

[1] Bradley's view is that the spatio-temporal diversities in a non-relational whole, 'as it comes first', do not 'wear a relational form'; and that they are mere relational matter, in so far as the sense of 'passage to and fro between the terms' is here absent. CE 654, 661.

[2] Russell, *Our Knowledge of the External World*, 58. Bradley would call them 'adjectival relations'. See PL 22.

[3] CE 648.

thought or opinion about it', 'though the assertion is something which involves thought'.[1] Now, it is not easy to see how any fact can self-consistently be *regarded* as being quite independent of thought. One possible escape from this compulsion is suggested by Bradley's notion of immediate experience. But here, in feeling, we do not have any relations as such. Moreover, Russell nowhere seems inclined to accept Bradley's view of feeling. Even if we leave aside all philosophical controversy, would it look natural to deny that our perception of the fact in question includes awareness of three clear diversities, Napoleon, Josephine and the relation of marriage? But if we bring in distinctions, can thought be wholly kept out?

Be that as it may, it seems safe to conclude that, in his criticism of Bradley's theory of relations, Russell commits errors of both commission and omission. He errs in believing, first, that Bradley uses 'existence' and 'reality' interchangeably, so that to regard relations as 'unreal' is at once to treat them as non-existent; and secondly, that the reality of relations is (by Bradley) denied because they are regarded as a subsidiary, reducible aspect of the given. Further, he should have shown—what he has not (here) attempted at all—how Bradley's basic criterion: 'the real is that which satisfies the intellect' is wrong; and also, we insist, how and where Bradley actually falters in his arguments to bring out the unintelligibility of relations. Finally, as against Russell's charge, we would do well to remember that Bradley certainly concedes to them, as to everything else, a measure of metaphysical reality. All appearances are, to some extent, real; and relations, to Bradley, are a necessary appearance. With their help, we are enabled at least to *defer* contradictions.[2]

But we must now turn to Russell's arguments against Bradley in his *An Outline of Philosophy*.[3] They may be summarized as follows:

The question—what is there *between* the relation and its terms? —arises only if we suppose that a relation is just as substantial as its terms, or that it is merely a third term, not a genuine connecting-

---

[1] Russell, *Our Knowledge of the External World*, 61; 60–61.
[2] As to the view that a relation *is* (in a measure) real, see CE 649–50.
[3] Russell, *An Outline of Philosophy*, London, George Allen & Unwin, 1956, 262–64.

link at all. This suggestion, of the relation's substantiality, is easily worked up when we *describe* a relational fact in terms of language, say as: 'A precedes B'. Here, 'precedes' falls between A, B; and, as a word, it has to be connected with A, B. But—and this is what Bradley may be said to ignore—in the relation considered *as a fact*, there is, so to speak, no room at all between the relation and its terms, and so no 'regress' arises.

Now, Cook Wilson develops this protest with great force; and, in so far as we propose to attempt a detailed answer to *his* criticism, we may only make the following general remarks by way of attenuating the objections put forth by Russell:

To protest that a relation is not as substantial as its terms can only mean that it is not a separate thing. But, where does Bradley posit such a separateness? He, on the other hand, insists that to be in touch with the terms, or to relate them positively is the very essence of a relation. It is precisely this activity of 'rela*ting*' which, we are told, distinguishes a relation from immediate experience, though the fact of 'related*ness*' or actual unity is a contribution of feeling. '*Relations are nothing if not conjunctive*; but what is merely conjunctive so far does not belong to immediate experience, and cannot in that character enter into feeling.'[1]

It is true that, in the chapter: 'Relation and Quality', a relation is spoken of as 'a solid thing', or as 'something itself'; but here Bradley's purpose is only to oppose the idea that a relation could be a mere 'unsubstantial' atmosphere, not to suggest that a relation merely falls between the terms without connecting them. The two sides of the matter are, in principle, one. A relation must needs be something in itself if it is actually to connect the terms.[2] Bradley's real view indeed is that a relation is both (somehow) related to—and partly independent of—its terms. This alone conveys the full meaning of his insistence, implicit in AR and manifest unmistakably in CE, that a relation holds the terms apart.

Whether in the details of actual argument, as distinguished from a formulation of his view generally from the outside, Bradley in fact lapses into any of the two extreme alternatives—the absolute independence of the relation from its terms, or its being merely one of their attributes—may, for the present, be regarded debat-

[1] CE 655. Our italics.
[2] AR 27–28.

able; but, as to the view which he *professes*, it is to us unquestionable that he does not accept any one of these alternatives as the whole truth about a given relation. This is borne out clearly by the following words of his:

> '... The relation can hardly be the mere adjective of one or both of its terms; or at least, as such it seems indefensible ... (It) is not the adjective of one term, *for, if so, it does not relate*. Nor for the same reason is it the adjective of each term taken apart, for then there is again no relation *between* them. Nor is the relation their common property, for then what keeps them *apart*? They are now not two terms at all, because not separate ...'[1]

We have, in the above, taken the liberty of including Bradley's footnote (AR 27). Perhaps it is his failure to notice this footnote[2] which prevents Russell from appreciating the whole point of Bradley's view.

We are at a loss to understand how, in the face of the above passage, Bradley could be said to hold that a relation is as 'substantial' as the terms—in the sense of being something real *wholly apart* from them; that a relation may be actual, with yet doing any 'relating' at all; or, finally, that it is a mere property of the terms.

But, it may be contended that during the course of actual argument Bradley lapses unconsciously into the error of regarding 'relation' as a separate, substantial entity; and that the contradictions and the 'regress' which he talks of arise only if the relation is so regarded. Our defence of Bradley would here proceed as under:

Bradley insists continually that a relation must (somehow) affect or connect the terms. Again, the contradictions, to which the relational form is in his view subject, arise not if the relation is posited as a third term, but *only if*, what seems necessary, the relation is thought to be *both* as connecting and yet as (relatively) distinct from the terms.

It is here important to mark Bradley's precise view of how the alleged regress arises. He does not say that if two sticks are to be

---

[1] *Ibid* 27. Our italics.
[2] Cf. Russell's citation of Bradley's passage, *An Outline of Philosophy*, 263.

THE RELATIONAL FORM

bound together by a piece of string, we in fact need another piece with which to tie the first to each object, and so on for ever; and he is not open to the charge that, on his view, it should therefore be impossible to tie two things with a bit of string. He only says that if two things are actually found tied up with a string; and if neither aspect of the situation is ignored—that is, neither the distinctness of the thread and the sticks, nor the fact of their being together—the question certainly remains legitimately open as to how, or due to what 'relating' factor, they at all came to be together. And, Bradley would insist, if the factor sought for is itself distinct, as it has got to be, our understanding of *how* the two diversities could at all be together is never, in fact, *complete*; and the demand for new connecting-links may for ever continue, and legitimately so.[1] Is it in any way improper to wonder *how* two successive links in a chain at all came to be together? True, there is only a spatial relation, no third 'link', between them. But,

> first, Bradley does not claim to *show* us a third, *existing* link between the two given ones, but only wonders (theoretically) *how* they could at all be together without any new connecting factor; and

> secondly, are the two specific links spatially together wholly by themselves, or merely by chance?

The essence of Bradley's view is simple. If two things found together are distinct, each from the other; if, to use his own words, they do not run into each other directly; and if, therefore, the reason of their being together is not provided entirely from within them, are we not called upon to search for fresh connecting-links because of which they are together? Conversely, could there be any warrant for such a search were what is presented to us a mere, undifferentiated continuity?

How, in the abstract, no regress would (in Bradley's view) arise were the relation separate from, or merely juxtaposed with the terms, is a point which we propose to discuss later. In fact, our entire discussion so far will become clearer as we proceed.

---
[1] What is, in Bradley's view, *impossible* is not that there should be any relation at all, but that it should be *finally* intelligible.

b. *Cook Wilson's objections*

We may now turn to Cook Wilson's criticism of Bradley's treatment of relations.[1] As we have already seen, Bradley maintains that we are forced into an endless positing of relations when we try to understand how a relation stands to its terms. Cook Wilson denies this categorically by saying that no such process really issues 'from relating the relation of two terms to the terms of the relation themselves';[2] and that to imagine that it does is a 'fallacy'. This fallacy, Cook Wilson continues, is based on a wrong presupposition:

> "The presupposition of this (that is, Bradley's) fallacy is that if two somethings are different from one another they must stand to one another in a relation which is different from either, not identical with nor included in the separate nature of either. In other words, r is not identical with A or B nor a part of what is already understood in A or B. So far from being always true, this presupposition can be shown to be never true where A and B are in fact properly described as related.'[3]

(a) The protest may be summed up thus. Where A and B are properly described as being related, the relation (r) is (or can be) identical with the terms, or is (at least) a part of what is already understood in them. And if, so to speak, no ideal distance separates the relation from the terms, how can a *new* relation be wedged between them? Cook Wilson therefore concludes that 'the idea of relation cannot be applied, as is proposed, to a relation and a term of that relation itself', and that Bradley's question: 'what is the relation between r and A?' is hence 'an unreal one'.[4]

(b) Cook Wilson further cites actual instances with regard to which this question cannot intelligently be put.[5] We may select

---

[1] Cook Wilson's essay, 'Relation and Quality', included in A. C. Ewing's *The Idealist Tradition*, Glencoe, The Free Press & the Falcon's Wing Press, 1957, 285–88.

[2] *Ibid* 285.

[3] *Ibid.*

[4] *Ibid* 286.

[5] We hope to be able to argue that Bradley's continually abstract way of dealing with the problem is in no way harmed by a consideration of concrete instances; and that Cook Wilson's complaint, that throughout the chapter: 'Relation and Quality' Bradley does not consider even a single concrete instance, is no real objection to Bradley's view.

for notice the most plausible one of them. Consider a surface as related to its volume. Would it here be proper to ask: what is the relation of the surface to its relation with the volume of a body? Let us see:

'What is the definition of a surface?' It is: a surface is the boundary of its volume. That is, the relation—of being the boundary of a volume—is necessarily involved in, or is rather identical with the surface. So, there is no sense in asking: 'How does the relation stand to the surface?' The surface *is* this relation; and another relation cannot be inserted between the two, simply because there is, so to speak, no ideal room between them. Thus, concludes Cook Wilson, the very first step of Bradley—the initial question in response to which the infinite process is said to arise—is fallacious. The question is 'obviously unreal, for it contains everything necessary to its own answer; it puts as a question what is no question to the person asking it'.[1]

Now, Bradley's answer to the above will be as follows:

(i) First, in the instances which are supposed to be hostile to his view, is the relation merely included in, *or* is it identical with the term? A choice is here necessary; for, the alternatives have different meanings. Cook Wilson himself seems undecided. Thus, in his essay, wherever he suggests that the relation is identical with the term, he immediately follows it up with the attenuating alternative that the relation is at least a part of what is already understood in the term.[2]

How are we to decide as to whether the relation is merely included in, or is identical with the term? Obviously, we have to reckon with both theory and fact. Now, theoretically, a term can never be *identical* with the relations in which it stands, or which it includes. To think—and we are so far talking of mere *theory*—that a thing stands in, or includes, some relations is necessarily to mark it off, however feebly, from what is beside or within it. Bradley would say that it is this theoretical compulsion which

---

[1] Cook Wilson's essay, 'Relation and Quality', *op. cit.* 287.

[2] Thus see: 'The presupposition of this fallacy is that ... r is not identical with A or B *nor a part of* what is already understood in A or B.' *Ibid* 285. Our italics.

Or again: 'The relation r ... is *either* identical with A ... *or* at least something always included necessarily in what is already understood by A.' *Ibid* 287–88. Our italics.

never allows Cook Wilson to feel really sure that the relation is *identical* with the term which includes it. And, when we turn to fact, we find that the verdict of theory is only confirmed. A man is not exhausted by his friendships. Nor is an *actual* surface really identical with its relatedness to volume. Every surface has in fact a sensible particularity which is not only quite as integral to its being as the relation in question, but is for ever incapable of being resolved into the relation.

It seems to us that the arguments of Cook Wilson are vitiated by a clear failure to mark off the manner of theory, necessarily abstract, from the wholeness of fact. Thus, when to his own question: 'what is the *definition* of a surface?' he answers, rightly enough: 'A surface is the boundary of a volume', he fails wholly to appreciate, first, that the question, in so far as it seeks only a *definition*, necessarily leaves out a great mass of *fact* about the surface, for example, its colour, smoothness etc.; and, secondly, that the relation provided by the answer is identical only with the *definition, not with the whole fact of a surface.*

To put it in the manner of Bradley, Cook Wilson commits the mistake of supposing that the answer to a question which takes shape by abstracting from fact can give us complete knowledge of actual reality. The fact of an existent surface as being the boundary of a given volume is not identical with the mere idea of a surface as involving a relation to volume taken abstractedly. The illusion that a surface is wholly identical with its relation to its volume is generated by a wrong start. The opening question should have been: 'what is a surface?' and not: 'what is the *definition* of a surface?' But even if we start by putting the second question, the *distinction* (we repeat) between a term and its relation cannot be cancelled. In saying: 'A surface is the boundary of a volume', we necessarily grant to 'surface' a measure of ideal independence from the relation: otherwise, there will be nothing to be related, and the relation itself will disappear. In our understanding of what a surface is, the relation of boundary to volume is of course included, but that which includes is not ideally one with that which is included. A relation that overruns and swamps or rubs out its terms is neither actual nor tenable theoretically.

To conclude: both in theory and in fact, a surface is something

THE RELATIONAL FORM

(in itself) which is the boundary of a volume.[1] In speaking thus, we make provision not only for what is demanded by the idea of a relation, but for the fact that the relation does not really exhaust the particular called surface.

(ii) What stands reaffirmed as the result of our arguments above is the irreducible distinctness of terms and relations. Now, once this is accepted, Bradley's question: '*How* does the relation stand to its terms?' at once becomes natural and necessary. Consider the situation as it now is. First, A and (r) both defy complete resolution into each other. In other words, they do not run into each other directly, or without reserve. Qualification of the whole by its parts is here not thorough. Secondly, A and (r) are (yet) found together in fact. We should not forget that the specific theoretical demonstration to which Cook Wilson objects occurs where, having shown the impossibility of qualities *without* relations, Bradley turns to consider them *as taken together*. Now, if both the aspects of the situation are taken into account, Bradley's predicament seems justified. That A and (r), or (some) quality and (some) relation, have each a hard core of self-existence, and yet are *always* found together—does this not at once make it theoretically necessary to posit a new link between the two?[2] To put it differently, if A, being in some measure resolutely defiant of (r) does not by itself satisfactorily explain its togetherness with the relation; if (r) too always retains its distinctness from A; and if, above all, the two are yet *always* found together, must we not look for a new link to improve our understanding as to how A and (r) could at all stand together?

Two points are here to be borne clearly in mind. First, the togetherness of A and (r), which Bradley throughout assumes in this specific demonstration, does not mean the mere juxtaposition of two alien entities. It rather means the necessary co-presence of a term with *its* relation and of a relation with *its* term. This is the lesson which Bradley expects us to learn from his earlier arguments

---

[1] This is the spirit of Bradley's affirmation: 'The qualities must be, and must *also* be related.' AR 26. Or again: ' . . . In order to be related, a term must keep still within itself enough character to make it, in short, itself and not anything diverse.' CE 634.

[2] This link may either be made to fall primarily *between* A and r or introduced *within* them as a relatedness of diverse aspects. In either case, as we have seen, there is, in Bradley's view, no escape from an infinite regress.

as to the impossibility of qualities without relations, and of relations without qualities. Secondly, the new relation—say (r′)—is required to further our understanding of the togetherness of A and (r); it does not make this given *fact* unnecessary.

The transition from 'A–r' to (r′) would be impossible were there no difference at all between A and (r); for, the question of 'togetherness' just cannot arise with regard to (or within) a single point of bare self-sameness, nor even in the case of a mere, undifferentiated continuity. Again, it would be unnecessary if A and (r) could explain their togetherness wholly by themselves; and self-inconsistent if, in the very process of its birth, (r′) cancelled its terms, A and (r), because thereby it would only commit suicide, a relation being impossible without some terms to connect. The facts, on the other hand, are that A and (r) are never really identical and that—as quality and relation in general—they not only always come together, but remain, in part, resolutely different from each other. Now, this discordance in the very heart of things—that they are both necessarily self-existent and self-transcendent—is to thought unacceptable; and we have to overcome it by supposing, after Bradley, that A and (r) are both *partly* self-existent and *partly* self-transcendent. The contradiction is thus shelved—though not finally overcome—by ascribing self-existence and self-transcendence to different parts *within* the individual being of A and (r). But this is at once to loosen the seeming solidity of both A and (r) into fresh terms with a new relation wedged between them.[1] *This* new relation is (r′).

The realization that this new relation may be posited as being *within* the terms enables us to perceive another flaw in Cook Wilson's argument. He seems to deny the possibility of (r′) merely on the ground that there is no ideal room whatever *between* A and (r), say, between a surface and its being the boundary of a volume. But (r′) is not intended to be an external link put *merely between* A and (r). No relation, in Bradley's view, can be merely external, though it cannot be wholly internal either. And (r′) has to be posited as a relation which, to explain their outer togetherness, loosens the terms from inside, as it were, and there

---

[1] Thus Bradley says, while speaking of the necessary self-existence and self-transcendence of a quality: '... *without* the use of a relation it is impossible to predicate this variety of A.' AR 26.

makes room for the clear diversity of self-existence and self-transcendence. If we do not keep this in mind, our own interpretation of Bradley will be harmed in two ways. First, he will come to appear as admitting, at least on occasions, the reality of merely external relations, against which, on the contrary, he repeatedly protests. And secondly, the connection between his dialectics of 'quality and relation' in AR and his demonstration of the relational form *as an appearance* in CE will become obscure.

It would perhaps be helpful to dwell a little longer on the truth that (r') is not merely external to A and (r), specially because Cook Wilson talks continually of (the impossibility of) finding (r') *between* A and (r). Admittedly, Bradley does not (positively) mention that (r') is (also) internal to A and (r) precisely where he carries out his demonstration in question.[1] But it is important to note that, throughout this specific demonstration,[2] Bradley never once uses the word: 'between'. On the contrary, he here appears clearly opposed to the conception of relation as a mere 'medium', because such a view prevents the relation from becoming a genuine 'connexion' which, as distinguished from a mere conjunction, is grounded essentially in the inner nature of terms. Moreover, if, as only seems proper, we take his argument that a relation must be both something in itself and be something to the qualities *along with* his earlier contention that diversity cannot be ascribed to anything without putting a relation *within* it,[3] the internality of (r') at once becomes obvious.

It is true that, if not in the chapter, 'Relation and Quality', at least in his essay on Relations in CE, Bradley stresses that a relation must 'hold the terms apart', or fall *between* them. But even there he speaks continually of the inner, ideal diversity of the terms necessitated by the fact of their being in relation; so that the relation, so to speak, bites into the terms, and is thus not *merely* between them. Bradley's complete meaning is had only when we also take the word 'hold' duly into account. That a relation *holds* the terms *apart* means, first, that it keeps the terms distinct, not that it keeps them spatially separate; and, secondly, that in so far as it actually *holds* them or keeps them together, the relation,

[1] *Ibid* 27.
[2] *Ibid* 27–28.
[3] *Ibid* 26.

in order to make this togetherness (relatively) intelligible, invests them with an inner duality—of self-existence and self-transcendence—which means that it is by no means wholly extrinsic to them.

We may now sum up the net result of our argument. A and (r) are irreducibly distinct; yet they invariably go together. This is a contradiction, which is, for the time being, overcome by introducing new relations within both A and (r)—relations necessitated by the need to hold the distinctness of A and (r) with their 'togetherness' *intelligently*. Bradley's positing of ever newer relations is therefore necessary, unless, of course, we ignore—and so do not try to circumvent—the immediate contradiction involved in regarding A and (r) as being both self-existent and self-transcendent.

A return to the specific instance cited by Cook Wilson will only confirm our conclusion. To speak of fact, is it unnatural to ask: how is the surface in its entire sensible detail related to its being the boundary of a volume? Is the connection between the actual surface and its being the boundary of a volume immediately clear? Or, does the fact that a surface is always the boundary of a volume explain the other fact, equally undeniable, that a surface always has a unique sensible character? If not, it is both legitimate and necessary to wonder: 'How could the relation stand to a specific surface, which it clearly does?'

Cook Wilson's attempts to reinforce his conclusions with an appeal to other concrete instances can be similarly dealt with, and so a brief notice of them should here suffice:

'A equals B.' Here, equality may be taken either in general, or as the specific equality of A to B. Now, Cook Wilson contends, if we ask: 'How does Equality (in general) stand to A?' Our answer will be: 'Equality links up A with B'; so that we come back to (r), and no new relations, as an infinite process, emerge. But, the argument seems to be fallacious, and that as follows:

When we ask: 'How does Equality (in general) stand in relation to A?' no explicit reference to B is immediately involved; and this question is not exactly the same as: 'How does Equality stand in relation to A *which is equal to B*?' The emphasis in the first question is on Equality and *A*. And, if we want to know the relation between *these* two, we must, for the time being, leave B out of consideration, and give some such answer: 'Equality is a universal in which the particular, A, participates' or 'Equality enters into—but is not exhausted by—its connection with A'. But such answers, which alone are true to the real point of the question under review, at once give us the new relation of 'participation'. Surely, the relation between a particular and a universal is not the same as that between two particulars.[1] Even if we accept Cook Wilson's own answer that the relation of Equality (in general) to A 'is the *kind* of relation which A has to B', we do not come back to the actual relation between A and B, merely as such, but to this relation *as an individual expression of Equality in general*, so that a new relation between a universal and its specific embodiment is at once brought to a focus.[2]

Nor is our conclusion in any way harmed if equality is considered as *particular*. What is the relation of A's-equality-to-B to A? Cook Wilson's answer is: 'It is A's equality to B, or r.' But this answer too misses the distinctive emphasis of the question. What we here want to understand is the relation of (r)—as particular—to A. The emphasis is meant to be on (r) and A, to the (relative) exclusion of B. Certainly, B does not disappear when we put the question; but it is just as true that the question, as it is put, requires us to confine our attention to A and (r). Cook Wilson dissipates the distinctive emphasis of the question by spreading it, in the answer, equally over A, (r) and B. It is theoretically by no means futile that, in accordance with the visible emphasis of the question, we here think primarily of A and (r). For, when we ask: 'What is the relation to A of A's equality (to B)?' a direct and meaningful answer would be: 'This equality is one of the relations of A'; in which case, again, we get a new relation, of a substance to one single relation

---

[1] Cook Wilson is not unaware of this distinction, but he fails to acknowledge it. Thus he says: 'The answer, then, is simply a statement of what kind (viz. R) the relation r is. Thus we have not gone outside the nature of r itself nor reached a new relation (r').' Cook Wilson's essay, 'Relation and Quality', *op. cit.* 286.

But, we protest, in speaking of r as related to A through the universal 'R' we have certainly gone beyond our original understanding of r as the specific A–B relation.

[2] Thus, as is necessary to meet Cook Wilson's protest, the statement that A stands in the relation of r' (particular-universal) to r or A's-equality-to-B, *is* new, and is certainly not a part of the original statement: A equals B. Cf. *Ibid*.

of it, or of partial expression or transcendence, which is not *visibly* contained in the mere statement: 'A equals B.'

A more familiar example will bring out our point clearly. If it be asked: 'How does my friendship (to my friend) stand to me', the ready answer would be: 'It is one of my sentiments or relations.' The new relation here suggested is that of a man's personality to one sentiment which by no means exhausts his total being. The individual is, so to speak, never wholly poured out into his friendship; and, what is in Bradley's view an additional point of note, the friendship is not *wholly* deducible from the man's own nature.[1] We cannot rationally pass on from the one to the other, without taking into account a number of extra factors which we quietly ignore as being merely extraneous when we speak of the relation, but without which the relation could never in fact be.[2]

Even if we agree to formulate the question in a way which Cook Wilson would welcome: '*How* does A's equality *to-B* stand to A?' the proper answer, whatever it be, should not be false to the precise kind of puzzlement involved in Bradley's use of 'how'. 'How' here means: 'What is the theoretical pre-condition (or justification) of A's standing in its relation to B?'; and the correct answer to it may roughly be put thus: 'A enters into a relation of equality with B, because of the prior participation of both A and B in a common kind.' This answer, we may note, gives us a new connecting-link which is not merely a distinct something, but is affirmed *theoretically* by understanding as it seeks to enlarge itself. The link, we may add, is not *found* as given. The transition to this new relation would not be possible if by 'how' in the question we mean something which is merely to be found as a fact, rather than to be affirmed as a theoretical necessity. Why Cook Wilson repeatedly lapses back to (r), instead of passing on to (r'), is due to the fact that, whereas Bradley continually understands 'how' in the question: '*How* does *r* stand to A?' as a symbol of the search for a theoretical condition of the relation which *is* there, Cook Wilson, in effect, always asks: '*What* is the relation between (r) and A?',

---

[1] Or, we repeat, the term is, in part, a resolute Other to its relation.

[2] Cf. '... It is false that you can ever go anywhere from one idea or more as simply themselves. Everywhere (a) a whole is involved, and everywhere (b) you abstract and your conclusion is abstract.' CE 668.

'what' being understood as 'what is *actually* the relation between (r) and A?';[1] and in so far as the actually existent—as distinguished from what is, in the main, theoretically necessary—is obviously (r), the transition to (r') appears improper,[2] and no regress arises. The 'how' is by Cook Wilson reduced to a mere 'what'.

Bradley insists that, in metaphysics, we are concerned primarily with theoretical necessities, not with the mere discovery of facts; and his inability to present (r') as a visible entity would not worry him. His task is completed as soon as the legitimacy of the question: 'How does (r) stand to A?' is admitted. We, however, hasten to add that we have so far found no reason to believe that Bradley's contention is not supported by fact.

(c) In the end, we turn to consider the last remaining argument put forth by Cook Wilson. He says that the distinct reality of (r') 'cannot be proved by saying that (r') is the difference between A and (r)'. For, what is the difference between A and (r)? 'To this question', he says, 'the only possible answer is that A is A and not the relation of A to B, and that the relation of A to B is the relation of A to B and not A. Thus the so-called difference is a way of relating the same facts as before and therefore a mere verbal difference'.[3]

Now, Bradley's answer would here run thus:

The difference between A and (r) certainly is 'that A is A and not the relation of A to B'. And this too is unquestionably true that (r'), if it is to be really new, must differ from both A and (r). But, from all this how does it follow that (r') consists *merely* in the difference between A and (r)? Cook Wilson here attributes his own idea to Bradley, and demolishes an attitude which the latter never assumes. When Bradley maintains that (r') is something *new* his meaning is not that it is something merely different from A and (r), but (also) that it is something positive in itself. It is spoken of as a '*new* connecting relation',[4] a 'bond of union ... which also

[1] Thus, Cook Wilson says: 'We have to ask *whether* there is indeed a relation between A and r and *what* it is.' Cook Wilson's essay, 'Relation and Quality', *op. cit.* 286. Our italics.

[2] Thus, considering equality as particular, Cook Wilson says: 'If then ... we go on to ask *what is* the relation of A to r, we can only reply that the relation to A of A's equality to B(r) *is* that it is A's equality to B.' *Ibid.* Our italics.

[3] *Ibid* 287.

[4] AR 27.

has two ends'.[1] The point here simply is that, if it is regarded as being merely different from the terms, a relation cannot be credited with any cementing-force of its own; in which case, it would leave the terms merely apart instead of (also) relating them and would thus be untrue to its own essential function which consists in relating.

We may take an example to bear this out. Suppose two persons grow jealous of each other, because of their fondness for the same (third) individual C. Here, jealousy (r') affects A, B through another relation of fondness (r). And, what is important to note, the relation of jealousy (r') does not consist merely in the difference between A, B and their fondness for C. Did it consist merely in this difference, it could not be the source of the positive antagonism which now threatens to turn A, B into each other's enemies.

We conclude, then, that Bradley's doctrine of the unreality—or unintelligibility—of relations remains unharmed by the criticisms of Russell and Cook Wilson. It has been developed by Bradley also in CE—at greater length, admittedly, but with no essential difference. Only, there he talks of the relational form, and infers its 'unreality' from its incapacity to hold unity and diversity[2] rationally as one. The terms are distinct, each from the other, and from the relation. When we try to understand how they could yet be held together, which they clearly are, our thought is forced into an endless positing of ever newer relations.

c. *A modern protest*

The suspicion may, however, persist that Bradley's insistence on the need to posit ever newer relations is not borne out by the evidence of fact. This is indeed the main complaint of Passmore who protests:

> that 'an infinite regress', which is Bradley's main reason for condemning the relational form, arises only if a relation is considered in the 'generalized form characteristic of philosophy';

---

[1] *Ibid* 28.
[2] 'Every relation must contain a diversity in the form of individual terms; and, on the other hand, unless the relation is one the relation is destroyed.' CE 648.

that, even if a 'regress' does in fact arise, it is no 'hard' or 'knock out' philosophical proof; and

that even if we accept Bradley's demonstrations as to the infinite process which is alleged to ensue when relations are sought to be understood, we are by no means logically compelled to accept his metaphysical conclusions.

These objections, and our answers to them, may now be formulated individually and at some length:

(a) To Bradley's contention that an infinite process ensues when we attempt to understand how a relation stands to its terms, Passmore's objection is that no such regress arises in an *empirical* case. Thus, to take an example, as soon as we are told that many philosophers use a similar style in their writings because they imitate the same philosopher, 'our puzzlement might certainly vanish' and we may not be forced into any 'regress' at all.[1]

Now, it is obvious that if the above contention is correct, Bradley's argument will have to be dismissed as being untrue to fact; nay, his entire attitude to the relational form, and the idea of the Absolute based (indirectly) on it, will forthwith become seriously questionable. Bradley would, however, insist that the regress must arise if we try to understand a relational complex in its wholeness, and that if it does not arise, it is either because we do not genuinely try to understand, or, in understanding, we blink some aspect of fact.

Let us turn to the instance cited by Passmore. Does it really suggest what he thinks it does?

Many philosophers employ a similar style of writing. Here, puzzlement arises only when (or because) we contrast the similarity of style with the distinctness of the writers in question. If the similarity in question obtains only between two authors, it is not so likely to cause puzzlement. Even in this case, however, we may well look askance at the situation provided the similarity is remarkable; which would mean that it contrasts finely with the distinct individuality of the authors involved. This contrast is brought to a focus when we find *many* philosophers using the *same* style, and so our curiosity is here readier and keener.

Now, it is easy to see that the puzzlement is not in the situation

[1] Passmore, *Philosophical Reasoning*, 22.

as such, but is experienced by us when we try to understand it. What, however, may not be so easily realized is the need that if we at all make the attempt we have to be consistent. We should not quietly accept what, on some other occasion, we seek solemnly to explain. Our attitude to fact will be internally self-consistent and objectively proper only if we do not cease to wonder unless that precise feature of fact is removed which first caused us puzzlement. Here, what first makes us wonder is, we have seen, the oneness of style jutting out, as it were, against the distinct plurality of those who employ it. Does this contrast really disappear when we are told that all of them imitate some other individual philosopher? It does not; and, to speak objectively, puzzlement would be just as proper with regard to many individuals' imitation of the same philosopher as with regard to their employment of the same style of writing. There is no tenable *reason* why the latter situation should be regarded as puzzling, and the former, not. We have, in both, a clear contrast of what is common with the distinctness of men to whom it is common, and if in one case we experience no wonder it is only because, sacrificing consistency, we suddenly decide to ignore one unchanged feature of fact—the distinctness of terms from one another, and from the relation. The 'regress' stops only when we ignore the evidence of fact; and it must continue if we try to hold on to the latter.

Thus, to return to our 'example', the realization that many writers imitate the same philosopher does not satisfy us ultimately. Why should they imitate him?—this is a perfectly legitimate question. In case it is sought to be answered by saying that they imitate him because they like his style or treat it as a model, our wonder is by no means silenced necessarily, and we may justifiably ask: why should they all like his style? Does it contain any intrinsic excellences which serve as grounds of general appeal; or is it merely because they just belong to his school of thought? It may be impossible, *in fact*, to carry on such questioning indefinitely. But, we must note, first, that there is no intrinsic absurdity about the process, and, secondly, that the practical inability to carry on a process which is theoretically necessary does not justify, but merely compels, our cutting it short. Bradley's 'infinite regress' duly exposes a compromise which is, in practice, found helpful.

(b) Passmore's second objection shows him agreeing with Waismann that, logically, no philosophical argument is really conclusive, or that no argument ends with a Q.E.D.

Now, the relevance of this objection is here as follows. Bradley's 'infinite regress' arguments with regard to relations do not *conclusively* prove what he thinks they do—that relations are unintelligible, because self-contradictory, and that (therefore) they give us but appearance, not reality. In other words, the second objection can be reduced to the third, to which we now turn.

(c) This brings us to Passmore's general criticism of Bradley's treatment of the relational form. It runs thus:

An infinite regress would ensue if a relation is regarded as 'a third entity' which only falls between the terms, or as a mere actual quality of one or other of the terms. But this 'does nothing to show that there is a self-contradiction involved in the notion of relation'. On the other hand, it only means, first, that relations cannot be explained in Bradley's sense of 'explanation'; and secondly, that 'relations cannot somehow be got rid of out of the world, by being treated as a sub-species of things, or as a sub-species of qualities'. Relations are not 'derivable from some more fundamental feature of things'. And it is only when the attempt 'to understand relation' is identified with 'deriving them from something more fundamental' that they come to appear 'unintelligible', which they in fact are not. Finally, from the admission of an infinite regress nothing really follows as to the self-contradictoriness of relations or as to the nature of 'Reality'.[1]

We may now examine the objections just outlined:

Passmore, like Russell, maintains that an infinite regress will emerge only if absolute separateness is first posited between the terms (one or both) and the relation.

This, however, needs some clarification. The 'positing' of a separateness of the relation from (its) terms, one or both, will not by itself give rise to an infinite regress unless it is seen to clash with the actual togetherness of what we call the relation and its terms. If they are in fact separate, the 'positing' is no mere supposal, but a truthful acknowledgement of fact; but this would mean that

[1] Passmore, *Philosophical Reasoning*, 34–35. This summary of Passmore's argument perhaps appears awkward at places; but it is faithful.

there is nothing to impel, much less to compel thought to tie up the pieces by positing ever newer links between them. Passmore should therefore be taken to believe that what sets the regress going is the clear opposition of ideal 'abstracting' by actual togetherness in the region of fact. This clash between fact and, let us say, one possible idiom of theory may be readily admitted; for, things are, in fact, inter-related.

But, what does this imply? Passmore thinks it only suggests that this idiom of theory could, with profit, be given up; for, he would add, it is only when we abstract relations from given reality, and treat them as a mere aspect of the latter, that self-contradiction and infinite regress seem to infect the notion of relation, investing it with a false suggestion of unintelligibility. To sum up, relations *cannot* be 'explained' only if, as by Bradley, they are isolated from reality; otherwise, there is no difficulty about them. Bradley would, however, protest as follows:

As to the inter-relatedness of things in fact, there is no doubt at all. But, equally indubitable for thought is the necessity of marking off a relation from its terms. That a relation does not merely fall between the terms, or that it is not a mere adjective of the latter, is, as we have already seen, Bradley's own professed view. A relation, he insists, is nothing if it does not in fact relate: it is not merely put along with the terms, but really connects them. But this emphasis on the unity of the relational fact is only one aspect of the matter. Another equally important aspect is the distinctness, relative admittedly, of the relation from its terms. When we say: 'a relation really relates', is it possible, without lapsing into meaninglessness, not to distinguish at all between the 'relation', its 'relating', and what is related? It may at once be objected that this way of speaking makes unnecessary ontological commitments, and that a truer way of putting the matter would be to say that relatedness is the basic manner of things. The alternative here suggested also appears demanded by Passmore's protest against treating relations 'as a sub-species of things', or 'as a sub-species of qualities'.

But suppose we decide not to subordinate relations to anything, and give up, as desired, all effort to derive 'them from something more fundamental'. Does this makeshift in any way rub out the distinction between the relation and its terms? 'The relation R holds A and B together';[1] this certainly makes the relation appear as including—and, therefore, not as subordinate to—the terms. But the distinctness of R from A, B is in this way by no means effaced.

In fine, a relation has of necessity to be distinguished from the terms; yet, in fact it clearly goes with them. It cannot in fact be *without* its terms; but neither, to thought, can it *be* the terms. The relational fact is for thought a unity of distincts. To be true to given unity, thought must heal the divisions it makes; but, to be true to its own idiom, it must not fail to mark off the link from what it links. It is, we have seen, precisely this native self-contradiction in the notion of relation—that it relates the terms, but is yet distinct from them—which initiates the regress and keeps it astir.

In the end, we may note that Bradley nowhere regards relations as a mere sub-species of things. Nor does he ever try to rub them out of existence. Rather, he regards them as the essential form in which the bulk of our experience actually comes to us. What he only protests against is, we repeat, their claim to ultimate reality; and this he argues by demonstrating their self-contradictoriness.

d. '*Together and apart*': *the spatial schema*

We hasten to admit, however, that particularly in the form it assumes in CE, the demonstration in question seems open to one clear objection. Bradley's argument here is briefly as follows:

A relation holds the terms apart, by falling *between* them; for otherwise, the terms coalescing will, so to speak, crowd it out of existence. But how to reconcile the unity which 'holds' with the apartness of that which is held, is for thought a problem insoluble.

Now, it may at once be suspected that the difficulties are here due merely to an unwarranted use of the spatial schema of 'together' and 'apart' or 'between'.[2] But, let us see if it is really so:

Consider an instance. A and B are related. This may be taken to mean that a relation obtains or falls *between*—and connects—A and B. Let us try to avoid the spatial 'between' by saying that a relation, say R, includes both A and B, and holds them, as it

---
[1] Bradley himself anticipates and examines this alternative. AR 17–18.
[2] Bradley's view here is that it is only 'in a highly reflective form' that a relation involves 'spatial character' or schema. CE 669.

were, merely from the outside. Now, a relation which *contains* A and B is certainly in some way related to both A and B; but how does it connect *A with B*, unless, as if by chance tossing, the two, as included in C, come to rub against each other, in which case the relation of A to B, as their point of contact, comes directly to fall between them—precisely the suggestion that we wanted to avoid? In fact, A's being related directly to B can only mean that A, on its side, transcends itself (ideally) and points towards B, and that B does the same with regard to A? But, if this self-transcendence of each is *towards the other*, their involvement or relation, distinct from what they are as terms, falls clearly *between* them. The 'apart' follows logically from the 'between', for if—as is, we have seen, theoretically necessary—the relation is to be given a locus *between* the terms, the two must not coincide or coalesce, so as to provide some (ideal) space for the relation; and this means that it holds them apart. There thus seems to be no escape from 'apart' and 'between'.

It is important to note that, as Bradley employs them, the necessity of these images is, in the main, theoretical. Surely, it is impossible even psychologically to ascribe differences to the self-same point. A man 'cannot imagine a thing as being at once round and square, black and white; he cannot mentally make two straight lines include a space, without destroying their straightness'.[1] But, is the law of contradiction valid for thought merely because we see, in the mind's eye, two distinct objects trying in vain to occupy exactly the same part of (ideal) space? Bradley would answer firmly in the negative. That which compels us psychologically is not, merely as such, tenable metaphysically. The latter (we have seen) is the irresistible for thought. Thought must distinguish; and, to *this* end, it must hold diversities apart. In metaphysics, no fact, whether psychological or physical, can as such be allowed to dictate a criterion to thought. 'Between' and 'apart' are, of course, spatial images, but they are here demanded by thought's own primal need to distinguish. To us it indeed seems clear that Bradley's use of spatial images is, as a rule, dictated by the demands of thought, and is not a mere psychological device. These images have a vital theoretical function to perform. Some of the more

[1] Stout, *A Manual of Psychology*, London, University Tutorial Press Ltd., 1947, 601.

difficult passages in AR and CE—specially the ones which try to understand the nature of contradiction, the extended character of the real, the difference between relational matter and relational form, and the incurable self-inconsistencies of the latter—become easily intelligible if we visualize and hold on to, as a constant point of reference, the spatial schema which Bradley employs in terms of such images as 'side by side', 'couple them apart', 'relaxing its unity' or 'distended' unity, 'collide and repel', 'hold together distantly', 'clots' and 'fluid', and 'between' and 'apart' or 'passage to and fro'.[1]

e. *The relational form—a necessary 'appearance'*

It indeed seems necessary to emphasize that Bradley's formulation of thought's characteristic plight is by no means as forced as at first sight it may appear to be. If it be protested that qualities and relations may, with impunity, be accepted as the original disposition of content in given reality, and that his entire dialectic is (therefore) a mere web conjured up in wilful deviation from the real as it actually is, Bradley would answer readily as follows:

Our task in metaphysics is not merely to accept the given as a relatedness of distinct parts, but to understand *how* the two aspects of unity and diversity—heightened in their distinctness by the emergence, or accentuation, of new differences in the given—could be held intelligibly together. And it is precisely when we attempt this task that difficulties emerge. Specially because it itself is an attempt to hold differences as one, thought can ignore neither the unity or relatedness nor the 'qualitied' or differentiated character of the given. But when, in response to its own inner impulse, as also with a view to understanding what is given, it tries to see if (or how) the one and the many can self-consistently be held as one, it is kept tossing without respite from one set of terms and relations to another in unending incomprehension. What is more, its inability consistently to hold unity and diversity can perhaps be realized even without indulging in dialectical subtleties. In fact, a mere look at the way in which thought actually works is here enough. In practice it habitually ignores one of the two aspects, unity or diversity, just as it suits its purpose of the moment, caring little for consistency. Thus, when we speak

[1] AR 18–19; CE 633, 647, 654, 669.

generally of things as related, their individuality may be merely skimmed; and when we dwell upon one object, the tendency is to blink its unity with what it seems merely to exclude.[1]

This brings us to a consideration of Bradley's explicit view that the relational form is a necessary appearance. Its necessity should by now be obvious, provided we accept Bradley's conception of the metaphysician's attempt to 'understand' given reality. But, that it is still an 'appearance' is no less patent. We have seen how a collision between its relational way of working and the goal which it pursues infects the very essence of thought. This, however, is not the only way to show that the relational form is a self-contradiction, and a passing reference may be made to the following other remarks of Bradley which are here relevant:

(a) A relation gets its terms, necessarily distinct, by discarding the manner of feeling. But on the other hand, the assurance—no less essential for the existence of a relation—that the differences are actually held as one is provided by feeling, not by thought which (we have seen) cannot in its own distinctive way hold diversities together. And in so far as the distinctness and the unity of the terms are both alike indispensable for it, a relation, we may say, is compelled both to transcend and to acquiesce in feeling:

> 'You can have the terms ... only so far as (in order to have the relation) ... you abstract from the former mode of unity on which ... (to keep your relation, which requires some unity) you are forced vitally to depend.'[2]

The relational form gains its distinctive character by seeking to leave out that without which it cannot yet exist; and the attempted independence is at once a contradiction.

(b) To put it differently, the existence of a relation clashes with the way in which it functions. As it exists or occurs in experience a relation is identical with the whole relational situation. In Bradley's view, such a situation means nothing but an actual relation considered in all its features—its individual mass of detail, often sensible; the sense of passage that it involves; the emotional

---

[1] Cf. AR 28; CE 638–39.
[2] *Ibid* 637. It may be noted, in passing, that Bradley is opposed to the view that we have *immediate* experience of mere relations of various kinds. *Ibid* 655.

tone which may accompany it; its relative occupancy of, or strain on attention; its frequency of occurrence or range of influence; and, above all, the continual sense, may be implicit, that the (distinct) terms in fact hold together.[1] To illustrate, the perception of two bright eyes as set in the face below the forehead, and at some distance from each other—surely, this relation as experienced, and not merely as thought of, is not just a strip between the two eyes; 'it is not merely the terms, or a bare form of union between them', but is rather the entire relational fact, presented, with all its sensuous detail, as one individual whole. But, as it is seen to relate or to function, the relation is less than the whole of relatedness. The terms now appear as distinct existences, each against the other, and both against the relation which holds them apart. The wholeness or non-relational quality of experienced fact is thus in part transcended, and the relation comes to appear as a mere element in and against the whole.

The dilemma here is briefly this. If we try to hold on to the unity which is actual, our awareness of distinctness is weakened, and our experience tends to change into the manner of feeling. If, on the other hand, we acknowledge the diversity, unity suffers. And if, as an attempt to avoid one-sidedness, we try to do justice to both unity and diversity, the task, we have seen, cannot in fact be accomplished so long as thought continues to work in the way it has to. The existence of a relation demands a unity which its working tends to dissipate; and in so far as our awareness of a relation is at once an experience of its working and its existence, we are left wondering if, to shed off the discord, the relation could exist without functioning or function without existing.[2]

The consideration that, as the essential form of thinking, a relation is always less than the whole of experience in which it is in fact grounded, has a vital bearing on Bradley's attitude to the relational form in general. It leads him to the view that no relational construction can give us the whole truth about given reality. In the region of fact the truth of this view is easily borne out. Thus, when we speak of a toy on the cornice, most of the details of the situation—say, the size and colour of the toy—may be easily ignored. But—and this is what we have always to remember—even

[1] *Ibid* 674–76.
[2] Cf. *Ibid* 637.

where we speak of a relation between ideas, the terms are abstractions from an ideal whole in which they both participate and without which the relation in question could not really occur. Thus, the ideal transition from 'cause' to 'effect' would be impossible were not the idea of the cause linked up with the other ideas of distinctness, priority, change and power or efficiency.[1] It is true that in practice a cause (or an effect) may appear simple and self-existent; and that, in so far as the terms of a relation insist on having their own measure of individuality, such abstraction is for thought unavoidable.[2] But this neither justifies nor compels indifference to the truth that, though the relational form is necessary, no relations—not even necessary ones—are as such adequate to the whole reality.

The way in which its terms are abstracted from their respective wholes determines whether a relation is, on the whole, external or internal. If a term is wrenched away from its setting and merely conjoined with something else—say, as when we imagine a blue man—the relation would appear merely external; for, in spite of the togetherness into which they have been forced, the terms are not directly suggestive of each other. If, on the other hand, the terms are distilled as symbols of the essential character of the whole in which they participate, as when we speak of the good man pursuing a moral ideal, the relation is internal.[3] Some relations are therefore clearly more internal than others, depending on 'how much of the fact' has by relational perception been 'fixed within an individual term'.[4] But in so far as every term is in some way an abstraction from a wider whole, the truth that it is always in fact related to what may seem to be merely beyond it—or that being-in-relation is the very essence of things—should (in Bradley's view) never be ignored.

---

[1] Cf. *Ibid* 668; AR 46.

[2] 'If we are to understand, the way of abstraction and analysis is necessary.' CE 664.

[3] Whether any relation can actually be merely internal is, of course, a different matter.

[4] Cf. CE 646. It may be noted in passing that, in Bradley's view, a relation as such has no 'degrees'. It either 'is there or is not there'; and that we can speak of its 'degrees' only when we take into account the situation in which it occurs and from which it is an attempted abstraction. *Ibid* 675.

THE RELATIONAL FORM

3. RELATIONS AS 'INTERNAL'

An examination of Bradley's doctrine of the essential internality of relations may now be attempted. This will be no digression from the task in hand. For our conclusion, following Bradley, would be that a relation, though essentially internal, can never be merely so; and that the attempt to understand how a relation can be *both* internal and external to the terms only reaffirms the unintelligible, because self-contradictory, character of the relational form.

Our discussion here may proceed along the following main lines of inquiry:

(i) What does the doctrine of 'internality' say?
(ii) How is it relevant to the metaphysics of Bradley?
(iii) His positive arguments in support of the theory.
(iv) His (negative) demonstration that no relations can be *merely* external.
(v) Is the causal relation 'internal' or merely 'external'?

(i) A word now as to what the theory in question says. It holds that, instead of being an extraneous bond merely superimposed upon the terms, a relation is grounded, if only partly, in the nature of what it relates; or that 'the character of the terms appoints and limits the relations in which they stand';[1] and, finally, that 'everything, if we knew enough, would turn out to be internally related to everything else'. On the other hand, 'those who believe in external relations usually hold a qualified position, saying that some things are related externally, others not'; and that, at least in some cases 'relatedness and independence are quite compatible'. The point of controversy between the rival theories simply is 'whether a term could be what it is apart from the relations it bears to others. ... A relation is internal to a term when in its absence the term would be different; it is external when its addition or withdrawal would make *no* difference to the term.'[2]

(ii) Now, it is easy to see that if everything is in fact related internally to everything else, the metaphysician's task of understanding reality 'somehow as a whole' is at once facilitated. This,

[1] Blanshard, *The Nature of Thought*, London, George Allen & Unwin, 1955, Vol. II, 482.
[2] *Ibid* 451.

however, is not the only way in which the doctrine is relevant to Bradley's metaphysics. His entire dialectic of qualities and relations could, in a way, be said to be grounded in the theory of 'internality'. The realization, that the relational form is in essence self-discrepant, comes partly as a result of our inability to understand self-consistently the *necessary* togetherness of terms and relations; and it is, in Bradley's view, precisely this necessity which the doctrine in question, in the main, emphasizes.

A considerable part of the controversy, whether relations are internal or external, turns around the meaning that we give to the 'nature' of a specific term. A *thing's* 'nature', we may say, is indicated by the way in which we define it logically. Bradley's concern, on the other hand, is with a term *as such*. He holds, quite generally, that it is the very essence of a term to be self-transcendent or that without its relational context a term just cannot be. In so far as this simple insistence of Bradley is in general ignored by his critics, we think it necessary to elaborate it as follows:

Consider a complex where the relation seems to be merely 'external': the book is on the table. The book and the table are the terms, and 'on' stands for the relation which obtains between them. But, holding on to fact, are the book and the table ever found without any relation of, say, 'alongside of', 'in front of', 'upon' or 'below' between them? And does any one of these relations anywhere exist as a mere link with but two ends of its own, that is, without falling between—and relating—actual terms distinct from the relation? True, the terms of a relation, as also the relation between them, can both easily change. But what is utterly impossible (we have seen) is to find a relation wholly without terms or a term wholly without relations. Now, if their mutual involvement is so unremitting, how shall we express this truth except by saying that terms and relations are internal to each other?

The suspicion may, however, persist that what we have said is a bit too general, and not really true of particular cases. But, the self-transcendence of terms in a *specific* relation is, in our view, quite easy to see. No two things can in fact be related to each other unless, transcending (so to speak) their visible bounds, they both already partake of some identical whole. This is precisely the point in Bosanquet's significant remark: 'Why is it absurd to ask for the distance from London Bridge to one o'clock? Surely because the one term is in space and the other in time.'[1] Bradley's view is that even if the relation be so obviously external as the one involved in comparing, say, virtue with a fountain pen, we have at least accepted 'the truth that existence or thought is an identity which somehow has within it these diversities, and that they are somehow connected in and qualify this unity'.[2]

If it be objected that the conception of a term's 'nature' advocated above gives us no distinctive knowledge about anything in particular, Bradley's answer would simply be that what is true of all terms as such cannot fairly be regarded as being wholly unimportant, and that the conception of 'nature' as logical definition in no way reduces the need to insist on the necessary self-transcendence of a term.

The second point, however, needs a word of comment. In defining a thing logically we necessarily abstract some of its features from what it actually is. The definition arrived at is supported throughout by this process of abstraction, and a reference to what is left out is all along necessarily *implied*, so that the 'nature' as defined is even now self-transcendent. It would here be improper to protest that the alleged 'reference' or relation does not in fact appear as a positive link in the mind's eye; for, we are in this case dealing professedly with ideas, not with images or sensible facts. It is a plain contradiction to posit an 'ideal' nature and to ask for visible connexions.

That definitions are both necessary and helpful is of course unquestionable. In a way, they may even be said to favour the doctrine of 'internality', as when the 'mortality' of Socrates is seen to follow directly from the very definition of man as mortal. But, does not our understanding of the man–mortality relation improve unmistakably, and does not this relation come to impress us as being more genuinely internal, when we pass on to take increasing notice of the individual's actual being and environment —say, of his involvement with the physical and the physiological which makes him so necessarily mutable? There is certainly some

---

[1] Bosanquet, 'The Doctrine of Relevant Relations', included in Ewing's *The Idealist Tradition*, 179.

[2] Cf. AR 520, footnote. Also see: '... The idea that, apart from its implication beyond itself in some whole, you could possibly starting from any kind of term, pass in any way beyond its limits is to me a radical error.' CE 646.

point in Bradley's repeated warning, which is generally ignored, that the larger interests of understanding always require us to have a look at what is, by a theoretical construction, necessarily left out.

(iii) It is obvious that our defence of 'internality' is as yet very sketchy. But, a closely reasoned—and, in our view, convincing—vindication of the doctrine has already been attempted by Blanshard in his reply to Nagel's objections;[1] and, for our purpose, the following simple remarks should do, primarily by way of formulating and defending *Bradley's* arguments in support of the doctrine:

(a) However we regard it, no object of experience is in truth self-complete.

If we turn to a diversity which is merely felt, we see at once that it is included in a whole, and is therefore self-transcendent. To deny this, on the ground that merely being found along with something else does not *prove* anything at all, would be clearly improper. No question of proof as ideal demonstration can here be permitted; for, we have already agreed to go by the evidence of mere fact. This we did when we decided not to idealize the given, and to keep close to what is merely felt. So, when we *find* that the details of experience are in fact integral to a psychic whole, we must, to be consistent, admit that they are self-incomplete.

If, on the other hand, the detail in question be regarded as an object of thought or as a 'quality' it is, we have seen, clearly relational.

Of course, everything would here depend on whether difference is a relation at all. But, as Blanshard rightly contends, if likeness is a relation, difference cannot be anything else:

'Likeness and difference go together in our thought as having the same sort of being; but likeness is plainly a relation, and it would be odd if difference were not. And if it really is not, what else can it be? To call it a substance, or a quality, or an event, or a way of behaving, or indeed anything *except* a relation seems forced and unnatural. We must conclude that it is either a relation or some form of being that is unique; and this it clearly is not'.[2]

[1] Nagel's essay, 'Sovereign Reason', included in Ewing's *The Idealist Tradition*, 317–45; and Blanshard, *Reason and Analysis*, 478–90.
[2] Blanshard, *The Nature of Thought*, Vol. II, 477.

Bradley's own argument, we have seen, is that difference as *judged* is a relation. Why it is not readily acknowledged as such may be due to the fact that it is often misconstrued as the image of two points held apart in the mind with nothing between them. The emptiness is taken to stand for a total absence of connection. But the image is a sheer deception—an encroachment by sense upon the idiom of thought. To understand a thing as different is necessarily to distinguish it from something else, and if we compare two things, do they still remain for thought wholly apart and disconnected?

But, admitting that it is in some way a relation, how are we to know that difference is 'internal' rather than 'external'? Now, to this our answer readily is that it is clearly 'internal', in so far as, were it absent, the term would cease to be what it actually is. A circle is no circle if it does not differ from a triangle.

(b) If, as is frequently the case, we find it impossible to pass from a thing to some of its properties, the inability may be due only to the fact that our understanding of the object is so far incomplete. It would indeed be dogmatic to reject summarily the contention of Bradley that 'the merely external is ... our ignorance set up as reality'.[1] Is it not a recurring feature of scientific progress that what first appears as a mere conjunction is, by further investigation, turned into a connection of aspects inwardly affirmed?[2] And in cases where no inner bond has yet been found between a thing and some of its characters, can we really be sure that further research in the direction is impossible or unnecessary?

Bradley's appeal, we must remember, is primarily to a basic demand of our being, rather than to any evidence of fact. Thought insists irrepressibly that there must be a reason why any two things in fact go together.[3] Thus, with regard to the togetherness of Socrates and a snub nose, we find it difficult to believe that the total fact before us is a hyphenated compound of two originally self-existent entities—a Socrates without (such) a nose and a

---

[1] AR 517.
[2] Ewing, *Idealism, A Critical Survey*, London, Methuen & Co., 3rd Edition, 1961, 176; Blanshard, *The Nature of Thought*, Vol. II, 457–58.
[3] Cf. 'The intellect cannot be reduced to choose between accepting an irrational conjunction or rejecting something given. For the intellect can always accept the conjunction not as bare but as a connexion, the bond of which is at present unknown.' AR 503.

snub-nose alike isolated. Conversely, we tend instinctively to accept the more tenable hypothesis that all the features of the living Socrates are but differentiations brought about by participation in some physiological law which holds them intelligibly together. Again, as Nagel points out, it may well be that the specific shapes which a metal assumes in different circumstances are not inferable (only)[1] from its definition as a metal. But, we ask, will any other metal assume precisely the same shapes under the same conditions? Are we not immediately repelled by the suggestion that its *specific* degree of malleability has *nothing* to do with what the metal in fact is?

(c) The ideal of taking increasing recognition of a thing's relational context—with a view to reducing the extent of what seems merely external to it—or of a comprehensive, unified whole of all possible knowledge, has of course often been questioned. Nagel, for instance, points out that for a lady who is interested merely in having a beautiful appearance, it is quite unnecessary to acquire any such knowledge of (say) hair which is not strictly confined to the beauty parlour. Moreover, if a thoroughly interconnected knowledge of all that exists is in fact unattainable, and if the various branches of knowledge are at present doing well enough within their own special bounds, is not the ideal of a 'conjectural' totality of knowledge irrelevant to human reason?[2]

Now, if he is confronted with such objections, Bradley would say that the specificity of a practical task is by no means original; that it is a mere abstraction forced by convenience and aptitude; and that, therefore, the attempt to overstep its visible bounds may even be practically useful, provided the transition is not a mere jump. To illustrate, will not the lady who is worried about the beauty of her hair be well advised (also) to have an idea of how its roots are nourished? What is the warrant for assuming that beyond the present extent of our concern with an object not a step can be usefully taken? And to turn to theory, the ideal of a perfectly unified whole of knowledge seems highly desirable. Is not the very variety of viewpoints, from which the same object may in different sciences be studied, a pointer to the truth that within

---

[1] Bradley himself insists that no relation can be deduced entirely from its terms.

[2] Cf. Nagel's essay, 'Sovereign Reason', *op. cit.* 326–27.

no individual field is it completely known? And if—as is hardly challengeable—this inadequacy is theoretically dissatisfying, must not an attempt occasionally be made to harmonize the findings of the various sciences? The ideal of knowing a thing exhaustively, and from every conceivable point of view is admittedly unattainable; but the limit can always be pushed back, and—as a principle which impels knowledge to be continually progressive—the ideal is quite relevant to human reason. Nor is it proper to say that the perfectly unified whole of knowledge which serves as our theoretical ideal is merely 'conjectural'; for even scientific investigation does not, on the whole, warrant the belief that our knowledge of a thing is in no way improved by a study of what seems merely beyond it.

It may here be objected that, in so far as—upon Bradley's own view—whatever is experienced gains its individual distinctness by being contrasted with what is beside it, the attempt to include more and more of its context in our understanding of an object is from the start self-cancelling. Our view, however, is that the objection does not really establish what it may seem to. This may be argued as follows:

First, it is clear that a consideration of the context will here be motivated entirely by the desire for fuller knowledge. The larger, ideal whole arrived at will, at every step, be internally more organized; and the gain in internal harmony and inclusiveness, at once a growth in respect of understanding. Secondly, a perfectly organized understanding of *all* that can (in principle) be known about an object will never in fact be attained in the way our intellect normally works. If our passage from the 'thing' to its context is to be really intelligent, the intellect must, in some measure, abstract; and there will always in fact be a core of organized qualities, as compared to which the other, as-yet-uncomprehended characters or relations of the object will (continue to) appear as relatively external. In other words, what an increasing consideration of 'context' may be expected to accomplish in fact is not the total elimination of all difference between the object and its setting, but only a reduction of our present ignorance of what seems to be merely beside it; and this, to be sure, is one of the accepted ideals of knowledge.

If, 'per impossibile', our understanding of the object becomes so comprehensive as to embrace *all* its relations and characters, every statement describing the thing would indeed be analytical; but, we hasten to add, it would be by no means trivial. The ideal whole arrived at would be a rational synthesis, and no mere totality; and every individual statement about the object would now be no bootless perception of a part which merely *is* within the whole, but an intellectual realization of how the value of every bit of what we know about it arises from its membership in a common unity.[1]

(iv) It would, however, be improper to ignore the objections put forth against the doctrine of 'internality'; and we turn presently to the most powerful of them—the argument from an appeal to universals. In the hands of Nagel, it assumes two main forms:

(a) We may admit that a man's redheadedness and his other attributes are causally related. But, how does it follow that they are related to it even logically? And if they are not, they cannot be said to 'follow' from—and so are merely external to—redheadedness.[2]

(b) Again, redheadedness is found and *known as such* in different individuals. In other words, it remains unaffected by variations in its context. How can we then say that it is related 'internally' to what goes along with it in fact?

Now, the first form of the objection may for the present be ignored, not because we think it to be unimportant, but first because it involves the wider question as to the nature of necessity which cannot adequately be discussed within the brief compass of this essay; and, secondly, because whatever of consequence Bradley has to say on the question, if causation involves logical necessity, will be indicated a little later, when we turn to study his attitude to causation. With regard to the second form of Nagel's objection, Bradley's answer would, in brief, be this:

Redheadedness can be regarded variously. If we confine ourselves to its mere idea as a universal, its distinctness as such is maintained necessarily by its contrast with the ideas of plurality and change; which means that its relation to them, though

---

[1] For 'entailment' is not mere inclusion. Blanshard, *Reason & Analysis*, 483-84.
[2] Nagel, 'Sovereign Reason', *op. cit.* 336.

implicit, is clearly internal or necessary. To consider redheadedness as an actual fact, if we notice it unreflectingly no distinctions are made; and we cannot here be said to *judge* that the character in question remains itself in spite of variations in its context. But if, as Nagel believes, the fact of redheadedness is 'known' to remain selfsame in the midst of diverse context, the reference is obviously to a sensible feature which is *perceived* as standing out against contextual instability; and *this* feature, as it on the whole appears, certainly undergoes some change, however slight.[1] So, both as idea and as fact, the character of 'redheadedness' is in a vital way one with what it is contrasted with. The relation is internal.

A variant of this objection may also be considered. A number can be seen to slip into—and to come out of—different relations without itself undergoing any change. Are not its relations, therefore, merely external? 'The number 8, for instance, will always remain the same number in all the relations in which it can be placed to other numbers—such as 8×4, 8 plus 3, and $8-5\ldots$'[2] It may therefore be said that the 'internality' hypothesis is applicable only to relations between concrete terms, not to those which involve abstract universals.

Now, in both AR and CE, Bradley has made certain remarks which suggest the following answer to the objection just outlined:

First, the significance of a number depends on its relation to the 'whole world of number'.[3] Bradley would insist on this; for, it is, we have seen, his basic argument for the internality of relations—the one which is built around the original self-transcendence of terms. Relations are so internal to the notion of a number that it can never wholly shake them off, without losing all significance as a number, as distinguished from its mere existence as a character in print. Secondly, changes in the relational fact or situation which occur when two numbers enter a (new) relation can never be explained entirely by the relation itself, but are always in part determined by the specific nature of the terms. Thus, when '8 plus 2' gives us '10', shall we say that the terms do not make *any*

[1] Cf. AR 518-21.
[2] Aliotta, *The Idealistic Reaction against Science*, London, Macmillan & Co., 1914, 337.
[3] CE 667. Cf. Blanshard: 'The practice of using universals *as if* they were thus independent proves nothing as to whether they *are* so.' *The Nature of Thought*, Vol. II, 491.

contribution to the product? Is the product a result only of the process of addition considered in itself? And if we here admit, as we have to, that 8 and 2 both contribute to the product, it would be inconsistent to hold that they are still self-complete. To insist that they have not undergone any change would really be to talk of such '8' and '2' as have not been added up. Here, about the number which is said to remain unaltered by the relation which it enters, Bradley rightly says:

> 'Yes, so far as you abstract and keep your abstraction; but this is (ex hyp.) just what you *don't* do when you predicate. And so far as you *don't*, it's false that ... (the number) ... is one and the same simply.'[1]

It may, in such cases, be extremely difficult to describe the precise changes suffered by a term when it gets involved in a new relation. But a theoretical necessity is not cancelled by a mere practical inability. An inability of the kind here referred to 'is not a ground of disproof, unless you assume that differences nowhere may be asserted unless the exact and particular point of diversity can be specified'.[2] The assumption, we may add, cannot fairly be made. For, to illustrate, even though it may not be known where precisely a term ends and its relation begins, is it not both needful and proper to posit some difference between a term and its relation?

Bradley's considered opinion is that what makes it plausible to talk of *merely* external relations is only the failure to 'emphasize the difference between our abstractions and the concrete fact'. Thus, when we speak of a thing or a person as remaining unaffected by a change in the relational context, we are in fact talking of a mere character ideally abstracted; and 'what is not proved at all is that this character could *exist* independent and naked'.[3] This would, in brief, be Bradley's answer to those who protest that a thing does not change when its spatial relations to other things are changed,[4] or that on becoming a father a man remains exactly what he was before the event.

(v) So far, however, we have not at all considered such criticisms of the 'internality' hypothesis as seem to draw added strength

[1] CE 666.
[2] *Ibid* 664.
[3] AR 513.
[4] *Ibid* 517.

from an appeal to the verification theory of meaning. Perhaps the most penetrating account of such objections is the one given by Schlick[1] in favour of Hume's view that causation is mere succession. As to Hume's own arguments on the matter, we may only say that they no longer go unquestioned.[2] But the protest of Schlick may be dealt with at some length—first, because Feigl hails it as a convincing refutation of the attempts made by Ewing and Blanshard to 'assimilate causation to logical entailment', and secondly, because it is in our view quite possible to meet the challenge of Schlick by availing ourselves of Bradley's attitude to causation.

A general remark may be immediately made before we turn to discuss the issue in question. Feigl's contention that 'the rationalistic conception ... *identifies* ... the causal relation with the logical relation of implication or entailment.'[3] is certainly not true of Bradley, Blanshard and Ewing, all of whom are in fact expressly opposed to the *identification* of causation with logical necessity.[4]

Now, to Schlick:

He formulates 'the philosophical problem of causality' thus: 'What is the difference between the proposition: "E follows C", and the proposition: "E is the effect of the cause C" or "E is because of C"? In other words, what is the distinctive *meaning* of "because of"?'

Here, obviously, we are faced with a question of meaning or verification. The way in which a causal proposition is in fact verified is, according to Schlick, only one: we take into account the regularity of the sequence in question, and nothing else. It is this regularity which in practice enables us to mark off a causal sequence from a merely temporal one. An example will bear this out. If a medicine brings about a cure in every patient suffering from a

---

[1] Moritz Schlick, 'Causality in Everyday Life and in Recent Science', included in *Contemporary Philosophic Problems*, ed. Y. H. Krikorian and A. Edel, New York, The MacMillan & Co., 1959, 350–59.

[2] See, for instance, Blanshard's *Reason and Analysis*, Chapter XI.

[3] Herbert Feigl's article, 'Notes on Causality', included in: H. Feigl and M. Brodbeck, *Readings in the Philosophy of Science*, New York, Appleton-Century-Crofts, Inc., 1953, 408. Our italics.

[4] Thus, see PL 544–46; Blanshard, *The Nature of Thought*, Vol. II, 496; Ewing, *Idealism*, 172, 174; and Ewing's article, 'The Necessity of Metaphysics', included in *Contemporary British Philosophy* (3rd series), ed. H. D. Lewis, London, George Allen & Unwin, 1956, 154.

particular disease, we say it is the cause of the cure. If the cure comes off only in some cases, not in others, we say that it comes merely as a matter of chance, or that it only follows, but is not caused by the medicine: 'The word cause, as used in everyday life, implies *nothing but* regularity of sequence, because *nothing else* is used to verify the proposition in which it occurs.'[1] Schlick, however, hastens to admit that, in so far as even the most regular sequence is not actually seen to hold in every (future) case, we cannot claim to have any 'clear concept of causality'. 'Where there is no definite verification, there can be no definite meaning.'[2]

It is further contended that, far from being a process of logical reasoning, the act of understanding a specific causal sequence consists only in the perception of what comes between the cause and the effect, and that what we *find* between the two is no causal *bond*, but only the succession of events—only 'links', no 'linkage'. Thus, to understand the relation between a drug and the cure which it effects we have only to observe that it is injected into the veins, and comes into immediate contact with the blood particles; that the latter thereupon undergo a certain chemical change, and travel throughout the body, affecting and changing an organ in a particular way; and so on. It is these events which make the causal chain.[3] What further research may discover between any two of these contiguous events will always be yet another event, and no linkage or tie other than these events.

Schlick warns us that to insist on getting a 'linkage' besides these links is to commit a common mistake which leads us necessarily to 'the region of nonsense'—the mistake of pressing thought beyond its 'logical limit'. 'Whatever can be observed and shown in the causal chain will be the links but it would be nonsense to look for the linkage.'[4] The 'mysterious' causal 'tie', other than the intervening events, is 'not a concept, but a mere word' vainly seeking meaning in a region beyond verification. Even willing, it is added, is merely the close sequence of, say, one bodily event upon

---

[1] Schlick, 'Causality in Everyday Life and in Recent Science', *op. cit.* 352.
[2] *Ibid* 353.
[3] This contrasts finely with Bradley's view that causation is no 'phenomenal sequence' or existing link, and that it is essentially an 'ideal construction formed by our minds'. PL 537–38.
[4] Schlick's essay on Causality, *op. cit.* 358.

a mental one. There is nothing in between the two. We certainly see them glued together, but we do not see the glue itself.

To conclude: causation, according to Schlick, is everywhere mere regularity of succession. It is no internal connexion between events.

Now, our answer, in the manner of Bradley, may be put as follows:

(a) Consider, to begin with, the way in which Schlick formulates the problem. He asks: 'How does "E follows C" differ from "E is because of C"? Or, what is the meaning of "because of"?'

Now, our immediate protest here is that Schlick entirely ignores the process of ideal construction which enters necessarily into our perception: 'E follows C regularly'; and that the sequence in question is never in fact self-complete. Nothing is to be *found* entirely by itself—neither C nor E. Thus, to turn to Schlick's own example, at the very start we leave out every other factor except the 'injection'—such as the effect of some previous medicine, or of rest, or the patient's will to recover—which may all have already started the patient's process of recovery, or at least prepared grounds for it. And, at the other end, while considering the cure as the 'effect', we shut out all changes beyond a certain time-limit, which is again a limit drawn by us, so that any appearance of the old disease after this limit is called a relapse, not a continuation of the old attack. In other words, what we speak of as 'cause' and 'effect' are as events not self-existent; they are products of abstraction from actual reality. This exclusion of irrelevant material may be merely implicit, but unless it is resorted to we just cannot speak of (mere) E following (mere) C.

Further, what we have said is true not only of C and E, but of 'follows'. What follows the injection immediately is, at least in some cases, a slight shudder of pain; but this we entirely ignore. To us, it is the 'cure', rather than anything else, which follows—and is the 'effect' of—the injection. The whole truth about the case in question is clearly this. *We* decide to take the injection as the start of the process, leaving out the entire context in which it occurs; traverse the series of contiguous events which follows; stop short at some specific changes, collectively called cure; and then, leaving out all the intermediate events, ideally link up the injection with these changes (or 'cure'), calling it *their* cause, not of anything else.¹ The start, the traversing, and the close of the ideal process are all our fixations in the flow of events. As thus distinguished, they do not in fact exist, and it is incorrect to suppose that in perceiving the drug-cure sequence we merely slide along the flux of events passively. But, if this is so—if the cause, the effect, and the specific relation of succession between them are all, in the main, a result of our ideal manipulation—is it really proper to insist on (merely) *finding* the bond, if any, between the cause and the effect?

(b) The full force of this question cannot, however, be realized without first reflecting as to the precise way in which a specific sequence is understood to be causal. Bradley would here like to explain as follows:

First, to speak generally, we want to understand the given; and this need cannot be met without resorting to ideal construction. It is difficult indeed to accept Schlick's suggestion that *understanding* may be provided by the mere perception of what comes in between the 'cause' and the 'effect':

'... Suppose the whole mass of detail to be presented, suppose not the smallest detail to fail—is this huge congeries an explanation? Or what is explanation? Does it not rather consist in finding within this mass the thread of connection?'²

The mere perception of intermediates is neither enough nor indispensable for understanding. Thus, to illustrate, what comes between exposure to cold and an attack of influenza may just be an hour of restlessness, but does this intervening fact in any way explain the ailment? Conversely, when the falling of an apple is said to be due to the law of gravitation, we certainly have some explanation, even though no intermediate details are here presented.³

The last point may be developed. If a causal sequence is 'understood' merely by observing what is found between the cause and the effect, as in the case of the drug-cure sequence, and if what comes between the two is always a *succession* of events,

---

[1] Cf. 'To experience a definite relation of succession demands the separation of irrelevant and relevant.' PL 539; 539–41.
[2] *Ibid* 541.
[3] 'Intermediate' is here to be taken in the sense of some actual *event* coming in between two other events. *Ibid* 541–43.

how are we to explain our understanding of, say, the 'impulse–action' sequence? The different elements of our experience in this case are: an implicit awareness that the self is continually involved; an experience of constraint; and, above all, a felt sense of interpenetration of content, so that whereas the impulse is felt as spilling into action, the latter may be seen to relieve—or for some time heighten—the impulse at work. These features, here, permeate our experience; they are no unitary events that only intervene. Yet the sequence *is* understood as being clearly causal.

Of course, the felt details of experience are here all subjective; and some may feel tempted to say that, in so far as they are merely psychological, they should be ignored. But to yield to this temptation would be clearly improper; and yet this is precisely what the positivist freely does. The philosophical attempt to discover the meaning of causation should, in our view, begin by considering all the ways in which the word 'cause' is normally used, even though, at the outset of our inquiry, we may have no idea at all as to where in the end the attempt will lead us. What Herbert Feigl proudly commends as a 'purification'—initiated by Galileo, completed by Hume and confirmed irrevocably by the positivistic treatment of causation[1] today—is perhaps only an arbitrary fixation of its meaning. For, to deny the involvement of causation as willing with the ideas of self, energy and necessitation seems no less improper than to credit gravitation with a will to determine bodies. In his attitude to the concept in question the positivist quietly ignores a whole region of inconvenient facts. What is, on the other hand, needed is a study of causation in its full ideal range—that is, as involved with the ideas of activity, power, change and succession. That, as a result of this complication, causation is found in the end unintelligible is quite another matter. It certainly does not justify a dogmatic restriction of our enquiry at the very start. And, after all, as Schlick himself admits, the criterion of regularity too does not enable us to arrive at a 'clear idea of causation'.

Secondly, to turn once again to the instance cited by Schlick, the *specific* understanding that the injection is the cause of 'cure' is not provided by merely following the various physiological changes which happen between the two events. It rather accrues

---

[1] Feigl, 'Notes on Causality', *op. cit.* 408.

thus. As we set out to traverse the chain of events, we already have a hypothesis on hand. Perhaps we are told, or we ourselves posit, that the cure of a particular ailment may follow the administration of a particular drug. Our attention, when we come to actual verification, is therefore from the beginning set on two events, the injection and the 'cure', as against the rest; and we want to verify the connection between *these* two. It is this prior orientation which determines where in verifying we start and where precisely we end. And our survey of the chain of events is no passive process; it is rather an active manipulation of the series on the basis of an ideal connection that we have already made, however tentatively.

(c) This connection is certainly 'mythical' if we look for it in the flux of events; but if our aim be at knowing how the perception of a specific sequence at all becomes possible, it is there undeniably —as an implicit pre-condition. When the entire chain of events, from 'injection' to 'cure', is unfolded before our eyes, 'understanding' of the causal link is provided not by the observed as such, but by the realization that what is seen confirms—though it does not reproduce—the link that we have already made. Our mind here moves in some such way. The ideal link is there; in actuality too we find the cure following the injection; hence the ideal link is verified. What is confirmed is always an ideal link and what really constitutes verification in such cases is the observation *not merely* that the specific intermediates come regularly, but that they come between the two ends of a connection which *we* have fixed by way of specifying our concern. Bradley adds that, in so far as it is consequent upon a process of 'ideal decomposition and reconstruction', the expectation that a specific causal sequence will recur in future is never merely psychological. What we expect is not the mere recurrence of a sequence, but that events in future will conform to, or verify an ideal construction we have made.

(d) Regularity of sequence is in fact neither indispensable nor by itself enough for the perception of causal sequences. Consider an instance. A man writes his *first* poem today. No regularity is here involved; and yet what is produced is clearly the effect of an efficient cause. Conversely, in spite of its inexorable regularity, the day-night sequence is not (ordinarily) regarded as a case of causal succession. Why is this so? Schlick's answer is: simply because day and night are not analysed into a series of natural events.

But, we ask, why not? Why are not 'day' and 'night' in this way analysed? To say that our normal experience of them is one of an unchanging stretch of time would be clearly untrue to fact. Nor would it do to say that whatever sense of change is here experienced —say, at sunset or at sunrise—is not clearly differentiated, and that succession is here absent, and so causation too, in so far as the two are identical. For, it would do nothing to answer the question as to why the change here perceived is not analysed into a succession of events. In our view, the explanation is simple. We do not here resort to any ideal manipulation just because we do not seek to *understand* the sequence of changes. Our concern with day and night is merely practical. This is why we do not seek to distil out of these temporal changes any ideal connection on the basis of which they could be arranged in terms of the cause-effect relation.

(e) Merely as they come to us, together or successively, facts and events do not satisfy us. We want to understand how they are connected, and it is this which necessitates the relational movement of thought, of which the perception of causal sequences is an important individual expression. Conversely, minds which are not really astir to understand an experienced sequence of events may not at all regard it as being causal, even if it repeats itself with unfailing regularity.[1] The events repeated must (in idea) be abstracted and connected before they can be *understood* as being causally related. And, whether we consider the subjective or the objective aspect of experience, the 'connection' must be 'internal' in a sense which is different from the one implicit in the idea of mere succession.[2] It is clearly untrue to common sense to hold that when we talk of two events as cause and effect, we regard them as detached items in a mere series, rather than as so internally connected as to provide for some order in given reality.

(f) The connection, we repeat, is affirmed by our attempt to *understand* things. As such, it is ideal. This does not, however, mean that it is merely imagined. For, first, it is essential theoretically—as implicit in the need to understand the given which is (in Bradley's view) everywhere self-transcendent; and, secondly, if

---

[1] In Bradley's view, 'the repetition serves merely as a help to the abstraction' (PL 540); and to unite facts by an ideal principle is clearly to reason. (*Ibid* 539).

[2] Ewing, *Idealism, A Critical Survey*, 183.

we insist on 'visible' verification, it is warranted by the consideration that some actual sequence answers to it in the region of sensible fact. It is, of course, true that the bond is not as such a part of actual existence. What we find as given is never a straight and clear-cut link between two isolated particulars, but always diversities embedded in a mass of relations and attributes. But, merely because of this, the bond cannot be dismissed as unreal. It is vain to 'look for' it if we seek merely to find it as a part of given reality. But, to insist on its reality is yet quite tenable, for it is clearly *implied* in Nature's intelligible orderliness.[1] It is by no means unchallengeable to believe that whatever is real must as such be a visible item of existence, or that our actual world is subject to no such necessity as is, in the main, grasped by reason, and not by the senses.

(g) Finally, it is true that facts succeed each other so closely that they may be said to crowd out all alien intruders. But, and this is precisely what Schlick seems in general to ignore, to understand is not to remain wholly confined to the given as such; and if we talk at all meaningfully even of a mere succession, we idealize facts forthwith, abstracting them from where they are found, and connecting them ideally. Here, in the idiom of understanding, it is not merely not absurd, but is positively essential that the 'linkage' should differ from the 'links'; for, thought (we argued) must preserve the mutual distinctness of a relation and its terms.

4. CONCLUSION

To conclude: every relation is, to Bradley, essentially internal, in so far as it necessarily contributes something to, and is itself grounded in the character of the terms. Yet, we hasten to add, his opposition to the idea of *merely* internal relations is just as complete.[2] A 'merely' internal relation would be one which does not at all depend on anything beyond the terms, or one in which the terms are related wholly in themselves. But this is, we have

---

[1] PL 540-44. From the fact that we do not see any connection between two events, it does not logically follow that there is no such connection. Ewing, *Idealism*, 175.

[2] CE 642.

seen, inadmissible. 'Our terms cannot make a relation by passing themselves over into it bodily. For in that event their individuality, and with it the required "between" would be lost.'[1]

In the main, however, Bradley's effort is directed against the hypothesis of *merely* external relations.[2] Those who advocate this theory rarely, if ever, acknowledge the need to explain the given togetherness of diversities. But, should they at all decide to make an attempt in this direction, it seems that the only way open to them is to make

> 'a covert appeal to experience in the form of mere feeling . . . But any such appeal must be at once illegitimate and suicidal. For the unity of feeling contains no individual terms with relations between them, while without these no experience can be really relational'.[3]

Bradley therefore insists that a relation is both external *and internal*.[4] His idea of 'essential' internality only means that the words, 'and internal', can in no case be left out, and that all relations are grounded in the original self-transcendence of the terms.

But, if this is so, if a relation is both 'internal' and 'external', it is, we have seen, in the end unintelligible. Bradley's conclusion therefore is that the *entire* relational form is an appearance, and that it cannot claim to give us ultimate truth and reality: 'The whole "either-or" between external and internal relations, to me seems unsound.'[5] It does not, however, follow from their ultimate falsity that all relations are equally self-contradictory. Bradley takes pains to point out that, though ultimate truth can be granted to neither, the doctrine of the essential 'internality' of all relations is preferable to that of *mere* 'externality'. Even generally, the place of 'internality' is in his thought pivotal. Both feeling and Absolute experience are (in his view) characterized by an interpenetration of content which is wholly inexplicable on the hypothesis of mere externality.[6] Thought's typical manner, he insists, is to glide

[1] *Ibid* 644.
[2] AR 513.
[3] CE 643.
[4] *Ibid* 641.
[5] ETR 238.
[6] Cf. *Ibid* 240.

across diversities, the very content and meaning of which shows them as mutually involved. The 'externality' hypothesis, on the other hand, tends to make 'implication' unintelligible.[1] In spite of all his protestations to the contrary, will not even an avowed advocate of this doctrine hesitate to accept as valid an argument which is put as a mere string of disconnected statements? Finally, contradictions which are involved in the idea of a relation as being grounded partly in the terms are not as blatant as those which infect the hypothesis of mere 'externality'. It is only as a result of dialectical thinking that the 'falsity' of our favoured doctrine is clearly revealed. The rival theory, on the other hand, is immediately repellent. It reduces the given to a mere mass of brute, irrational conjunctions.

But, if the very way of thought is in essence self-inconsistent, is there any point left in our pursuit of Reality? Yes, there is; for our conclusion is not merely negative. The ideal of individuality is vindicated in our very dissatisfaction with the relational. If only indirectly, thought presses for its own transcendence in a whole which is both all-inclusive and supra-relational.[2] The doubt, of course, persists: is the whole that we desire *at all* accessible to the working of thought? But, we must somehow be enabled to answer this question affirmatively, if only in part. For if this cannot be done, the alternatives left with us are, we saw, unacceptable. They are: acquiescence in mere feeling or an acceptance of what is but imperfectly individual as the final reality. It is, however, by no means enough to stress our plight or to hope for its redress. The very adequacy of thought to reality may in some (other) ways be questioned; and, prior to any discussion of the Absolute of Bradley, the relation of thought to reality must be examined at some length.

---

[1] *Ibid* 259.
[2] It is in this sense that, with all its imperfection, the relational form is 'a necessary step' towards our idea of the Absolute. AR 522.

V

THOUGHT AND REALITY

The dual character of Bradley's thought, that is, its emphasis on the notion of a perfectly self-consistent Reality, as implicit in the very act of 'rejecting the inconsistent as appearance'; the faith that the metaphysical criterion so far employed is 'intellectually incorrigible'; and, above all, the central idea in his conception of the relation of thought to reality—these are clearly manifest in the following categorical words of his:

> 'To think is to judge, and to judge is to criticize, and to criticize is to use a criterion of reality ... in rejecting the inconsistent as appearance, we are applying a positive knowledge of the ultimate nature of things. Ultimate reality is such that it does not contradict itself; here is an absolute criterion. And it is proved absolute by the fact that, either in endeavouring to deny it, or even in attempting to doubt it, we tacitly assume its validity.'[1]

The suggestion here is that by applying the law of contradiction to given reality we are able to lay bare the true 'nature of things'. But, is this really so? Does the law at all hold of facts?

It is obvious that if Bradley's view is to stand, questions such as these must be answered affirmatively. Could it somehow be proved that the law has no real relevance to things, two conclusions would forthwith emerge: first, that it is absurd to call things 'unreal' merely because they do not conform to the law; and secondly, that where, as in Bradley's metaphysics, this law holds absolute sway, the biggest affirmations, the Absolute itself, can hardly be credited with any bearing on our actual world. On the other hand, the 'relevance' in question cannot be taken for granted. Quite a few modern thinkers deny it completely. What is more, the protest is today grounded in a general opposition to all 'a priori' construction of the universe, and in the concomitant emphasis on verification. Our discussion of the matter may therefore proceed

[1] AR 120.

as under—within a wider theoretical framework, covering quite a few other issues:

(i) Thought and Reality: the viewpoint of science.
(ii) Logic and Reality: the problem as to the ontological relevance of the law of contradiction.
(iii) Fact and the 'a priori'.
(iv) 'Ontologizing' in Bradley.
(v) The Verification theory: the positivistic criticism of Bradley's utterances, and his own attitude to the theory.

If, as a result of our discussion of the above issues, Bradley's attitude to thought and reality is found in the main tenable, his employment of the metaphysical criterion to determine the measure of reality possessed by the individual 'appearances' will cease to appear arbitrary in principle; and it would then seem not only proper, but needful to give some attention to the doctrine of 'degrees' as well.

1. THOUGHT AND REALITY: THE VIEWPOINT OF SCIENCE

The normal exercise of thought aims at understanding some aspect of given reality. It seems equally natural to say that existence is not essentially hostile to our attempts to understand it. The dichotomy of 'inner' and 'outer', of thought and reality is to common-sense artificial; for, in actual experience, content is seen to pass freely from the 'objective' to the 'subjective', and vice versa. A sound heard for long may become a part of the felt, subjective background.[1] Conversely, 'our emotional moods, where we could hardly analyse them, may qualify objects aesthetically'.[2] Bradley invites our attention to the fact that in 'the blind pressure and the struggle of changed sensations'[3] the content of fact is everywhere seen to overflow its 'that';[4] and that when its inner material is thus seen to go beyond the visible bounds of the object, without yet being severed from it, thought is compelled to regard

---
[1] *Ibid* 79.
[2] *Ibid* 80, footnote.
[3] *Ibid* 424.
[4] This is so even when, to use Bradley's words, facts are 'let alone', that is, even if they are not subjected to any deliberate process of analysis or construction.

the given as being relational—that is, as a unity of differences (now) held apart. Thought is thus a legitimate furtherance of the native 'ideality of the given finite';[1] it is, in this sense, internal to reality.

But, even if thinking about reality is accepted as a legitimate and necessary endeavour, how does this warrant Bradley's further assumption that systematic thinking may, on the whole or in the end, be expected to reveal a corresponding order in concrete reality? Does not objectivity demand that, instead of positing an inherent order in reality, we should merely classify facts and let them speak for themselves? This is indeed the attitude of men like Mach and Pearson. But, as Cohen and Polanyi point out, even scientific thinking is not done in this way. Drawing abundant support from the theory and practice of science, and from the introspective utterances of the scientific mind itself, they protest effectively against the belittlement of the role of ideal construction in scientific discovery and method, and argue powerfully in favour of the hypothesis that all scientific work necessarily presupposes an order in nature which *is* there whether we understand it or not, and which is in principle intelligible.[2] Does not a rational principle of making distinctions enter into the process of classification itself, if, as Pearson himself admits, the process means the collection only of 'relevant and crucial' facts? Classification, however thorough, is in fact never enough. The scientist pursues system. He tries to grasp the significance of a thing by seeking to understand it as an integral part of a whole, or as the instance of a principle. He is as sensitive to contradiction as any one else; and science progresses by subsuming lesser systems under a more inclusive one.[3] True, no logically developed science can so far claim to have given us a perfect system, but the ideal of system still holds valid, as revealing the imperfection of the particular sciences, as also the task which they have yet to accomplish.[4]

---

[1] 'Given' here stands not for fact considered in itself, but for 'experienced fact'. Cf. 'Fact which is given . . . changes in our hands.' (AR 146). 'Finite' too is significant. Whatever is given 'at any one moment' is limited (*Ibid* 78); and so is, in Bradley's view, determined—and made to shuffle—by what is left out.

[2] Cohen, *Reason and Nature*, 201.

[3] *Ibid* 113.

[4] Ewing insists that the ideal of system is still powerfully operative in science, and that the criterion of our accepting a hypothesis is logical coherence in a system rather than practical convenience.

A passing reference may here be made to Cohen's well-reasoned view as to the applicability of thought to reality. Scientific laws, he contends, are not mere 'convenient short hand symbols for groups of separate facts that have nothing real in common'; rather, they stand for connections which *are* there. In spite of Mach's protest, harmonic functions do enable us to understand vibrating strings. If nature appears to deviate from our theoretical constructions, it only means that there is something wrong in our thinking, not that reality is intrinsically inaccessible to thought.

Polanyi's protest against Mach's positivistic emphasis on extreme scientific objectivity is exceptionally well-supported by evidence from the history and practice of science itself. His main conclusion is that 'the intuition of rationality in nature ... (is) a justifiable and indeed essential part of scientific theory'; and that it is wrong to think of science as 'a set of statements which is "objective" in the sense that its substance is entirely determined by observation, even while its presentation may be shaped by convention'. The theory of relativity, he tells us, demonstrates clearly 'the power of science to make contact with reality by recognizing what is rational in nature'. It sprang out of an intuitive perception of rationality in nature, unaided by earlier observations.[1]

Yet, it would be improper to blink the strength of the opposite view. Besides Schlick and Poincaré—who voice the popular view in saying that 'mathematics and logic do not point beyond themselves'—there is Einstein to affirm that the laws of mathematics are certain only in so far as they do *not* refer to reality, and that the logical-formal, as distinguished from objective or intuitive content, alone forms the subject-matter of mathematics.[2] The whole issue is, in fact, subject to such an intricate mass of controversy that only the following simple remarks can here be made without much risk:

First, the theoretical necessity of regarding reality as a system is perhaps admitted even by those scientists who want to keep the

---

[1] Polanyi, *Personal Knowledge*, 11; also 4–16.
Here, Reichenbach disagrees. He maintains that 'Einstein has always acknowledged Mach as a forerunner of his theory' (see Reichenbach's article, 'The Philosophical Significance of the Theory of Relativity' in *Readings in the Philosophy of Science*, 203). But Polanyi's argument seems overwhelming. See *Personal Knowledge*, 9–13.

[2] Einstein, 'Geometry and Experience', *Readings in the Philosophy of Science*, 189.

'a priori' entirely away from the region of fact. Thus, we have it on the authority of Reichenbach that, on an admission of Einstein's own, the theory of relativity could not be found had its author not been 'so strongly convinced of the harmony of the universe'.[1] Again, when Reichenbach avers that the method of modern science can be completely accounted for in terms of an empiricism which recognizes only sense perception and the analytic principles of logic as sources of knowledge,[2] are we to understand that these sources feed the enterprise of knowing in absolute separation from each other, or, what appears saner to believe, that the laws of logic are allowed to coordinate—and organize—and thereby correct the deliverances of sense? And what is the warrant for allowing the method of science to sway the working of philosophy?

Secondly, the philosopher who refuses to accept the suggested dissociation of necessity from fact has his own legitimate way of arguing. Indeed, it appears that, unless by 'factual content' we mean merely 'a forecast of our sensation', every proposition could be said to involve a reference to reality considered as a system of fact. A numerical proposition: '7 plus 5 = 12' assumes the validity of the whole system of number which, in turn, is grounded in the actual fact of plurality and difference in the world. The fact that 'after all mathematics has proved to be eminently applicable to empirical subject matter' seems clearly irreconcilable with the view that the propositions of mathematics do not bear any relation to factual content.[3] 'The most formal propositions are those which apply to all kinds of entities, and reference to such possible application is essential to their meaning'.[4]

2. LOGIC AND REALITY

Our primary concern here is, however, with the laws of logic. Do *they* convey any information about facts? Quite a few modern philosophers, we admit, would like to answer this question categorically in the negative. But, those who protest against this severance of logic from reality have their own arguments to

---

[1] Reichenbach, 'The Philosophical Significance of the Theory of Relativity', *op. cit.* 197.
[2] *Ibid* 210.
[3] Blanshard, *Reason and Analysis*, 428-29.
[4] Cohen, *Reason and Nature*, 196.

advance—arguments which, in our view, cannot be easily dismissed. Cohen draws our attention to the fact that, though they are meant primarily to regulate our *understanding* of the real world, the laws of logic, even as they are commonly formulated, 'rather make affirmation of existence: whatever is, is; nothing can both be and not be; everything must either be or not be. Would it not be better to call these propositions invariant laws of being or existence?'[1] Nor is it possible to ignore Blanshard's disagreement with the view that logical laws apply exclusively to thought and language rather than to things. He argues at length how, on every one of the three views of their nature advanced by Prof. Popper, the laws of logic must be interpreted as saying something about our actual world. Again, he maintains that their ontological relevance is in no way harmed by the general protest that they are not propositions, but rules of symbolism. The logician may start by stipulating any arbitrary rules, but once he sets out, as he must, to find out what these rules entail, he cannot avoid crossing over into the region of reality.[2]

Bradley's view on the matter is clear and categorical. He contends that the laws of logic are not bare forms which we can

'so take in hand. The principles of Identity, of Contradiction and of Excluded Middle, are every one material. Matter is implied in their very essence. For without a difference, such as that between letters A and B, or again between the A in two several positions you cannot state or think of these principles. ... And the nature of these differences is clearly material.'[3]

Therefore, even if it is formulated in a way which seems merely formal, say as: 'B and C cannot belong to A at the same time' the law is not absolutely devoid of reference to fact, for difference, which is here clearly present, refers necessarily, if only implicitly, to the fact of plurality. Bradley sees it clearly that, in so far as it is in thought continually *assumed*, the validity of the law of contradiction cannot be proved; but he hastens to add that it can neither be

---

[1] *Ibid* 203.
[2] Blanshard, *Reason & Analysis*, 427, 424–27.
[3] PL 519–20. Blanshard wonders if these strictures of Bradley against formal logic have anywhere been satisfactorily met. *The Nature of Thought*, Vol. II, 372, footnote.

disproved, and that it is therefore a necessary assumption.[1] It indeed seems impossible to conceive of a suspension of this law; for, the very word 'suspension' would then mean both what it normally does and its opposite.[2]

We are, on the whole, inclined to agree with Blanshard's assurance that Bradley's affirmative attitude to the ontological relevance of the law in question remains unharmed by such developments in philosophy as the 'appearance of linguistic theory of "a priori" statements, of a conventionalism that would justify logical rules pragmatically as means to desired ends, and of "alternative systems" of logic'.[3]

Yet, such an enormous mass of philosophical argument—arising, in particular, from the various theories of Necessity and Implication, and from the positivistic alienation of fact from necessity—is in this context available that, due to limitations of both space and ability, only a simple defence of the ontological applicability of the law of contradiction can here be attempted, partly in terms of a general statement of our view of the matter, and partly by examining Ayer's attitude to the law.

Does the law hold of fact? We believe it does. But, doubts in this connection are difficult to dispel. Is not a logical law too general to give us any information about particular fact? We are here reminded of Wittgenstein's cryptic remark that 'while "it is raining" gives us information about fact, "it is either raining or not raining" gives us none'. But, we ask, what is it to convey information? Does it merely stand for the attempt to describe a particular, sensible object? Is no information conveyed *at all* when we formulate or discover a general rule which the idiom of fact can nowhere contravene? Or again, if a law applies to every manner of fact, does it, merely because of this, tell us nothing about concrete reality?

But, the objector may persist, why must the law hold *of* anything at all? Why can't it be said merely to hold *in* the region, or to illustrate the use, of linguistic symbols? Now, supposing that we concede this, what does it prove? It hardly succeeds in making

---
[1] AR 491–92.
[2] Cf. Blanshard, *The Nature of Thought*, Vol. II, 423.
[3] Blanshard, *Reason & Analysis*, 424. This view of Blanshard is no mere affirmation; it comes as the conclusion of a detailed, critical examination of the matter. *Ibid* Ch. VI.

the law self-referrent. That which illustrates the use of symbols, linguistically or otherwise, certainly holds of a particular region of ideal construction. Everything would then turn upon the possibility of proving that this region is not a fact; and the attempt may be resisted stubbornly by one who dwells within the articulate system to which the symbols belong. Even if, for the sake of simplicity, we confine ourselves to linguistic symbols, and to fact understood as what is external and observable, our protest stands. Is not linguistic usage itself a fact? Is its validity determined only by the internal consistency of its constituent words and phrases, and not at all by their ability to capture, and to conform to the idiom of fact? It may be ingenious, but it does not seem natural to work for the view that linguistic usage is not a fact or that it is developed in utter indifference to fact. Every convention has its use; and one of the prime functions of language is to hold on to, and to convey the apprehended character of fact.

Now, to a brief examination of Ayer's view:

With regard to the following formulation of the law: 'Nothing can be coloured in different ways at the same time with respect to the same part of itself', Ayer says that, though it does convey some sense, 'I am not saying *anything* about the properties of any *actual* thing ... I am expressing an analytic proposition, which records our determination to call a colour expanse which differs in quality from a neighbouring colour expanse a different part of a given thing. In other words, I am *simply* calling attention to the implications of a certain linguistic usage.'[1]

The contention here is, in general, this. If nothing is by us said to be coloured in different ways at the same time with regard to the same part of itself, the reason merely is that we have decided to describe two adjacent colours as belonging to different parts of a thing. Or, in uttering the proposition under review, we are only conforming to a linguistic convention, and are not acknowledging any truth compelled by the inherent nature of things. It is not any truth about the actual world, but merely a settled way of talking, which is revealed by the (so-called) law.

To facilitate discussion, Ayer's view may be sub-divided into the following main ideas:

[1] Ayer, *Language, Truth & Logic*, London, Victor Gollancz Ltd., 1958, 79. Our italics.

(a) By the proposition in question, nothing is said with regard to the properties of any actual thing.
(b) We are here dealing only in language, not with things. Only a linguistic usage is being explicated.
(c) This usage is a matter of mere convention. It is merely our decision that when two neighbouring expanses of different colours are seen, they will be regarded as two different parts of the given thing.

We turn now to an individual examination of these points:
(a) To begin with, it may be admitted that (in quite a few cases) the law says nothing with regard to the properties of any *actual* thing, if the latter is taken to mean a present object. The law is, by its advocates, believed to apply to everything which is or could be. It is, therefore, harmless to admit that in using the law we do not (always) talk of any actual, presented object. But, we ask, how does this admission disprove the general ontological relevance of the law? If, as here, something is said with regard to each and every thing, it is surely curious to hold that nothing has been said about anything at all. Again, unless they are regarded as empty sounds or mere characters in print, the words 'be', 'different', 'time' and 'part' in the proposition under review refer necessarily to existence and its features.

So far, however, we have merely followed common sense. Let us now discuss what is distinctive in Ayer's view.
(b) The proposition runs thus: 'Nothing *can* be coloured in different ways ... same time ... same part.' Ayer reduces the word 'can' to 'can be said to be', so that the proposition, upon his view, becomes: 'Nothing can be said to be coloured in different ways ... same time ... same part.'[1] And when we ask him, 'why this compulsion?' his answer is: because of an agreed way of talking, or because of the linguistic practice that, as a matter of mere habit or usage, and not because of any compulsion by the nature of things, two extents differently coloured are said to stand for different parts of the thing. In other words, Ayer's view is that we first agree to talk in a particular way, and then, when

[1] Thus, Ayer merely abjures fact in favour of a way of speech. But, suppose we insist on the *factual* impossibility of lumping two different colours as such into the self-same part. Would *this* impossibility be a matter of mere speech?

the relevant situation occurs, apply this 'convention' to it, so that, far from revealing any secret within things, the proposition in question only shows how we habitually talk about them. But, the crucial questions are: Is the convention formed entirely at random? Does a consideration of fact in no way conduce to the origin and continued acceptance of this 'convention'?

(c) If it is merely a matter of *my* decision to speak in a particular way, can I decide to refuse to speak of the two adjacent colours as belonging to different parts of the thing? Conversely, can I decide to speak of a thing showing only one colour as having, here and now, two different colours in its different parts? That would be extremely inconvenient 'because the plurality of my words would be in constant conflict with the singleness of fact. I should be using two names when I could see from the nature of the case that one of them would always be impertinent. Thus, our determination or convention is anything but arbitrary; it is an attempt to conform our speech to the apprehended character of fact'.[1]

To conclude, the vital link between fact and the proposition under review is not removed by saying that the latter is a mere linguistic convention. The full truth, however, is that language is here arranged not only with an eye on fact, but—as Bradley would insist—in response to an essential theoretical demand. The comprehensiveness of his view is indeed striking. He takes into account the evidence of both fact and thought. In the region of fact, different qualities nowhere belong to any one aspect of existence. And that they *cannot* thus belong is realized in and by thought, by virtue of the impossibility of thinking without 'distinguishing' or holding diversities apart. The irresistible quality of the law is implicit in reflection:

> 'In order to *think* at all you must subject yourself to a standard, a standard which implies an absolute knowledge of reality; and while you doubt this, you accept it, and obey while you rebel.'[2]

The law is valid metaphysically not because it translates a suggestion from given reality, but primarily because it is an irresistible compulsion felt by thought which concrete reality 'seems' merely

[1] Blanshard, *The Nature of Thought*, Vol. II, 420.
[2] AR 135. Our italics.

to subserve.[1] It is because of this double reason that we cannot run counter to the proposition: 'Nothing can be coloured in different ways ... same time ... same part of itself.' The law of contradiction is no linguistic convention. It is thought's primal demand and reality subserves it.

Can we, in idea, ascribe differences to a point which has no internal diversity? Do we ever find two colours occupying the selfsame part of a thing? If not, are we still justified in regarding the law of contradiction as a mere convention?

Bradley is convinced that, far from being hostile to thought's demand for non-contradiction, given reality is itself a witness to the impossibility of holding differences in the selfsame point. We may refer, in this connexion, to an abstruse passage[2] where, in the true spirit of metaphysical inquiry, Bradley tries to push thought as far as he possibly can. Here he wonders: why is it that whereas a thing can certainly have a colour *and* a smell, it cannot have two colours in the same part of its being? The question, we admit, is not quite as radical as Heidegger's well-known one: 'Why should there be anything at all rather than nothing?' But, in so far as it asks for the 'why' of the relational manner in which things may often appear to us, it is basic enough and again, because it does not seem to be as unanswerable as Heidegger's extreme question, it is perhaps more legitimate than the latter. In any case, Bradley's answer is striking, if only because it seeks to argue, though but tentatively, the ontological validity of the law of contradiction. His argument here is briefly this:

A thing cannot have two colours in the same part of its being, though, if they are put alongside of each other—in different parts of the thing—they will co-exist without difficulty. And, to speak generally, diverse qualities, such as colours and smells, belong to different aspects of the thing. Does this not suggest that differences can, in fact, belong to a thing only when they exist alongside of each other, or, we may say, only when they inhere in different aspects of the object, and not if they are sought to be lumped into the selfsame point? The real is differentiated, but only by holding

[1] Thus see: 'It *seems as if* a reality possessed differences, A and B, ... and ... in order, without contradiction, to retain its various properties, this whole consents to wear the form of relations *between* them.' *Ibid* 18. Our italics.
[2] *Ibid* 18–19.

differences apart or relationally. And, in so far as to hold differences apart is to prevent them from pressing into the very same point, which would be contradiction, the idiom of fact, we may say, seems only to subserve the native demand of thought.

It is, we have seen, only by relaxing its unity, and by taking the form of a relational arrangement, that an object is able to hold differences. Whatever is said to be differentiated must, in the abstract, be regarded as big enough to hold diversities apart or relationally. The relational form circumvents discord by widening the bounds of the object. Harmony and inclusiveness go hand in hand. This is alike true of thought and reality.

If it be asked: 'Is the law true of things *in themselves?*' our answer, following Bradley, would be, first, that the attempt to *know* things wholly in themselves—that is, without any involvement with thought—is impossible; secondly, that ideal construction could yet be kept to the minimum, as in simple perception; and, thirdly, that reality as perceived (we have seen) seems clearly to conform to the law.

3. FACT AND THE 'A PRIORI'

The attack on 'contradiction' is, however, but a part of the wider empiricist thesis that there can be no 'a priori' knowledge of reality, and so no deductive metaphysics. Starting from Hume's classification of all significant propositions into tautologies and empirical propositions, the logical positivist alienates necessity from fact; reduces the former to a matter of mere linguistic convention; and denies the possibility of 'synthetic "a priori" ', and hence also the possibility of a metaphysics which seeks to 'ontologize' or to establish propositions of existence or non-existence in a purely 'a priori' way. Now, it is here obviously not possible to reflect on all these issues in individual detail. But, some general remarks may well be made to indicate that the prospects for a vindication of metaphysics are today not as bleak as they once were. This should serve incidentally to lend some point to the view of Bradley.

Hume's classification of significant propositions is no longer found unquestionable,[1] and the possibility of 'synthetic "a priori" ' is, by quite a few thinkers, today seriously vindicated. Nor can the

[1] See, for instance, Passmore, *Philosophical Reasoning*, 1–4.

positivistic conception of necessity as a matter of mere convention be said to stand unchallenged. And, with regard to the proposition: 'all "a priori" propositions are analytic', Ewing and Blanshard pose questions which, consistently with his attempted dissociation of necessity from fact, the positivist should find it hard to meet. Is this proposition itself a mere convention which could, with impunity, be brushed aside? Again, does it belong to the class of empirical probabilities or to that of tautologies? If we regard it as belonging to the former, a necessary proposition which is synthetic *may* at any time turn up. If, on the other hand, we regard it as a tautology, the proposition in question cannot be said to hold of propositions; for, described as 'a class of sentences' by Ayer himself, propositions are facts. Ewing insists that 'the principle that there can be no synthetic *a priori* propositions must itself be synthetic *a priori* if it is to be known and to be of any interest'.[1]

The positivistic view of logical constants—say, its reduction of 'if' to 'and'—clashes with Bradley's insistence on the necessity of understanding *why* two diversities at all co-exist. If, with a view to regarding it as a piece of tautologizing, we agree to replace: '*If* Socrates is a man, he is mortal' with 'Socrates is a man *and* he is mortal', what do we gain? Is this novel view truer to facts; or, does it enable us to understand them better? Facts, it is obvious, do not bear it out. The two attributes, 'humanity' and 'mortality' do not go as lightly and separably together as, say, 'humanity' and 'living on a diet of cabbages and peas'. It is the internal relatedness of the former pair which the 'if' in its normal sense seeks to heighten, and which its reduction to 'and' serves merely to ignore, if not to cancel. Nor is the acceptance of the view in question of any help to understanding. A thing is not *understood* merely by being put along with the others. To understand is necessarily to perceive (or to posit) some internal link between the details of the given. The mere fact that diversities are (or are put) together will never satisfy us. We must get some insight as to why they are together, and the 'why', Bradley insists, must not fall wholly outside of them.

Finally, in spite of stubborn opposition from within the field of both science and philosophy, the question of synthetic 'a priori' propositions is by no means finally closed.

[1] Ewing's article, 'The Necessity of Metaphysics', *op. cit.* 145.

Blanshard gives us a whole list of them,[1] out of which we may select one for notice: 'whatever is red is extended.' Is it analytic? In denying the predicate, do we here contradict the subject? We do not; when we deny that what is red is extended, we do not say: 'what is red is not red.' We deny only the togetherness of 'extended' with 'red'. Blanshard finds it easy, and even necessary, to rise from this consideration to the view of necessity as residing in system. Our purpose is, however, served by the realization that the proposition in question is, according to Ayer's own criterion, synthetic. What is more, 'when one says that whatever is red is extended, one ordinarily supposes oneself to be talking about all possible red things, including all the red things that have existed, do exist, or will exist'. If it be contended that 'whatever is red' stands for a universal and that, therefore, it cannot be said to refer to particular fact, our answer would be that the objection springs out of an acceptance of the false idea of an abstract universal. Our point is borne out clearly by Blanshard's lucid words:

> 'It is true that a priori statements deal with as suches, but these as suches may exist and be given. When I look at this specific shade of red, I am seeing what is at once given (since it is no construct or inference), existent (since it occupies space and time), and universal (since this shade could appear in other instances). If, in looking at it, I judge that whatever has this shade is extended, I mean to make the statement about this instance and all like it. . . . Indeed the attempt to draw a line between the universal and the existent is fundamentally wrongheaded, for unless universals were present in individual cases, it would be meaningless to call them cases at all . . .'[2]

4. 'ONTOLOGIZING' IN BRADLEY

Our direct concern is, however, with Bradley. What is the precise element of synthetic 'a priori' in *his* work? Is he justified in legislating with regard to matters of facts on purely 'a priori' grounds? Is his 'ontologizing' legitimate?

[1] Blanshard, *The Nature of Thought*, Vol. II, 407.
[2] Blanshard, *Reason and Analysis*, 303.

Now, questions such as these may be answered as follows:

(a) The 'a priori' element in Bradley's work is, of course, unmistakable. His governing principle, the law of contradiction, is no product of a survey of facts. Again, he would gladly sacrifice 'a great historical fact' if it is seen to clash with a 'high abstract principle'. His opposition to sense-perception as a deliverer of truth and reality contrasts finely with the present-day positivistic attitude. The view that sensory observation is 'the smallest guarantee or test of truth' is, according to him, a 'wretched superstition' which reveals 'that completest blindness to the experience of every-day life which is possible only to a vicious a priori dogmatism'.[1] 'The book is red' is, by Bradley's standards, a judgment of the poorest sort.

(b) It would, however, be wrong to believe that he merely ignores the 'facts' of sense or the arguments advanced to support their claim to truth. Bradley's more important theses are fairly well supported by an examination of the empiricist arguments. Consider, for instance, his rejection of pluralism. It is based, on the one hand, on a refutation of the view that the unit of thought is a psychological existent, an image; and, on the other, on the reasoned impossibility of securing uniqueness of reference within the singular judgment, and on a demonstration of the impossibility of merely external relations. Bradley also argues, though not very thoroughly, as to how demonstratives and proper names both fail to ensure uniqueness of reference. Another argument of his against the possibility of asserting particular fact, his protest against the unitary analysis of the proposition, is fairly detailed. It is true that in this connexion he makes some assertions which may appear to ignore simple distinctions. Where he maintains that all S–P statements are really Identity–Statements, we may indeed feel impelled to accuse him of confusing the 'is' of identity with the 'is' of predication. But, as Wollheim rightly points out, far from being unaware of it, Bradley rejects the distinction only after an examination of the various possible interpretations of 'A is B' —the Nominalist view, the Equational interpretation of Jevons, and the class membership interpretation.[2]

(c) We must indeed be clear about Bradley's attitude to sensible

---

[1] CE 70.
[2] Wollheim, *F. H. Bradley*, 75–81.

fact and existence. He certainly 'ontologizes',[1] but only in the traditional sense—that is, if ontology be understood as the *logos* of *to on* or *ta onta*, or as 'an intelligible account of all that is'. If it be understood as an attempt to deduce the existence of specific kinds of things from self-evident principles, the charge that deductive metaphysics is impossible does not apply to Bradley at all; for, he neither questions the existence of the things that are nor tries to prove the existence of any new things.[2]

Attention may here be drawn to some points of detail. First, Bradley does not seek to give us any sensitive information about the world.[3] He even maintains that, in metaphysics, a philosophy of Nature should abstain 'wholly and in every form from speculation on genesis'. 'Its idea of evolution and progress would, as such, not be temporal. And hence a conflict with the sciences upon any question of development or of order should not properly arise.'[4]

Again, he openly admits that starting 'from the mere intellect' we cannot anticipate the detailed features of given reality.[5] Thought's relations, he insists, 'are in part the result of perception and mere psychical process'. It is, of course, true that thought can proceed systematically and 'without a break'; but at no point in its working is the reference to what-is entirely suspended. Thought's most harmonious systems do not 'come out of bare thought'. Moreover, 'why connexions in the particular are just so, and not more or less otherwise—this can be explained *in the end* by no faculty of thinking'.[6]

Finally, to turn to the crucial point, we should never forget that, as already pointed out, what Bradley denies is not the existence of

---

[1] Stout maintained that Bradley had done the maximum which human ingenuity could achieve in the field of ontology. Russell, *My Philosophical Development*, London, George Allen & Unwin, 1959, 38.

[2] Bradley certainly tries to argue the reality of the Absolute. But 'reality' here does not stand for existence. (Cf. AR 442). Moreover, the Absolute is, in Bradley's view, already there. To argue for its reality is therefore not to try to bring a *new* thing into being.

[3] Except, of course, the truth of its inner relatedness which, we may note, is (by Bradley) affirmed as much on the strength of argument as a matter of mere fact.

[4] AR 441.
[5] *Ibid* 427.
[6] *Ibid* 425. Our italics.

things, but only their claim to ultimate or metaphysical reality. If his precise intent is kept in mind, the protests of Russell and Lazerowitz could all be reduced to the curious accusation that Bradley tries to see if things are self-consistently *thinkable* without investigating their *perceptual* character.

To conclude, Bradley's criterion is surely 'a priori'. But, in so far as the ontological relevance of the law of contradiction is hardly questionable, and in so far as the law is here actually applied to given reality, and that again with a view to determining only the intelligibility, not the perceptual constitution of things, the metaphysics of Bradley is neither a vacuous wheeling of thought upon its own axis, nor a trespass of thought into the domains of science. And yet it may be regarded as being, in its own way, essential—provided, we should add, his conception of 'understanding' is found in principle acceptable.

5. THE VERIFICATION THEORY

The empiricist of today may, however, protest against the very assumption on which Bradley's entire metaphysical superstructure is based. How is self-consistency superior to verifiability as a criterion of meaning and truth? The question is obviously of vital importance to us; and an attempt may be made to answer it in the order indicated below:

a. The present status of the verification theory;
b. Bradley's criticism of this theory;
c. The positivistic criticism of Bradley's metaphysical utterances.

a. *The theory: its status today*

The verification principle—which has been the main ground of denying meaningfulness to metaphysical statements—is no longer held unquestionable. It has been subjected to powerful criticisms by Ewing and Blanshard, Marcel and Heidegger. What is more striking is the gradual dilution which it has suffered at the hands of the logical positivist himself. Its claim to be the sole arbiter of meaning is today not accepted. Passmore's reasoned conclusion is that 'Hume and the positivists after him have failed to produce any general argument to show that certain expressions are meaningless'.[1] What an expression means is largely a matter of convention; and what is meaningless today may well become meaningful tomorrow—by finding some usage.

Some of the more important arguments of Passmore may here be outlined, primarily because they seem to lend indirect support to Bradley's view on the matter:

What has the verification principle to say against metaphysics today? It cannot say that there is, in point of fact, nothing corresponding to a metaphysical expression; for, to make this protest would at once be to object to the use of such essential phrases in science as 'the first men to land on the moon' or 'the first men who lived on the surface of the earth'. It should rather contend, as Schlick rightly suggests, that it is *logically* impossible for anything to correspond to what a metaphysical statement seeks to express. But, how can the logical impossibility of producing 'samples' be proved? Passmore suggests the following three ways:[2]

First, the statement in question may be shown to involve an explicit contradiction. This can be easily done in the case of such expressions: 'that which is both intelligible and unintelligible'.

Secondly, we may show that the meanings of the constituent words are so 'refined away' by the expression in question that 'there is no longer any possible way of discovering whether anything answers to this description'. Thus, the word 'experience' in 'the Absolute is Experience' does not direct us to anything in particular. We are at a loss to think of something that could answer to it.

Thirdly, we may succeed in pointing out 'an incompatibility between the nature of description' envisaged in the statement 'and the possibility of its applying to a particular case'. This is possible in the case of such statements: 'This is a transcendental being.' Here, the 'this' is patently incompatible with 'transcendental'.

Now, with regard to the above, we may be allowed to make the following observations:

The first and the third ways base the logical impossibility of finding 'samples' on the contradiction, explicit or implicit, involved in the statements in question. The second does not *seem* to do so.

[1] Passmore, *Philosophical Reasoning*, 98.
[2] *Ibid* 90–91.

But let us see. Why is it impossible to find anything corresponding to Absolute Experience? Why does not the word 'experience', as here used, direct us to anything specific? *That* it does not so direct us will, again, not do; for, from the viewpoint of spiritual realization, it may be sincerely claimed that corresponding to the word *as thus used* there is actually an experience which *is* absolute.[1] The positivist can only contend that it is logically impossible for 'anything' to correspond to 'absolute experience'. But this, in turn, can be argued only if we oppose the particularity implied in 'anything' or 'sample' to the universality 'described' by '*absolute* experience'. In fact, while objecting to the 'metaphysical' use of the word 'God', Carnap himself suggests that there is no way of determining whether anything satisfies the definition of 'God' as given by metaphysics; that this is so because a statement such as: 'an event is the work of "God"' clashes with the supposition that God is the unconditioned, the omnipotent; or that, in brief, the entire idea stands on a 'logically illegitimate combination of words'.[2]

To sum up: the three possible ways of arguing the *logical* impossibility of finding 'samples' seem alike grounded in our inability to accept self-contradiction.

But this at once makes it clear that by itself the verification principle cannot prove the logical impossibility of finding 'samples', and that, to accomplish this end, it has to take the help of the principle of contradiction.[3] If the positivist decides to go by the verification principle alone, the only thing he can rightfully do is to wonder vaguely as to *how* could samples ever be produced answering to such-and-such a description. If he seeks to ground the 'how' in logical certainty, the appeal to the principle of contradiction is, we have seen, inescapable. And if, on the other hand, he remains confined to mere psychological uncertainty, nothing is *proved*.

---

[1] Thus, see Śaṁkara's description of the state of mokṣa. S. Radhakrishnan, *Indian Philosophy* Vol. II, London, George Allen and Unwin, 1951, 636.

[2] Carnap, 'The Elimination of Metaphysics' in *Logical Positivism*, ed. A. J. Ayer, 66.

[3] Passmore admits that the verification principle has here to take some help from somewhere, but he does not explicitly say that this help must come from the principle of contradiction. *Philosophical Reasoning*, 87, 91.

Finally, may not the 'how' with regard to the task of finding 'samples' be understood in a way which considerably increases the possibility of an ultimate verification of metaphysical utterances? It may be taken to express a willingness-to-learn, as distinguished from the mere keenness to argue; a prompting of the will, rather than mere intellectual unrest. A decision to resolve the 'how' in *this* sense would commit one to a discipline of life which may lead him up to actual experiences that correspond to, and verify some of the profounder assertions of metaphysics and religion. We must indeed insist that verification of some of the loftiest utterances of abstract metaphysics may be provided by the higher reaches of Man's moral and religious experience.[1]

The limitations of the verification theory, and the difficulties with which it is beset, are today well-known. But, from the viewpoint of Bradley its chief limitation is its bias that whatever claims to be real or true must be verifiable as an object of sensuous experience.

Ewing's protest that 'we must join issue with the positivist movement . . . in insisting that experience is not limited to sense-experience'[2] gains added support from Ayer's own admission that all experience is not necessarily sensuous: 'A logical positivist would not say that it was inconceivable that any one should have . . . non-sensuous experience of value.'[3]

Drawing our attention to the fact of 'a disclosure . . . in which I come to myself and realize myself as more than the observable behaviour I display',[4] Ramsey argues powerfully that even human

---

[1] Thus, 'jīvanmukti' or liberation during life, is an attainable ideal according to a powerful section of Hindu religious thought. Again, we have it on the authority of Sri Aurobindo that 'states of consciousness there are in which Death is only a change in immortal life . . . and this not in abstract conception only, but in actual vision and in constant and substantial experience'.
Sri Aurobindo, *The Life Divine*, Calcutta, Arya Publishing House, 1939, Vol. I, 79.
[2] Ewing's article, 'The Necessity of Metaphysics', *op. cit.* 163.
[3] Ayer, 'The Principle of Verifiability', *Mind*, XLV, 1936, 201.
[4] Ramsey, 'Possibility and Purpose of Metaphysical Theology', *Prospect for Metaphysics*, 167. For a deeper suggestion of the possibility of attaining to a primal awareness of the Self as the distinctionless source of the 'I-thought', see Arthur Osborne's account of Paul Brunton's 'dialogue' with Raman Maharshi in *Raman Maharshi—and the path of self-knowledge*, Bombay, Jaico Publishing House, 1962, 19–21.

behaviour cannot be adequately described in terms of observables. The 'I', in such cases, is not merely indicative. The question: 'Is there any moment of self-awareness which is wholly without any objective element?' can be answered by pointing, in particular, to the experiences of men of spiritual realization. For us, common men, it is but occasionally that the 'penny drops' and we experience those 'fallings from us, vanishings'[1] which mark a temporary suspension of our objective concern with things. But, for them, self-awareness can be such a continual manner of being as is replete with what the existentialists call 'authenticity', and as is, in addition, in no way inconsistent with psychological alertness and integration. The contention that such experience is not sensuous would do nothing to disprove its reality. It would only bring to light the inadequacy of the theory under review.

It is improper to reject a metaphysical statement merely because nothing can be immediately shown up to correspond to it with the sharpness and particularity of a sensible object. Even in science, confirmation is often but relative; it may not be 'a straightforward matter of being confirmed or being unconfirmed'. Again, the latest developments in empiricism seem to prefer the contextual theory of significance to operationism and the verification theory as ways of expressing the epistemological significance of science. Considering the older form of empiricism—the one associated with the names of Locke, Hume, Mach, James and Russell—along with the work of more recent thinkers like Quine, Carnap and Bergmann, Pasch strongly suggests that 'the original empiricist principle that, in order to be empirically significant, every idea should be derived from experience may be translated as the principle that the ultimate antecedent framework of every cognitive context should be experiential'.[2]

But, if the emphasis is to be on the experiential *context* rather than on any isolated fact or experience, significance will have to be determined variously in different regions of experience. It is precisely this truth which Polanyi emphasizes. A method of verification which the contents of one region seem duly to demand may be entirely inapplicable to another sphere of reality; and to subject all our diverse experiences to the same kind of verification

[1] Wordsworth, Ode to Immortality.
[2] Pasch, *Experience and the Analytic*, 259.

is obviously improper. The true manner of the verification of an experience is to be sought from within the individual articulate system to which it really belongs. The seeming meaninglessness of metaphysical propositions may be due to the fact that the positivist uses a language 'that is apposite to one subject-matter ... with reference to another altogether different matter'. And this cannot but cause bewilderment. 'The comparatively modest attempt to describe atomic processes in terms of classical electromagnetics and mechanics has led to self-contradictions which appeared no less intolerable unless we got eventually accustomed to them'. The truths of religion, in particular, fall largely outside the scope of objective ascertainment. Verification is here an 'indwelling,' a personal and emotive participation in what is experienced as true, rather than a merely intellectual, 'ab extra' assessment of the given; it is, in Polanyi's words, validation rather than verification. 'Proximity to God is not an observation, for it overwhelms and pervades the worshipper.'[1] The verification theory is surely not adequate to Truth as a whole.

b. *Bradley's strictures*

Bradley does not explicitly make the distinctions referred to above. But he is quite aware of the general truth that in the realms of art and morality ideas are not verified in the same way as in our more practical and scientific pursuits. He concedes that every special science is free 'to adopt one sole principle of validation', but protests that natural science has no right to transgress its own limits, and to assert with regard to *all* phenomena that they have been, or can be explained by that one sole method.[2] Verification insists on observing; but is truth true merely because (or when) it is observed? Is there nothing in truth and beauty, and in reality at large, except what appears of them in our experience? Every idea, say that of privation or failure, is not verified as a *realized correspondence* of the ideal with the sensible. But if, on the other hand, verification is taken to mean the mere having of an experience, however incommunicable, the most insensible of our experiences cannot, from the outside, be rejected summarily. Love invests its object with an abiding sense of deep, inward contentment; and

[1] Polanyi, *Personal Knowledge*, 198.
[2] AR 439–40.

this felt inwardness is doubtless real, even though it is not observed.[1]

Bradley's main objection to the verification theory, however, is that it is improper to prefer sensible verification to coherence as a criterion of truth. The arguments which he here advances may be summed up thus:

The demand for verification is rooted in the felt instinctive need that truth must be irresistible. But, which of the two can fairly be regarded as being more compulsive—the sensibly given or the systematic? That coercion can be exercised by relations between ideas, just as well as by the mere existence of outer fact, is obvious. On the other hand, in so far as the need to supplement and check the initial findings of sense with subsequent observations is in general always there, would it be improper to suggest that the idea of mutual agreement or coherence is of great help to us in avoiding error, or that sense-observation as such is not the final or sole deliverer of truth?[2] The net perceptual character of an experience is, as a rule, determined (also) by factors which may seem to be merely beyond it.[3] But, with this realization, the possibility of error is at once seen to creep into a fact of perception; and it may truly be said that the significance of perceptual awareness depends vitally on the question as to how well it agrees with, or how much it contributes to, the existing body of knowledge.

That knowledge cannot be had in absolute separateness from our actual world; that to this world we have repeatedly to return to 'gain new matter and maintain the old'; and, finally, that the order which it appears to have is not entirely contributed by the subject, all this is by Bradley openly admitted. But it does not, in his view, warrant the conclusion that judgments of sense can ever be absolutely infallible. Ideal construction enters necessarily into the very constitution of a fact, if it is to *mean* anything at all;[4]

---
[1] ETR 73–80; 103.
[2] Cf. *Ibid* 206.
[3] In Bradley's view, a setting is never in fact entirely shut out. A perceptual fact must be a fact for observation and it must give me the feeling: 'I am here and now having a sensation or complex of sensations *of such or such a kind.*' *Ibid* 205. Our italics.
[4] Cf. 'And why, I ask, for the intelligence must there be datum without interpretation any more than interpretation without datum?' *Ibid* 204.

and our task is to keep in touch with the world of sense, continually and ever more fully, and at the same time to understand it—in other words, to hold it in thought ever more harmoniously. At least in part, statements are 'verified'—and facts are significant —exactly as they cohere with one another. If what is verified is accepted *by the mind* on the evidence of senses, our intellectual demand for self-consistent understanding can in no case be irrelevant to verification.

It is here important to mark what Bradley really means by coherence. Admittedly, it is a demand of *thought*. But, first, as we have seen, the demand is supported by the manner of given reality itself in so far as it is differentiated; and, secondly, the movement of thought as it pursues consistency is warranted by the native self-transcendence of facts in the flux of experience. Moreover, it is not to be separated from comprehensiveness. Coherence is system, that is, knowledge made as wide and consistent as it can be. The assumption that the true and the real is that which satisfies the intellect *in this double sense* is certainly less easily questionable than the verification hypothesis. Bradley in fact insists that individuality is a more tenable criterion of truth and reality than mere correspondence. Why should the truth of an idea be judged by its (mere) conformity with fact, unless the two naturally demand each other to make up the wholeness of Truth? But if they do, mere correspondence can hardly satisfy us. Our ideal is at once seen to be different. It is to ascertain how fact and idea could be held as one; or, to rise from continual self-transcendence to final self-existence.

c. *Ayer and Bradley*

This at least is *Bradley's* ideal. Most of his important metaphysical utterances spring primarily out of his desire to understand facts—as a whole, and harmoniously. His emphasis is continually dual—on given reality and on understanding as discursive. Even with regard to the Absolute he insists that it is what we everywhere experience, though nowhere fully. And our *idea* of it as the supra-relational Reality is reached not through any capacity of intuition, but through a self-critical dissatisfaction of thought with its own relational form. So, Ayer's protest against metaphysics that it affirms the possibility of securing 'knowledge of a transcendent reality' through an exercise of 'intellectual intuition'[1] is wholly irrelevant to the view of Bradley.

Bradley protests explicitly against the idea of a Reality which does not enter at all into sense-experience. Only he always takes care to add that such experience can never exhaust reality. And this is a view which cannot fairly be questioned. It seems, in a way, warranted by the distinction which Ayer himself draws between strong and weak verification. Taken in the 'weak' sense, the principle demands that a proposition claiming to be verifiable should be such that experience can render it (only) probable. Here, the question with regard to a (metaphysical) proposition merely is: 'would any observations be relevant to the determination of its truth or falsehood?' But, the attempt to explain what the word 'relevant' may here be taken to mean at once tends to make the criterion 'far too liberal'. Thus, from the very start, our insistence on sensible verification causes us uneasiness; and when we try to mend the principle suitably, we detract at once from what alone made it initially acceptable—that is, its definiteness, seemingly final.

And consider the reason because of which Ayer finds it impossible to accept verification in the 'strong' sense. His argument here is briefly this. It is a fact that the general propositions of law and propositions about the remote past are both factually significant and yet not conclusively verifiable. The principle that a sentence can be factually significant only if it expresses what is *conclusively* verifiable is therefore self-stultifying; 'for it leads to the conclusion that it is impossible to make a significant statement of fact at all'.[2]

Now, two remarks may here be made. First, in the argument outlined, the acceptable form of the principle of verification seems itself determined by the need to avoid contradiction. And secondly, the contradiction here referred to is no mere collision in the abstract; rather, it consists in denying one of the two sides of a situation which in fact holds them together, the factual significance of certain propositions and their being (only) inductively verifiable. Need we still doubt the inexorable necessity of the law of contradiction and its relevance to fact?

[1] Ayer, *Language, Truth and Logic*, 33.
[2] *Ibid* 38.

Nor is Ayer's analysis of Bradley's individual utterances any more convincing. He is obviously referring to Bradley when he says that it is nonsensical to condemn our everyday world as a world of mere appearance, as opposed to reality, for the simple reason that 'no conceivable observation or a series of observations, could have any tendency to show that the world revealed to us by sense-experience was unreal . . .'[1] But, when Bradley dismisses the sensible world as 'unreal', his criterion (we have seen) is not 'observation' at all. Nor is he troubled by the observed actuality of things, which he openly admits. Unfortunately, Russell, Ayer and Lazerowitz have all lost sight of a simple point in their keenness to overthrow the metaphysics of Bradley. *His* viewpoint is throughout theoretical. If we forget this and adopt sense-observation as our criterion, we at once feel tempted to agree with Ayer that the following utterance of Bradley is but a pseudo-proposition:

'The Absolute enters into, but is itself incapable of evolution and progress.'

For, we cannot 'conceive of an observation which would enable one to determine whether the Absolute did, or did not, enter into evolution and progress'.[2] Here, the mistake, we protest, lies clearly in trying to use a kind of verification which is wholly inapposite to the proposition in question.

But, our defence of Bradley could here be deeper. Do the words 'conceive of an observation' mean merely the act of projecting an observed observation into the future? Ayer would himself not answer in the affirmative.[3] But then, do they stand for visualizing a possibility on the basis of some theoretical necessity? To this, again, Ayer would probably not assent; for, this is precisely what Bradley professes to do. Perhaps we are required to conceive of a (new) future *observation* on the basis of present ones. But the demand is illegitimate; for the Absolute as such is neither a sense-object nor a fact of psychology. And if it still be insisted that the metaphysician must direct us to an 'observation' which may lend some point to the proposition cited above, is not the matter rescued from the region of utter improbability by our daily

---

[1] *Ibid* 39.
[2] *Ibid* 36.
[3] See the way he rejects the older empiricist principle, *Ibid* 14.

experience that a path enters into movement, but does not itself move? Bradley himself is not slow to cite an analogy:

> 'For nothing perfect, nothing genuinely real, can move. The Absolute has no seasons, but all at once bears its leaves, fruit, and blossoms. Like our globe it always, and it never, has summer and winter.'[1]

How is then a metaphysical proposition incapable 'of being substantiated to any degree whatsoever by any possible observation'?[2]

6. THE DOCTRINE OF 'DEGREES'

Our next step needs a word of recapitulation. We have seen how our common world may be said to be 'real' even from the metaphysical point of view. It meets the theoretical criterion of individuality, though but imperfectly. The first suggestions of wholeness are, however, not good enough to satisfy critical inquiry; and a metaphysics such as Bradley's must face the following questions. Does anything meet the demand of thought *perfectly*? Or, is anything absolutely real? Again, are all things equally real? It is questions such as these that the doctrine of 'degrees' seeks, in the main, to answer. Its validity may be debatable, but the part it plays in Bradley's metaphysical scheme is, in our view, obvious. It seeks to redeem the balance from what may seem to be a merely negative tilt in the first section of AR. Contrasted with the Absolute, everything is unreal. Yet nothing is wholly so. Everything partakes of Reality. Did it not, it would merely lie outside of, and so delimit Reality.

The doctrine, we insist, is integral to his conception of metaphysical thinking. The attempt to see if anything is perfectly real reveals not only how the various regions of our experience fall short of, but the measure in which they conform to the criterion of reality employed. If our refusal to regard 'appearances' as being finally real is to have a warrant in reason, we must first indicate how the attempt to think them out is riddled with contradictions. And it is this attempt which tells us that things are self-incon-

---

[1] AR 442. Unfortunately, Ayer pays no heed to the context from which the sentence in question is abstracted.
[2] Ayer, *Language, Truth and Logic*, 136.

sistent and (or because) limited in different degrees, and that yet nothing is wholly so. How can a thing be entirely without all content? Even in order to *be*, it must be something; it must have some quality-content. Again, it must be itself—or, to an extent self-consistent—even in order to exclude other things. Everything must therefore be credited with some measure of inclusiveness and harmony or some degree of reality—some character of the Real. The alternative to the theory of 'degrees' would be a sweeping apotheosis or a summary flattening of all that is.

(a) But, we must explain. First, it is the individual 'appearances' which are said to have 'degrees'. Secondly, what is revealed in 'degrees' is individuality or the character of the Absolute, never the Absolute as such. This character is, in turn, a blend of two features—self-sufficiency and 'intenseness', both of which are to be ascertained by thought. A thing is self-sufficient in proportion to the degree of completeness with which it includes its own conditions. So, self-sufficiency may, upon Bradley's view, be equated with inclusiveness. 'Intenseness', as he uses the word, stands for internal harmony.[1] Thirdly, the criterion employed in the determination of 'degrees' is 'the idea of perfect Reality'.[2]

The second point is, however, beset with difficulties which must at least be noticed.

Bradley is emphatic that the Absolute as such has no degrees,[3] and that what is revealed in varying measure is only its character.[4] But here a question at once crops up: is it not self-inconsistent to suggest that an aspect of the Absolute, allegedly perfect, manifests itself in 'degrees', every one of which is necessarily imperfect? Now, Bradley's answer here would run roughly as follows:

The suggestion is without doubt questionable. We cannot in truth take our stand on the Absolute and say anything from its own point of view. But, the inconsistency here involved is, in a way, unavoidable. For, if we choose to avoid it, we get committed to alternatives which are much more unacceptable. We must then either abjure all idea of an absolute reality, which is (we have seen) to thought irresistible; or posit a complete hiatus between

---

[1] Cf. AR 390.
[2] *Ibid* 355.
[3] *Ibid* 318.
[4] *Ibid* 485.

what is revealed in 'degrees' and our absolute reality, which would at once cancel its claim to absoluteness by putting a limit to its inclusiveness; or, finally, hold that the Absolute itself is revealed in 'degrees', which would be immediately self-cancelling.

(b) Again, 'degrees', we are told, are of truth and reality. Does this coupling of *reality* with truth have any special significance? Yes, in our view, it has. The suggestion that 'reality' has 'degrees', if taken along with Bradley's open insistence that the Absolute as such has no 'degrees', conduces to the realization that, as already brought out in our second essay, by 'reality' Bradley does not always mean the Absolute. Surely when he says: 'no one ever means to assert about anything but reality', his meaning only is that in all our assertions we mean to qualify a 'that' by a 'what',[1] not that we are always talking about the Absolute as such. What is more, the 'and' is significant. Bradley nowhere means to identify truth with reality.[2] Truth is certainly *about* reality; but, in so far as it works through ideas and aims at qualifying existence harmoniously in terms of judgment, truth must for ever preserve the estrangement of the predicate from the subject, and is therefore never able to recapture the cohesion of actual existence.[3] Finally, it seems to us clear that the theory in question will be understood but imperfectly if it is taken merely to say that every proposition is partly true (or false), that is, unless its relatedness not only to thought, but to reality is duly taken into account.

We do not, however, wish to suggest that Bradley has tried to explain how the doctrine is to be applied to every individual appearance. As he himself puts it, his aim is only to give us 'a sound general view of Reality'. With regard to judgments, however, it is easy to say, if not to defend, what the theory in general holds. Every judgment says something specific. Yet no judgment is really self-complete. It is meaningful by virtue of referring to a wider region of reality which its own explicit content seems merely to shut out. This reference may well be implicit. Yet it is very much there, and is vital. But for it, Bradley insists, judgment would cease to have any meaning at all. To see if a judgment is

[1] *Ibid* 145.
[2] Cf. *Ibid* 492. It may be noted in passing that even the basic assumption of Bradley speaks of truth *and* reality, not of truth *or* reality. *Ibid* 491.
[3] *Ibid* 147.

true, and in what measure, we have to find out with how much of the reality (seemingly) shut out its explicit content agrees, and how well. Truth, in short, is not an intrinsic property of judgments; it depends on their agreement with the totality of facts and ideas. It consists in system. The greater the supplementation and rearrangement which a judgment needs before it can be accepted by reality, the lower is its place in the scale of degrees.[1] To put it differently, how much truth a judgment possesses is indicated by how much enlargement of our view it is able to withstand unaltered; and this, in turn, depends upon how much it already includes.

(c) We should add that an appearance can 'include' not only bodily, but ideally. It may 'usurp ground by its direct presence, but again, further, by its influence and relative importance'.[2] And it may harmonize differences not necessarily by juxtaposing them in space, but by making them appear as partakers of the same law or truth. This explains how a principle may include more content, and include it better, than a mere fact:

> '... the higher the principle, and the more vitally it, so to speak, possesses the soul of things, so much the wider in proportion must be that sphere of events which in the end it controls. But just for this reason, such a principle cannot be handled or seen, nor is it in any way given to outward or inward perception. It is only the meaner realities which can be so revealed, and which are to be verified as sensible facts.'[3]

The above reflections are, to us, important. They give us a clue to understand why Bradley's view is so completely opposed to the empiricist outlook of today. A principle as such may not be observable. But if it sheds light on a great mass of fact, should its impalpable character be allowed to detract from its significance? It appears difficult to say 'yes' except on the assumption that what can be observed is intrinsically superior to that which is not open to inner or outer perception. Is this assumption irresistible? Has the empiricist learnt to doubt his own prejudices?[4]

---

[1] *Ibid* 355.
[2] *Ibid* 318.
[3] *Ibid* 333–34. Also see *Ibid* 336.
[4] Bradley, however, puts this question to the pragmatist. ETR 73.

Here, in passing, a reference may also be made to Bradley's attitude to temporal existence. Existence in time is without doubt real. That which lasts longer is so far more real. The presented event is an important form in which experience comes to us, and the content of being-in-time is undoubtedly rich. But, to turn to what is Bradley's main challenge, does this mode of being contain *all* that there is, and is it able to hold everything equally well? Let us see.

Being-in-time may mean either being-present at a particular moment of time, or being contained in the entire temporal series. Now, in its first form, temporal existence is clearly not all-inclusive. The meaning of an idea, as distinguished from its occurrence as a psychic event, transcends the 'here' and the 'now'. What is, however, important to mark is that even the entire temporal series cannot be said to include every detail of human experience in such a way that nothing significant is left out. Change, simultaneity, succession—these are, as we know, the distinctive features of Time. But is the essential *significance* of scientific theories, and of aesthetic and religious experiences, at all describable in these terms? Does their verification or their overt expression really exhaust them? Or, at least in the case of moral and religious experience, is not the essence of the matter wholly missed when we speak in purely temporal terms? To illustrate, a noble resolution may be seen to endure; but how is duration a clue to its inwardness and quality? Much that is significant in life does not merely *happen*: and a time-measure is, to quality, often utterly irrelevant:

'To be nearer the central heart of things is to dominate the extremities more widely; but it is not to appear there except incompletely and partially through a sign, an unsubstantial and a fugitive mode of expression.'[1]

This is no mere phrase-making, but is theoretically important. Often, in life, truths are verified, not by holding them up as objects before the mind, but by realizing the inadequacy of their *objective* verification. Experience, in such cases, is very much

[1] AR 338.

there; but the way it 'verifies' is through an undoing of the constriction implied in perception, internal or external.[1]

(d) We may end our discussion of the doctrine of 'degrees' by considering a basic objection. Is it at all proper to apply the criterion of individuality to given reality? Could not metaphysics do with any other principle of worth?

Here, the following answer should perhaps serve:

First, our criterion does not seem hostile to common sense. Even ordinarily, '... we can experience and feel our nature as a whole, and, as against this whole, we can realize the inadequacy of any one side of life';[2] so that it does not appear forced to make wholeness a criterion of worth, and to credit every aspect with but a measure of reality. It is certainly a common attitude to rank those attainments and experiences higher which secure us insight into, or control over a wider stretch of the given. Conversely, when a trifle is dismissed as unimportant, our argument only is that it does not hold much or well. Nor is popular opinion averse to the idea of preferring that which holds content harmoniously. Mere indiscriminate doing is always assigned a lower rank than acting for a principle; and in moments of sanity self-discipline is thought to be superior to the chaos of mere impulses. From this it is only a step to say (with Bradley) that, in so far as it provides us with a fuller synthesis of the 'is' and the 'ought', religious experience has a greater measure of metaphysical reality than mere morality.

Secondly, is there any other standard which could enable us to have an idea of the comparative worth of *all* the different regions of experience, and to do justice alike to the sides of both idea and existence.[3] Presentation-to-sense will just not serve; for, it would prevent us from granting any reality to the more important truths of moral and aesthetic experience. Nor can pleasure be accepted as the sole criterion; for, the reality of pain is, upon this view, merely ignored. A plurality of standards, each serving for different aspects and occasions, will not do either; they would, in practice, often tend to clash. Moreover, the felt unity of our nature rebels

---

[1] It is here easy to cite supporting evidence from religious literature. But, even the single Upaniṣadic doctrine, that we know the true Self by becoming it, is enough to bear out our point.

[2] ETR 4.

[3] Cf. AR 354.

instinctively against the idea of keeping the different regions of experience entirely under the sway of separate standards.

7. THOUGHT'S NATIVE INADEQUACY

Our aim so far has been at a general vindication of Bradley's *positive* attitude to the relation of thought to reality. He holds not only that thought cannot fairly be kept entirely away from reality,[1] but that it can be made to deliver a positive knowledge of the general character of the Absolute itself. Yet, it would be a mere hasty recoil to believe that he regards thought as being in every way adequate to given reality, or as capable of describing in detail what may be accepted as the final reality.[2]

Let us deal with these aspects of his thought individually. Consider, first, the relation of thought to reality regarded as existence with character. If the rose appears to be red the dependence of its content or character on the subject is clear. '... The thing without the points of view, appears to have no character at all.'[3] This natural tendency of experienced content to go beyond the immediacy of its existence[4] makes directly for the perception that two distincts, a 'that' and its 'what', are held together, yet apart. We get a judgment, say: 'the rose is red.' A task is now set to thought. How can two distincts be held as one, which they clearly are in actual fact? This is a question, we have seen, which thought cannot finally answer. It is therefore inadequate to reality.

We may here consider (as instructive) a protest against Bradley's view that thought is less than reality. Ewing thinks that the view in question does not really make any point against thought, for an identity of the knowing self and the reality known is never our actual ideal of knowledge.[5] Our view, however, is that Bradley's view *is* significant, and that Ewing fails to realize its importance

---

[1] 'Reality is qualified by thought ... ' *Ibid* 350.
[2] Bradley's emphasis on the inadequacy of thought to reality is unmistakable:
'It is only by misunderstanding that we find difficulty in taking thought to be something less than reality.' *Ibid* 143.
[3] *Ibid* 20.
[4] Cf. *Ibid* 146: 'The essential nature of the finite is that everywhere, as it presents itself, its character should slide beyond the limits of its existence.'
[5] Ewing, *Idealism*, 211.

because he misses its true meaning. In saying that thought is less than reality, what Bradley wishes to stress is not the obvious fact that the two cannot become identical, but that thought cannot, in its own way, account for the actual togetherness of diversities in given reality; and this, we may add, is by no means obvious. The details of the way in which he argues this inability of thought may be questioned. But that is a separate issue. What we here wish to emphasize is only the real *meaning* of Bradley's view.

He, in fact, insists that an examination of the form of judgment serves only to reaffirm his view as to that specific 'inadequacy' of thought of which we have just spoken. But, this needs some clarification, specially because it may be held, as Ewing actually does, that the S–P relation is unintelligible only in the sense that it cannot be reduced to, or explained in terms of anything else.[1]

Now, to turn to Bradley's treatment of the matter, the subject and the predicate are, and must remain clearly distinct from each other. 'No one ever *means* to assert about anything but reality.'[2] On the other hand, the predicate 'red' is a quality distinguished—and so held apart—from the subject 'rose'; here it is ideal because it not merely overflows, but is actively loosened from its 'that', and is kept thus. True, it is also ascribed to the subject. The very aim of judgment is to reconstitute individuality. But the connection is here relational, so that the distinctive character of the predicate is insistently maintained. If we allow *this* to be ignored, the rose as thought of dwindles at once into the merely felt fact of a red rose. 'Red', if rewelded to existence, is the fact, not the idea of redness; it is no longer a predicate.[3] And if, in predicating we merely duplicate existence, why should we resort to predication at all?

Now, how can we hold the two, the subject and the predicate, rationally together? Or, how can we pass on from mere thought to truth? The only way open to us is to fill in the conditions, implicit yet operative, which make and keep the rose red. The rose must now be taken along with ever more features of reality. We have to

---

[1] *Ibid* 223. Bradley's view, on the other hand, is that this relation is unintelligible exactly as every other relation is so—that is, because of the impossibility of holding differences rationally as one, and that (further) a relation only implies, but is never identical with a substantial whole.

[2] AR 145. This is so, provided 'reality' is understood in a comprehensive sense, so as to include even the imaginary.

[3] *Ibid* 147.

say: 'The rose, taken along with this *and* that, is red.'[1] But this forced expansion of the subject is a process[2] which seems foredoomed to failure. *All* the factors which conduce to make the rose red can never be taken into account. Moreover, every 'condition' of the rose's being red which we consider is itself ideally loosened from its setting in reality, in so far as it is made a distinct object of thought; and the same problem, of holding differences as one, which we are seeking to meet with regard to 'rose' and 'red', now breaks up with regard to the factors newly noticed.[3] The fact of 'red' is a further impediment. It is certainly one of the conditions we are seeking; but, if thought is to retain its relational character, 'red' must remain for ever held *apart* from the rose. But even if, 'per impossibile', a complete totality of conditions could be secured, such a notice would still be merely ideal: it would not *be* the subject.[4] A system of relations has to be traversed, and so is not immediate. The subject as given is, on the other hand, non-relational. 'Thought, in its actual processes and results, cannot transcend the dualism of the "that" and the "what".'[5] The richest of our judgments, our most comprehensive truths, are all merely *about* reality: they are not identical with it. There is always some 'difference left between your thought and the thing'.[6]

To conclude: in its dealings with the real, thought seems subject to a dual disability. Its manner is hostile to the wholeness of fact; and its contact with the latter is but a point of departure. These two features are, however, in principle one. There is no *thinking* if we merely keep glued to the given. We must loosen the object (ideally) into terms held clearly apart. But this is at once to part company with the real, not in the sense of shutting it out of view,

---

[1] The two discrepant features of the subject in this case are its claim to immediacy and sensuous infinitude. *Ibid* 155–56.

[2] 'Because the given reality is never consistent, thought is compelled to take the road of *indefinite* expansion'. *Ibid* 145. Our italics. Bradley's true meaning here is that given reality is never *quite* consistent; for, if it is not at all consistent, his professed thesis that it is individual, or that it is a that-what togetherness collapses at once.

[3] This is what Bradley means by saying that truth is the attempt to heal the that-what looseness 'homoeopathically'.

[4] AR 158.

[5] *Ibid* 148.

[6] *Ibid* 151.

but in that of abdicating its idiom. Reality is certainly the subject in a judgment; but this is so only because it passes off, at once and necessarily, into the relational form. The wholeness of reality is thus thought's continual Other. If we try to reconstitute the cohesion of fact by undoing the predicate's estrangement from the subject, thought itself disappears; and if the disjunction is retained, individuality eludes us. Once again, as we saw earlier, it is thought's *manner* which clashes with its end.

8. MEETING DIFFICULTIES

But, it may be urged, why should thought strive after individuality when it knows that the attempt is suicidal? Our answer is that thought rests on individuality; that it grows through an increasing cultivation of this character; and that the pursuit in question is therefore no mere suicide, but is akin to that transcendence of the specificity of a demand which is at once its consummation.[1] In realizing its end thought sheds off its native defect of relativity; but the liberation is at once a transcendence of its 'special' nature. This may be brought out at some length.

Though but poorly, thought as judgment is able to hold differences as one, by holding them apart. But to hold differences as one is at once to *be* (in a measure) individual. What is undeniable is not only the distinctness of the subject and the predicate, but their being held rationally together, however tentatively.[2] What is more, the very growth of thought is an ascent in respect of individuality. The richer the inclusiveness of its syntheses, and the fuller their internal differentiation, the surer is the onward march of thought. Even apart from this, if—as seems natural to believe—thought's prime concern is to understand what-is, it must, in conformity with the unmistakable wholeness of its object, try to hold as one the differences which it finds or makes. And if, in the end, it finds itself unequal to the task, thought must press for such an absolute harmony of the diverse as answers to its ideal com-

---

[1] To illustrate, is not morality both transcended and consummated in religious experience which is super-moral? Cf. *Ibid* 153.

[2] This means that thought already has all the features of reality, though 'in an incomplete form'; and that 'in desire for the completion of what one has there is no contradiction'. *Ibid* 159-60.

pletely, if only by transcending its special nature, rather than stay content with its own imperfect attempts, or with mere feeling.

It is, however, clear that many difficult questions are here involved. Can thought at all visualize a harmony that is perfect? Is the idea of such a harmony even generally tenable? Is it possible and necessary? If not, there is nothing to protest against our staying where we are, or even against our retracing our steps.

This brings us to consider the relation of thought to absolute reality.

Now, to begin with, thought's fundamental law—the law of contradiction—is (in Bradley's view) an absolute *criterion* of reality. It is, we have seen, rationally unchallengeable; and, what is more, even the world of fact seems only to subserve it. But, what is that which quite conforms to this criterion? Evidently, it could neither be mere feeling nor anything relational; for neither, we have seen, is truly individual. It could only be a whole which includes all diversities, and which holds them, further, in perfect accord. This end cannot be achieved so long as the details insist on retaining their measure of self-existence. They must be made to—as, in feeling, they are found to—conduce without reserve to their mutual involvement. The dual need is met, Bradley believes, by the Absolute which combines within itself the comprehensiveness of a final intellectual synthesis with the immediacy of simple apprehension.

Surely, difficulties here abound; and we must clear them up if we are to argue that the Absolute is not a mere metaphysical fantasy. But, a detailed attempt in this direction will be made only in the next chapter, and here only the following problem may be noted:

If its confession of being inadequate to reality is intelligent, thought must have some idea of what reality is. But, if this is so, does it not become (in some sense) co-extensive with reality in the very act of insisting on its own limits? In fine, it seems self-inconsistent rationally to hold that thought is inadequate to reality?[1]

Now, whether 'reality' is taken in its ordinary sense or as the Absolute, our answer here is one: the claim, and the confessed incapacity to know do not refer to the selfsame point, and so there

[1] AR 154.

is no contradiction. What thought does know about given reality is *that* it is individual; what it does not know about the real is *how* it could be so. With regard to the Absolute as well, thought does not seek to cancel precisely what it affirms. What is claimed to be known is only the general character of the Ultimate, and what is admitted to be unknown is the detailed disposition of content therein. The claim is insistent, and, to Bradley, incontrovertible—that is, so long as we are not able to rid thought of its conviction that individuality alone can serve as a criterion of absolute reality, or to prove that feeling's immediacy or thought's relational manner *can* provide us with what we seek. And the sense of incapacity is a reasoned conviction. It comes as a sequel to sincere self-searching on the part of thought, Bradley's entire treatment of the relational form being an attempt in this vein. His main point is likely to be missed unless we heed his argument as to the radical incompatibility between what thought seeks and the way it sets about its task.

The idea of the Absolute is, however, still quite obscure; and it is with the intent of lessening its vagueness that we turn to the next chapter.

VI

THE ABSOLUTE AND ITS APPEARANCES

According to Bradley, the highest reality is the Absolute. But, why should we at all talk of such a reality? Again, how can we describe it, and its relation, if there be any, to the world of appearances? It is to questions such as these that our discussion in this chapter is, in the main, directed.

First, a word as to the reasons why we should at all talk of the Absolute. The metaphysician is led up to it as the goal of his inquiry—that is, as a perfected individuality which culminates thought's attempt to avoid contradictions in 'understanding' given reality. But, some concern with 'reality' is perhaps shared by us all. The word—and whatever it stands for—cannot dogmatically be banished from discourse; for the actuality of experience, of things-being-presented-to-us, cannot be denied. And yet, unless we suddenly stop thinking, things and experiences which come to us cannot all be regarded as being equally real:

> 'You can scarcely propose to be quite passive when presented with statements about reality ... (or) take the position of admitting any and every nonsense to be truth, truth absolute and entire.'[1]

We must discriminate. But how? Bradley would say: by employing the criterion of self-consistency; for, it is this which appeals to our reason most readily. Things must be intelligible, if their claim to reality is to be acceptable to the intellect. There is no getting away from this.

Now, given reality, we have seen, is nowhere perfectly individual; and did it not everywhere show a looseness of content from existence, thought would remain merely external to it. But, though legitimate, our recourse to thought does not entirely rectify the situation. No intellectual scheme answers perfectly to the ideal of theory. What, then, is the alternative? Shall we reject the very

[1] AR 120.

idea of a higher reality, and say that we know only the phenomena? Or may we, in the alternative, accept the idea in question, but reject entirely the claims of thought to know anything positive about the Reality to which this idea refers?

Rejecting both these alternatives, Bradley insists that his idea of the Absolute is the truly satisfying ideal of theory. To the question if we know anything about the higher reality, his confident answer is:

'I am so bold as to believe that we have a knowledge of the Absolute, certain and real ...'[1]

'The Absolute, though in detail unintelligible, is not so in general, and its general character comes as a consequence from a necessary principle.'[2]

What is here maintained is, in brief, this. We have a general idea of the Absolute. In so far as it follows from a principle which is theoretically irresistible, this knowledge is positive and real; but, in so far as it does not extend to the details of the Absolute, it is incomplete.

Bradley protests emphatically against the suggestion that we cannot have *any* knowledge of 'first principles' or absolute reality.[3] Is not some such knowledge implicit in thought's natural tendency to reject the self-inconsistent as appearance, or again in our awareness that thought cannot itself provide what it none the less seeks? Our dissatisfaction with the self-contradictory character of the relational form seems directly to suggest the idea of a suprarelational harmony where 'each aspect would of itself be a transition to the other aspect', at once and intrinsically, turning synthesis into self-completion, and analysis into self-explication.[4]

But the objector may persist. May not every distinct region of experience be allowed to have its own standard of truth? Now, even if we answer this question affirmatively, the claim of non-contradiction to be an overruling test of truth is in no way harmed. There are no rigid divisions in being and experience; and, in what may be called a border case, the question will surely arise as to

---

[1] *Ibid* 3.
[2] *Ibid* 497.
[3] Cf. *Ibid* 119–20.
[4] *Ibid* 507.

whether the different criteria could be employed without collision. And again, within its own special field, every standard, whatever it be, must be used self-consistently. Nor will it do to contend that in saying: 'reality is such that it does not contradict itself', we are not giving any positive information about reality. For, first, all negation may (in Bradley's view) be said to rest on a positive ground; and, secondly, it seems curious to hold that in knowing what a thing does or does not do, we know absolutely nothing about what it is.[1]

If it be directly asked as to what the Absolute (in general) is, Bradley's answer would be: it is one supra-relational, all-harmonizing whole of Experience, which, though affirmed theoretically in the course of metaphysical inquiry, answers perfectly to the common demand of every aspect of our being[2]; and which is, further, manifest everywhere in the region of experience, though nowhere fully. The idea of such a Reality is here not claimed to be a readymade Truth revealed in intuition: it is regarded as an affirmation of *theory*. So, it is not only permitted, but necessary to examine the arguments in which Bradley's view is grounded. The following problems may be here dealt with at some length:

1. How the Absolute is one or all-inclusive: the protest from asymmetrical relations.
2. What does it mean, and is it proper to say that Reality is Experience?
3. How is the Absolute related to Appearances?

1. THE PROTEST FROM ASYMMETRICAL RELATIONS

An important objection to Bradley's idea of the Absolute as the One, all-inclusive Experience is provided by the fact of asymmetrical relations.

Let us bring out the precise point of the protest. An asymmetrical relation, say, 'A is the father of B', implies a unique, irreversible order. Now, it is difficult to see how such a *specific* order could be provided for in a whole. For, if we speak of a whole which is qualified by the child-parent relationship, we fail entirely

---
[1] *Ibid* 121-24.
[2] Or, to the demand for individuality.

to specify that A is the father of B, and not vice versa. And yet, Bradley's ascent to the Absolute from the side of the relational form depends vitally, if not exclusively, upon the demonstration that every relation points to a totality in which it is *included* and grounded. How can we include an asymmetrical relation in a totality without relieving it of its unique irreversibility? But, if this character is ignored, the very essence of the matter is left out, and the relation is not really included. The alternative is to keep saying, 'A is the father of B'. But, in that case, there is no transition to any inclusive whole: we remain where we are, and the theoretical ascent to the Absolute does not at all begin.

Wollheim's formulation of this difficulty, though it does not consider the latter 'vis a vis' the Absolute, may here be quoted with advantage:

> '... Whereas it might seem plausible to say that "A is close to B" can be interpreted as "The unity AB contains or is qualified by propinquity", to say that "A is greater than B" can be interpreted as "The unity AB contains or is qualified by diversity of magnitude" clearly will not do—for this suggested rewriting of the proposition leaves quite undecided the question whether A is greater than B or B is greater than A. With asymmetrical relations there arises a "distinction of sense"—i.e., which way the relations go—and this cannot be done justice to on a monistic interpretation of relations.'[1]

Wollheim thinks that even in CE Bradley has not really been able to meet this difficulty raised by Russell. Our view, however, is that if Bradley's brief argument in CE is considered *along with* his dialectic of quality and relation in AR,[2] the difficulty ceases to appear insurmountable. It is true that *from the side of the whole* or the unity AB, the irreversibility of an asymmetrical relation seems to remain unaccounted for. But, what exactly is this unity AB? And does Bradley really proceed from the side of the whole?

Now, as we shall presently see, the first question is answered by reflecting as to *why* Bradley speaks of a relation as embraced within a unity; and this enquiry must begin with the remark that he starts by wondering as to how a given relation could stand to its

[1] Wollheim, *F. H. Bradley*, 119–20.
[2] And also, we may add, along with certain remarks in the Appendix of AR.

terms which it, in fact, relates, and which are yet distinct not only from it, but from each other. In the more important parts of his work Bradley does not straightway assert that a whole contains, and is qualified by, relations; he *argues* that they cannot be understood except by positing a larger whole, of terms and relations, in which they are grounded.

Consider, for instance, the relation referred to above: 'A is the father of B.' The relation is admittedly asymmetrical. But Bradley's question is: how does the relation obtain between the two? The answer may be attempted either in the abstract, or with an eye on fact.[1] If we adopt the former way, the whole, affirmed or demanded by the question as to how a relation stands to its terms, will be but *ideal*, and to expect such a whole to provide *visibly* for the specific sense of direction involved in the relation in question, or even for the concrete particularity of the terms themselves, is clearly improper. And if we decide to go by fact, the whole arrived at will be a mass of specific conditions; and *such* a whole will be seen to provide clearly for the uniqueness of the relation. Thus, to speak concretely, does this uniqueness remain wholly unaccounted for if we say that A married a particular lady; that the two lived together; and that, as contrasted with her, and by virtue of having provided for the maintenance of both the lady and the child, A is the *father* of B? True, *all* the conditions which have gone into the making of this fact can not be easily ascertained. But the point only is that the fact, as it seems, is not self-complete; that it is grounded in a set of conditions; and that when they are actually taken into account, the irreversibility of the relation is clearly provided for *and is not left out*.

What has to be noted clearly is that, if we talk in merely abstract terms, the conditions or factors included in the whole will naturally remain unexpressed, and so will the uniqueness of direction hidden within them:

'... When it is objected against me as a Monist that all that I as such have a right to is the terms and the whole, while the order or direction is in neither—my answer is that *no* whole is really a simple whole, and in every whole are always conditions

[1] Cf. 'Logically *and really*, all relations imply a whole to which the terms contribute and by which the terms are qualified.' AR 521. Our italics.

unexpressed, and that in these conditions falls the difference required here, and here is the reason why ARB and BRA are incompatible (that is, *when* and *where* they are so).'[1]

The unity of A and B, *if we seek to understand it*, is not the mere linkage of A with B, both taken simply as they seem to be, rounded and self-complete.[2] Abstractly, it is an ever-widening whole of terms and relations—a process of which the necessity has already been brought out. *This* unity of A and B is richer than their togetherness as merely individual terms, and it contains—invisibly, because abstractly—the conditions of their being together. Bradley's meaning is, in our view, precisely this when he says: 'Relations are *unmeaning* except within and on the basis of a substantial whole.'[3]

The mistake committed by those who follow Russell in criticizing Bradley on this score is, in brief, this. They miss the necessary, theoretical manner in which the whole is affirmed, regard it straightway as a mere container, and as merely *ideal*, and then expect it to provide *visibly* for the specificity of the relation (alleged to be) included therein.

A legitimate objection to Bradley's view that a relation is self-transcendent or that it is, by thought, seen to transcend itself into a whole which includes it—should proceed from the side of a *given relation*. But, is not an asymmetrical relation self-transcendent, both in fact and in idea? The unique irreversibility of the parent-child relationship is due to a host of factors in which it is, in fact, grounded.[4] And theoretically, Bradley would insist, an asymmetrical relation partakes, without reserve, of all those necessary features which constitute the essential meaning of a relation, and which make it seem so incomplete. What is implicit in the very idea of a relation is by now well known to us. First, the

---

[1] CE 672.
[2] Cf. 'Every case of terms in relation is an individual and unique "situation"—a whole, where any alteration on either side must affect the whole throughout and not leave that anywhere unaltered.' *Ibid* 664. But, of course, it is a whole from which, in practice, we are compelled continually to abstract.
[3] AR 125. Our italics.
[4] A fact abstracted from its setting 'has had its lines of attachment cut; it could theoretically be repeated anywhere, and therefore is the reverse of unique'. Blanshard, *The Nature of Thought*, Vol. II, 487.

terms are distinct, or are held apart, each from the other; secondly, in so far as whatever is distinct is so (partly) because of its being distinguished or compared, a passage both ways is involved in the perception of a relation; and, thirdly, a relation is in no case *identical* with its terms. Now, the distinctness of terms is, in the case of an asymmetrical relation, unambiguous. What may not be readily clear is that a passage is here involved *both* ways. But it certainly is. 'He is her father' at once implies: 'she is his daughter.' We may not here raise the question as to whether an asymmetrical relation is really a single relation. But this must be pointed out that it is not, so to speak, a case of one-way traffic. To be sure, an asymmetrical relation holds in one direction, and it does not hold in the reverse direction. But, the (relational) perception that it does not hold in the reverse direction is involved essentially in our awareness of the asymmetrical nature of the relation.

Finally, the distinctness of the relation from its terms is also unmistakable. It is with the fact of asymmetrical relations as his main basis that Russell argues, as a point against Bradley, the utter impossibility of reducing a relation to a mere property of its terms. How Bradley himself rebels against the idea of such a reduction has already been brought out in our fourth chapter. But, and this is the point we here wish to press, if we have, in the case of an asymmetrical relation, an actual togetherness of features which are so utterly diverse—the father from the daughter, and the 'forward', from the 'backward' direction of the 'passage'—is it not ground enough to justify Bradley's wonder as to how such diversities could at all be together, which they in fact clearly are;[1] and are we not forced inescapably to consider the wider setting of factors in which the relation is and must be grounded?

We hasten to add, however, that there is, in Bradley's view, no *direct* passage from a relational unity, however inclusive, to the Absolute. His speculative leap from the relational workings of thought to the supra-relational unity of the Ultimate may be questioned. But this is not relevant to the matter in hand. Here, we may rather reflect thus. Bradley does not profess to take his

[1] Their being together in fact is acceptable so far as we do not oppose the diversity to the unity; that is, so long as our mode of experience is mere feeling. From this viewpoint, again, asymmetrical relations are not ultimate. '*They* imply inherence, which does *not* imply them.' CE 671.

stand on the Fact of the Absolute, with a view to exploring how exactly everything is disposed therein, or to deriving everything *therefrom*; and the question as to how the plurality of the given, *in detail*, finds a place in the Absolute is surely irrelevant to Bradley's view of the matter.

To the question: 'Do asymmetrical relations at all find a place in the Absolute?' Bradley's answer would in brief run thus:

First, the one ultimate reality is *not* simple inherence; were it that, *any* relations, and not only asymmetrical ones, would disprove monism.[1] Secondly, as a matter of fact, an asymmetrical relation is grounded in a wider whole; and, in idea, its diversity clashes clearly with its given unity so that, as a theoretical compulsion, we cannot avoid going beyond the relation and including it in a whole which certainly contains—but, being merely ideal, does not of course display—the irreversibility of the relation. Thirdly, no detail of the given is *as such* included in the Absolute; so that it is vain to expect to *find* an asymmetrical relation bodily there.[2] There is, we have seen, no reason to suppose that such a relation is not (as relation) self-contradictory. But if it is so vitiated, can it rid itself of the taint except by transcending itself into a supra-relational whole?

In fine, we are certainly free to question, if we can, Bradley's basic views—the theoretical need to avoid contradiction; the self-contradictory nature of the relational form; the necessity, therefore, of positing a stage beyond, yet inclusive of relations; and the faith, finally, that, made likely by the fact of feeling, the supra-relational Reality actually *is*. But the mere protest, that a whole cannot visibly include an element which is unique, is valid neither of any actual whole nor of a whole ideally affirmed in the manner of Bradley; and, with regard to his *Absolute*, the protest is utterly irrelevant. Bradley, we may repeat, proceeds not from the side of the Absolute, but from the self-transcendence of fact and idea. The monism of Bradley will collapse only if we could somehow argue that there *is* a fact or relation which is not self-transcendent,[3] and not if we merely protest that the Absolute does not *seem* to include everything.

[1] *Ibid* 670.
[2] Nor is the Absolute itself a Fact open to perception. *Ibid* 671.
[3] Cf. AR 494.

THE ABSOLUTE AND ITS APPEARANCES

2. REALITY AS EXPERIENCE

Our next question is: how is ultimate Reality a (supra-relational) whole of *Experience*. Now, Bradley's argument here is, in brief, this. Everything, actual or merely possible, falls within, or itself is experience. The Absolute includes all that is: so it must itself be experience. Bradley is convinced that we can justly lay claim to this positive, though abstract, knowledge of the ultimate Reality.[1]

Now, in the light of the above, it is easy to see that 'reality' in 'Reality is Experience' may be taken to mean either given reality or reality as Absolute. This can be brought out in one other way. That reality is experience is, in Bradley's view, borne out if, as an experiment, we 'try to discover any sense' in which we can still continue to speak of a thing 'when all *perception* and feeling have been removed'.[2] The Absolute, on the other hand, is not open to 'inner' and 'outer' perception. None of the higher truths, we have seen, is *thus* knowable. Therefore, the reality which is found to be experience as the result of an 'experiment' cannot be the Absolute; it can only be given reality. On the other hand, Bradley's insistence on the Absolute as Experience is clear and recurrent. So we propose to discuss the doctrine in question with reference to both the senses of 'reality'.

Before, however, we actually address ourselves to the task, we would do well to bring out, if only in part, *why* Bradley advances this doctrine at all. This will serve to bring out how the present essay is related to the last one, by telling us something about thought and reality. An important dilemma which faces Bradley is, we have seen, this:

Thought is less than reality. But, in asserting this, we seem to commit a self-contradiction. If thought knows that it is less than reality, it must know what reality is; but then, how is it less than the latter?[3]

It is here that the identification of reality with experience may be seen to help. If reality is experience, it cannot fall wholly or for ever outside of thought. Whatever is experienced *can* be made an object of thought, if but from the outside and in general. But,

---
[1] *Ibid* 470.
[2] *Ibid* 127–28. Our italics.
[3] *Ibid* 492.

on the other hand, experienced reality is not mere thought. The real may come to us non-relationally, or as feeling. Willing and desiring are, from the outside, known to thought. It knows that their manner is, in the main, non-discursive. In other words, thought is aware of its other, and is, therefore, confessedly less than the whole reality.

There is no contradiction between the two sides. What is claimed to be known is (sentient) reality as a general object of thought. What is confessed to be distinctly other than thought is the (non-relational) form of many aspects of experienced reality. An object of thought is, so far as it is an object, within thought; but it need not necessarily be itself mere thought.

It must, however, be added at once that our difficulty persists—with regard to reality as the totality of facts, if not with regard to reality as sentient. How is this wholeness of what-is different from, and yet within thought? The answer—which is, in Bradley's own view, the main solution of the dilemma—may be put as follows. What thought, in the end, aims at is to be secured by including (in idea) all that there is, even aspects which are other than thought, in a harmonious whole. In so far as such a whole is also what we may mean by the word as it is ordinarily used, 'reality' as the totality of facts is within thought, because it is (in metaphysics) an affirmation of the intellect. But, on the other hand, because the whole affirmed is supra-relational, thought is here transcended. No side need be ignored, neither the immanence nor the transcendence of reality in relation to thought; for, the supra-relational, all-inclusive whole—which is the true metaphysical reality—is thought's own ideal, and in being consummated a special aspect is not merely left out.

We may turn now to examine the doctrine: reality is experience. Let us begin from the side of experience. What is Experience?[1] Common-sense would say that it is our actual condition in waking life, or that it is given and present fact. Experience is a blend of content and awareness. The two sides may well be distinguished, specially where the content is a physical object. But can we draw

---

[1] We have chosen to begin thus, because this question, as distinguished from that relating to the kinds of experience, is often ignored by those who subject the doctrine to a critical examination. See, for instance, Wollheim, *F. H. Bradley*, 201-04.

a clear line between the two? The attempt may be made either in fact or in idea. If we take the object away, and cease to imagine it, or to think of it, the specific awareness disappears; but the awareness which remains is by no means contentless. If, on the other hand, we try merely *to think of* the content as completely stripped off its linkage with awareness, the attempt is clearly self-inconsistent and so bound to fail. What would an object be if it is, in idea, divested of all its features revealed to awareness? Being and sentience seem to be indissolubly one: *this* is experience—a whole of feeling 'in which distinctions can be made, but in which divisions do not exist'.[1]

It is important to see that, as Bradley understands it, experience is not a mere shadowy tissue brought over from the side of the subject and superimposed upon the object. It is that original sentient unity *within which* we distinguish 'the experiencing' and 'the experienced', the self and the world; and because of which the distinctions cannot be exaggerated into actual separateness. Desire cannot be separated from the desired, nor thinking, from what is thought of. Here, however, it may be contended that the alleged impossibility of separating the two sides holds merely because of the ideal nature of the material. Desiring and thinking are ideal attitudes, and a visible line cannot obviously be drawn across what is merely ideal.

Let us, therefore, consider a physical object. Or, to talk loosely, leaving 'experience' we turn now to 'reality'. What is a fact as we 'find' it? Does it stand 'separate and on its own bottom'? Certainly not; it comes 'as a feature and aspect within one whole of feeling'.[2] This is true of all presented fact. We cannot say precisely where awareness ends and where the object's own intrinsic content begins. Not only the secondary qualities, but even the primary ones cannot claim complete independence of sentience. In point of fact, nothing exists entirely by itself. The very affirmation that a thing exists makes it an object of thought, and relates it to experience.

Bradley, therefore, concludes that the distinction between 'experience' and 'the experienced' is but relative. It depends on whether we look at presented fact from the side of subjective

[1] AR 128.
[2] *Ibid* 128–29.

activity or from that of content. But neither can be had, or said to *be* apart from the other. Reality, whether present or merely imagined, is experienced. 'The experienced' is 'experience' from the side of the subject. So reality is experience, not the 'experienced'. Bradley's argument, here, would probably be that if we describe reality as 'the experienced', reality as felt, as distinguished from reality experienced as an object, is likely to be ignored.

Our account of the matter so far is, however, inadequate, and open to many objections. It is to these that we now turn:

(a) In equating all reality with *experience*, do we not either ignore the solid facts of life or reduce them to something impalpable? Bradley's ready answer would be that we do neither, and that what we, in fact, do is only to protest against the one-sided apotheosis of mere fact or of mere sentience. Facts which are 'solid' in the sense of being wholly self-existent are nowhere to be had. Awareness enters inextricably into the very being of a sensible quality. Nor is experience anywhere wholly without content. Experience appears to be merely impalpable only because we artificially empty it of all content, exactly as things seem self-complete only by being abstracted, in idea, from actual experience. But, both are abstractions; and, in the end, impossible to hold. What alone is a fact is the indissoluble unity of content and sentience, or experience.

But the belief that experience is, so to speak, utterly airy, and that things are wholly self-complete is, with many people, so deep-seated that some more remarks on the matter may here be permitted. What is sought to be emphasized by this view is the visible, external and full character of a thing as contrasting with the invisible, internal and empty character of experience. But, though in practice it may seem necessary, the distinction is by no means absolute: it does not warrant a clear-cut separation of the two sides. 'Visible' stands for what is 'out there', in the things themselves, not merely that which is, or can be, *seen*; for smells and sounds are, according to common-sense itself, as much a part of things as their visible form. But are smells and sounds merely there, 'out' in the objects? And if not—if, that is, they depend vitally upon sentience—how are they merely external? Conversely, is the idea of a building merely internal? And again, is every*thing* full or compact exactly in the same degree? Surely not. A gentle breath of wind does not have the solid feel of a mountain: yet it is external like the latter. But if, with all its lightness, a breeze is a thing, why is a faint tingle of pain not so? And how does a vivid bit of fancy have lesser content than any one of these?

(b) Again, admitting that present fact is inseparable from sentience, how is it proper to regard things as *experience* rather than as 'experienced' or as 'objects of experience'? The difficulty may be met thus. Experience is the fusion of being and sentience. What is experienced is equally so. So, the experienced is experience. The difficulty in accepting this is due to a stubborn error. We first begin by accepting the fact of an experienced object. Then, when we are presented with the proposition, 'the experienced is experience', we begin to have our doubts; and by surreptitiously lifting the object clean out of its being experienced, we wonder as to how the thing's solidity could be the same as the ideal tissue discarded. But, the object thus abstracted *is not* the experienced; nor is the emptied ideality in any way experience.

If we hold on to this, that the distinction between 'experience' and 'the experienced' is but relative, quite a few criticisms of the theory under review seem to lose their sting. An instance may be cited:

Lazerowitz suspects that to say, as Bradley does, that 'feeling, thought, and volition (any groups under which we class psychical phenomena) are all the materials of existence and there is no other material, actual or even possible',[1] is too extravagant a claim 'to maintain in the face of fact'.[2]

Now, the suspicion is natural. How is a table *experience*? The difficulty is, however, dissipated the moment we realize that, for Bradley, 'experience' is, in the end, identical with 'the experienced'? What *is* the table apart from its experienced characteristics? And what *could* it be said to be apart from characteristics which are within experience? Lazerowitz fails to notice that Bradley does not only say that reality is experience, but strongly opposes the 'separation of feeling from the felt, or of the desired from desire or of what is thought from thinking'. The very 'ground' and 'foundation' of the doctrine, reality is experience, is, upon Bradley's own view, the contention that nothing is presented as real by

[1] *Ibid* 127.
[2] Lazerowitz, *The Structure of Metaphysics*, 199.

itself, neither the subject nor the object. Experience, we may repeat, is never without content; and content, in turn, neither is nor is thinkable apart from experience.

(c) So far we have been talking of presented fact. But, what shall we say of an absent object? How is an object, which is not being perceived or thought of at all, *within* experience, not to speak of its being identical with experience? Bradley's reply to the question would proceed thus:

It is certainly true that much is always left out of our actual experience. But what is thus left out is also intrinsically capable of being experienced, however imperfectly. How can we be sure of *this* in advance? The answer is: because the rival possibility—the possibility of anything as being wholly outside of experience—cannot self-consistently be asserted.[1] To hold that an object is outside of—or different from what we experience—is at once to make it an object of thought, and thinking *is* experience. It is also to temper the alleged total strangeness of the fact in question; for, difference, existence, and even the mode of possessing characteristics, are all known features of our everyday experience. Can we imagine anything in such a way that it may borrow nothing from known experience, no manner of 'existing' or 'appearing'?

It may, however, still be insisted that we should not, and we cannot, set an ideal limit to possibility, and that something may well *be* there without possessing any of the characteristics which are known to us. Now, even if we allow its intrinsic contradiction to go unnoticed, the insistence seems questionable. Every possibility must have some basis in known reality; and if, in the region of familiar existence, there is nothing entirely removed from sentience, nothing intrinsically impervious to the different modes of our experience, are we still justified in insisting on the possibility of there being something quite opposed to sentience?

But suppose we do not *assert* that a thing is wholly beyond sentience. May it not then exist quite outside of experience? Bradley's ready reply would be that, in such a case, the thing in question can in no sense be *believed* to be; for, it is in fact impossible to entertain a belief as to the existence of any such thing as is quite outside of our common modes of experience.

(d) Another objection to the doctrine is provided by Ewing.

[1] AR 129.

It is true that only such characteristics and relations can be ascribed to an object as have either themselves been experienced by us or which are at least 'definable in terms of characteristics or relations which have been thus experienced'. But how does it follow from this that 'physical objects are themselves of the nature of *experience* or that *all* physical objects are experienced'? There is no warrant for believing 'that the characteristics we ascribe to physical objects (are) all logically inseparable from the experience of them'.[1] Now, our earlier discussion has already prepared the ground for Bradley's answer to the above. It would run roughly as follows:[2]

It does not appear fantastic to say that physical objects are of the nature of experience if two considerations are duly borne in mind. First, as already brought out, 'experience' is not to be sundered from 'the experienced'. Secondly, when we ascribe a characteristic to an absent object, it *is* experienced, in so far as it is made an object of thought. We cannot say that the objects of our thought, however vaguely and loosely held, are *in no sense* experienced. To sum up, the criticism seems to lose a part of its sting the moment we resolve to guard ourselves against two erroneous beliefs—first, that experience is a mere contentless form, and secondly that, to be experienced, an object has to be close to the subject in actual fact.

(e) The theory in question may also be criticized by finding fault with the traditional epistemological argument on which it seems to depend. Our view, however, is that the questionable character of the doctrine made out by such criticism is at least tempered if the full details of Bradley's specific attitude are taken into account. Wollheim's account of the argument is as follows:

'Everything that we come across or accept as real, everything that we call a piece of existence or a fact, is always found *combined* with experience:

and if it is always *combined with experience,* then no meaning can be attached to the assertion that it could exist without experience;

[1] Ewing, *Idealism*, 405. Our italics.
[2] Our entire reply to the objection is here but tentative. The element of truth which Ewing's criticism could perhaps be said to contain will be brought out a little later.

and if it could not exist without experience, then it is indivisible from experience; and if it is indivisible from experience, then it is, or is nothing but, experience.'[1]

Wollheim's more important comments on Bradley's employment of the above run as under:

The initial premiss is acceptable: it is 'clearly true that everything that is experienced is experienced'. But, how do we pass on from this to the succeeding steps? Or, what is the warrant for saying that everything is experienced or experience? Perhaps this: we are asked to imagine some event, to hold it as an object in the mind's eye, and to see if it is anything but experienced; whereupon we find that it *is* experienced. The ideal experiment is then made the basis of the following affirmation: an unexperienced event is unimaginable, and therefore impossible. But, and this is the crux of Wollheim's protest, imaginability which is the true criterion of possibility or meaningfulness only means ability to be supposed or postulated: 'and to suppose or postulate an event is not to make it an object of experience.' In brief, Bradley reaches his conclusion 'only by exploiting an ambiguity in the meaning of "imagination" or some related concept'.[2]

We turn now to see if this objection is as tenable as it may appear to be. Consider, to begin with, the way in which the argument is said to open. Does Bradley anywhere say that everything is found (merely) *combined with experience*? In our view, he does not. So to speak would be to suggest that it is theoretically quite legitimate to *conceive* of 'experience' and 'thing' as being originally self-complete, and that in actual existence they are only *found* together. But this is, we have seen, precisely the suggestion against which Bradley explicitly protests.[3] Wollheim's positive objection to Bradley's view, however, is that to imagine an event is merely to postulate it, and that it is 'not to make it an *object* of experience'. Or, an event may be imagined to be without being experienced. It cannot, therefore, be said that a thing could not be apart from being experienced.

But, we ask, is all 'experiencing' necessarily the holding of

[1] Wollheim, *F. H. Bradley*, 201. Our italics.
[2] *Ibid* 203.
[3] *Ibid* 127–29.

content clearly as an object? And, is what is merely postulated *in no sense* experienced? To postulate something is without doubt an activity of thought; and is not thinking a mode of experience? Bradley insists that content which is not at all experienced, not even non-relationally, is absolutely 'unmeaning'.[1] Wollheim's other protest, the one which is directed against Bradley's transition from 'everything is experienced' to 'everything is experience', is attenuated by the consideration, already brought out, that the distinction between 'experience' and 'the experienced' is but relative.

(f) Yet another objection may be considered before we turn finally to sum up our views as to the net value of the theory under review.

Bradley says: Reality is Experience. But the bearer of experience is everywhere the self. Does it mean, then, that the finite self with its processes is the only reality? Does the doctrine preach solipsism? Is there no reality beyond *my* experience? Bradley answers firmly in the negative, and his argument is here as follows:

What is 'my experience'? Speaking from the viewpoint of structure and manner, 'my experience' is either immediate or relational. Now, if 'my experience' is understood as what is immediately given, as 'the "here" and the "now"', there are here no distinctions as such, not even the one between 'mine' and 'not mine'; and so, if we speak strictly, the experience in question cannot be said to be pre-eminently mine.[2] Moreover, in so far as it breaks up continually into the relational form, experience as immediate cannot be said to be the only reality. If, on the other hand, we take experience as relational or indirect, solipsism, according to Bradley, will again be found unacceptable. First, the identical self which is here said to be aware of 'objects' is not there from the very beginning of our experience. It is rather a construct which emerges as we live, and is by no means primary. Secondly,

> 'If I base myself on indirect experience, I must concede not only that there are certainly things other than myself, but also that there are almost certainly selves other than my self; and the reasons that I have for believing in the existence of these other

[1] *Ibid* 128.
[2] *Ibid* 224.

selves are not "sensibly" weaker than those which I have for believing in the existence of my self.'[1]

Certainly, reality is, in Bradley's view, experience. But we cannot, he insists, pass on from this to: the self is the only reality; for, experience cannot be equated with the self. The self exists as opposed to the not-self; it is the term of a relation. Experience, on the other hand, is not only relational, but non-relational. Again, what comes first is (in Bradley's view) unmediated experience; the distinction of self and not-self emerges only later within this experience. Finally, the self, as an experient that is opposed to what is experienced, is always transcended by the total experience. But, experience 'taken at full'[2] cannot be transcended.

To conclude: the self, with the experience that it owns, could well be the only reality were it utterly self-complete. But the truth, on the other hand, is that, however inclusive it be, the self always leaves out some content and gains its status by being contrasted with what it is seen to exclude. Solipsism is but 'the apotheosis of an abstraction'.

Yet, when all has been said for it, the doctrine: 'reality is experience' seems to us, in some ways, questionable. Our argument here may be outlined thus:

(i) Bradley regards Experience as the indissoluble unity of Being and sentience. This unity must be either relational or non-relational or both. It cannot be supra-relational, for this mode of unity is not, as such, open to us. Now, is the unity of Experience relational? If we say, yes, we come to regard it as *a relation* of being and sentience. But then, both the terms, upon Bradley's own view of the relational form, must be said to be relatively other than the relation. This would mean that being can be, nay has got to be, partly independent of sentience. But if we say this, it would be patently inconsistent with Bradley's main thesis: 'Being and reality are, in brief, one thing with sentience; they can neither be opposed to, nor even in the end *distinguished* from it.'[3] Perhaps,

[1] Wollheim, *F. H. Bradley*, 207. For a fuller treatment of Bradley's attitude to Solipsism see, *Ibid* 204–09. It is with this in mind that our argument here is so briefly presented.
[2] AR 465.
[3] *Ibid* 129. Our italics. Bradley, perhaps, would like to emphasize: 'in the end'.

then, the unity of experience is non-relational. This indeed seems to be Bradley's real view; for, he speaks of experience as being a unity 'indissolubly', and again as 'one whole of feeling'. But, here too we are faced with a difficulty. Experience as a non-relational unity is immediate experience; and, again upon Bradley's own view, such experience is self-transcendent. If that is so, the unity of being and sentience which is experience must be regarded as being continually open to the possibility of breaking up into the relational form; and our earlier objection is thus still seen to hold.[1]

(ii) Another criticism is suggested by the consideration, made out by Ewing and Wollheim, that to ascribe a sensible characteristic to an object, or to postulate an event, is not necessarily to *experience* the characteristic or the event. Our final view here is that, though it is difficult to say that these attitudes are not 'experiencing' in any sense, *they are not 'experience' in the sense commonly intended* when we talk of physical objects, or of events; and that this distinct sense of the word must be retained in the interests of intelligible discourse.

Consider an instance. Suppose a man ideally ascribes a smell to a flower the discovery of which is reported to him. In doing so, does he actually *experience* the smell? Clearly not, though the smell is certainly made an object of thought. At least in such cases, merely to think of a quality is *not* also to experience it. As a felt quality, the smell is here not experienced, though in some loose way it *is* made an object of thought. And it is clearly the former sense of 'experience' which is here relevant. Bradley is right in saying that if we try to *consider* it in utter separateness from sentience, a sensible quality loses all *meaning*. But, on the other hand, is it not true to say that the '*experience*' of such a quality loses its distinctive and natural meaning if it is considered apart from all sense-contact; and that if such contact is not there, the quality in

---

[1] To us, it is not quite proper to protest that, because Bradley does not take his stand on an argument, it is improper to *argue* against his view. (Cf. Ewing, *Idealism*, 405). True, in ETR (316, footnote) Bradley himself says that 'we have here a matter for observation and experiment and not for long trains of reasoning'. But then, what about the following?—
'Nothing is ever so presented as real by itself, *or can be argued so to exist without demonstrable fallacy*. And in asserting that the reality is experience, I rest throughout on this foundation.' AR 129. Our italics.

question is not being experienced? How is then *all* reality experienced or 'experience'?

A possible answer is that, even though all things are not experienced at any one moment, they can all be experienced, if only successively. But, the 'can' suggests many questions. To confine ourselves to physical reality, can we be sure that our powers and apparatuses of perception are adequate to all reality; or conversely, that everything in given reality is so structured as to be intrinsically within the fold of the perceivable? True, aided by science, our perceptive powers are growing everyday. But this certainly does not warrant the categorical assertion that *every* object can be experienced. The idea may indeed be entertained that, in so far as our knowledge of the nature and kinds of organisms with their modes of perception is still imperfect, the objects of Nature might have always been perceived, if not by human beings, by other unknown sentient creatures. But, this is no more likely than that there may be many unknown regions of physical reality which are wholly imperceptible. Both alternatives are mere possibilities which neither finally confirm nor utterly disprove the suggestion that all reality is capable of—or is in fact—being experienced.

(iii) Finally, it seems a clear exaggeration to say, as Bradley does, that 'even *barely* to exist, *must be* to fall within sentience'.[1] '*Barely* to exist' is different from 'to be *thought of* as existing'; or else, the word 'barely' is merely ignored. But, if this is so, what is the warrant for saying everything that exists in fact falls within sentience? Bradley's favourite way of arguing his view is to begin by asking us to show, or to assert this reality of an object quite outside of sentience.[2] But, if it is impossible, because immediately self-refuting, to point to an object, in fact or in idea, and yet to keep it entirely away from sentience, is it in any way proved that the thing *exists*, with respect to *every* detail of its being, *only for sentience*?[3]

We, however, hasten to add that, even if its extreme character be admitted as an obvious defect, the theory is by no means entirely ungrounded in reason or commonsense. Why does Bradley at all advance it? Is it merely because he is averse to materialism? No;

---

[1] *Ibid* 127. Our italics.
[2] *Ibid* 463.
[3] Cf. Ewing, *Idealism*, 22.

that is not the only reason. What Bradley tries to seek continually is wholeness or individuality, and he dismisses our common attitudes as unreal or untrue simply because of their one-sidedness. It would, for instance, be clearly improper, because one-sided, to regard given reality as merely sensible. Nor is thought our only mode of contact with the Real. Feeling, volition and desire have also to be taken into account. Experience is the only word which covers all these attitudes. Moreover, in describing given reality as experience, we provide also for the continual flux in the world around us, the recurring passage of content from the 'subjective' to the 'objective', or from feeling to thought, and vice versa. 'Experience' is, therefore, as good an 'integrator-word' for the metaphysician as 'Being' or 'Self'; and, what is more, it is free from that suggestion of inertness which the notion of 'Being' may seem directly to involve. Nor is commonsense in any way opposed to this comprehensive use of 'experience'. Our initial, natural reaction to the identification of the experienced with experience is indeed one of protest. But here we would do well to remember, first, that Bradley himself does not refuse to make the distinction, or to regard it as practically necessary, as distinguished from being ultimately tenable; and, secondly that, if it could be provoked to reflect even a little, commonsense itself would see it readily that experience is, in fact, never contentless, and that, speaking from the side of content, it *is* 'the experienced'.

Finally, in so far as *experienced* fact is everywhere individual—in the sense of being an actual, felt unity of differences—the doctrine, reality is experience, may be said to support our earlier suggestion as to how, even from the viewpoint of metaphysics, given reality may be regarded as being (in a measure) 'real'.

And yet, Bradley would add, the given is by no means the final reality. True, our experience everywhere is one of aspects in a felt whole.[1] The unity, we have seen, is not cancelled even where our thinking is most detailed. In this sense of an experienced whole which holds differences without being divided by them, what we experience is, as feeling, everywhere the Absolute, and this is an

---

[1] We have spoken of given reality differently, sometimes as relational, and sometimes as individual or 'felt'. The seeming discrepancy is perhaps resolved by the consideration, developed in our third and fourth chapters, that what is relational may be, from the outside, felt as one.

experience which we can nowhere wholly avoid.[1] But as we experience it, the whole is never really at rest; and, assuming that the Absolute is really there, we experience it everywhere imperfectly. Within the felt unity of the given there is a perpetual loosening of content, of idea from existence.[2] We can deny neither the visible unrest of content nor the experienced unity of being; and, in so far as, though being in fact together, the two are to thought so clearly different, we are compelled to reflect as to how, without any impoverishment, the 'that' and the 'what' could be held finally as one. It is this metaphysical wonder which, we have seen, leads Bradley to the affirmation of a supra-relational Absolute.

Attention may here be drawn to two considerations which follow from Bradley's insistence that the Absolute *is* experienced, however incompletely. First, to reach the Absolute, if only in idea, we do not have to ignore or reject the (inviolable) unity of our experience; we have only to affirm it finally, by absorbing within it—but as perfected—the relational form of thought which seems inimical to true individuality. Secondly, if the Absolute is supra-relational, and our concrete, experienced reality too is (in part) individual, 'reality' in its two senses, as 'Absolute' and as 'existence with character', may be used interchangeably, without utter neglect of principle, if not without causing confusion. Quite a few utterances of Bradley, such as: 'The real is individual', are thus dual in meaning, and so on the whole tenable, though not readily intelligible.

The Absolute, we are assured, does not leave out the essentially unified or felt manner of our experience, that is, the way in which 'reality' is directly 'given' to us. All content, says Bradley, is here intuited:

'... what for us is intelligible only, is more for the Absolute. There somehow, we do not know how, what we think is perceived. Everything there is merged and re-absorbed in an experience intuitive, at once and in itself, of both ideas and facts.'[3]

---

[1] Cf. AR 397.
[2] How this very instability may be regarded as a revealer of reality will be brought out later.
[3] AR 246.

THE ABSOLUTE AND ITS APPEARANCES

We may, in the end, consider if it is at all tenable to apply the word 'experience' to Reality *as Absolute*. An obvious objection here is this. Experience is 'personal' and so limited. We cannot therefore speak of the Absolute as Experience. If, on the other hand, we make 'experience' all-inclusive, it ceases to have any intelligible negative, and itself becomes meaningless.[1] This is precisely the point in Kant's insistence that every concept is applied, rightly or wrongly, within a limited field.[2] Again, 'all conceivable experience is experience of a sequence of events in time, the earlier events in the sequence determining the later'.[3] The Absolute, being supra-temporal, cannot therefore be spoken of as Experience.

Now, following Bradley, our answer to the above could be roughly as follows:

Everything here depends on how we interpret 'experience'. If there is anything like immediate experience, it is not proper to say that all conceivable experience is the experience of a *sequence* of events in time. The non-relational form of feeling is our daily experience; and when we apply 'experience' in this sense to the Absolute, we succeed in avoiding the suggestion that the final reality has nothing to do with our common world. Again, the contention that 'experience' stands for something personal and limited is true only of mediate experience, that is, of experience where the self is held in conscious opposition to the not-self. Moreover, Bradley would say that, even in the case of relational experience, the 'personal' character only means that experience belongs to the self, not that it is identical with, or is exhausted by the latter.

Nor is it true to say that 'experience' has no intelligible 'other'. As Bradley understands it, 'experience' is a felt whole which is not divided by the distinctions which it holds. Its intelligible other is any fact which is asserted to be presented entirely by itself.[4] Finally, Bradley would ask, is not experience the one common region in which every concept is intelligible? And if the Absolute is

---

[1] Cohen, *Reason and Nature*, 453–54.
[2] *The Nature of Metaphysics*, 138.
[3] *Ibid* 24.
[4] Whether such an abstraction is, in the end, defensible is quite another matter.

theoretically affirmed as the *all*-inclusive harmony, is not 'Experience' the most suitable term to describe it?

3. THE ABSOLUTE AND ITS APPEARANCES

Obviously, however, the suggestion that the Absolute includes all the appearances is beset with many difficulties. Some of them may be formulated in terms of the following questions:

How are all the Appearances included and *made good* in the Absolute?

How, in general, can we describe the relation of Appearance to Reality? Is the way in which Bradley's basic intuition envisages this relation intelligible and tenable?

a. *The Absolute as a perfect harmony*

The idea that the Absolute is a perfect harmony is, according to Bradley, the true ideal of theory. It stands for two considerations which are distinct, though allied: first, that the final reality is suprarelational, and, secondly, that it is all-inclusive. Both, we have seen, are demanded by thought. The attempt to *think out* how in detail the relational form may be transcended is, of course, self-inconsistent, and therefore futile. But, on the other hand, thought itself insists that the transcendence in question must somehow be accomplished. Besides, encouraged by the fact of feeling, we think it reasonable to say that the relational form could be transcended by tempering the self-assertiveness of details, so as to make every individual aspect conduce directly to the character of the other. The Absolute is not a totality of mere thought. Bradley insists that the relational form is here wholly transcended, though not left out.

The suggestion that the Absolute contains everything is equally an affirmation of the intellect. As for the individual appearances, he is convinced that none of them is truly self-existent, and that they are all not merely included, but consummated in the Absolute. Considered in itself, an appearance is self-transcendent. But in the Absolute, because of the very presence of all appearances therein, everything gains the entire supplement which it needs; confesses, as it were, to its utter relativity; and (yet) is at once consummated in so far as what could—from its own viewpoint—bring it to final self-completion, is already immediately there. If we take out from this Whole the smallest bit of content, its 'absoluteness' disappears; and this, not because of the mere loss of a limb, but because of a dissipation of essence. No appearance is now supplied with *all* that determines it; it remains self-transcendent, withheld from what it none the less demands; and the entire aggregate is but a collocation of the merely finite. Hence, says Bradley: 'Emphatically the Absolute is nothing if taken apart from any single one of its elements.'[1] It is only in so far as it is a supra-relational harmony—and, again, only because the 'externality of the manifold has (here) utterly ceased'—that the Absolute is, to Bradley, spiritual.[2]

We here think it essential to reiterate that this idea of a final harmony is not given to us, dogmatically and full-blown, at the very start of our inquiry. Nor is it developed in a kind of philosophical vacuum, in utter irrelevance to the idiom of fact. It emerges, by degrees, under the stress of thought's basic insistence that, besides being its own inherent demand, individuality is our end in every region of experience. The ideal of theory is consistent predication. Morality, again, aims (in the end) at a perfect harmony of the actual and the ideal in a supra-moral experience. And Art is distinguished everywhere by a claim to (relative) self-completeness. In brief, all our attitudes, theoretic or practical, aim at individuality; and it is, in Bradley's view, the impulse to hold more content—and to hold it more harmoniously—or, in a word, to be more truly individual, which explains the self-transcendence of every portion of our experience.

But, it may at once be asked, are the individual aspects of our experience in fact self-transcendent? Now, leaving aside the *argument* that whatever is finite must transcend itself into a bigger whole in order to overcome the contradictions which beset it, we turn at once to the evidence of fact:

To speak negatively and generally, the specific regions of our experience can nowhere be rigidly demarcated. It is not only the winsome objects of sense, but some shapely trains of reasoning that may strike us as being truly beautiful. Again, it may be im-

---
[1] AR 152.
[2] *Ibid* 441.

possible to *divide* religiousness from what is (merely) morally good.

Positively, consider any specific region of existence or experience. Admittedly, it has its own positive character. But, let us insist on it, or regard it as truly self-complete. In case the insistence is rational, it has to be argued that the thing's content is not determined by anything outside of it. We have, however, seen that when such an attempt is made, whether in fact or in terms of mere theory, the thing's claim to self-completeness is at once belied.

If we turn to moral experience, this truth is forced upon us more compellingly. The voluptuary extols sense to the status of Reality. The result is that, because of the very intensity and onesidedness of this effort, he is gnawed continually by the sense that much is left out. True, in fact and in action, he may find it impossible to step out of the chasm which he has chosen to inhabit and which he tries in vain to bridge; but in the few sane moments that may yet come to him, the realization is clear that the aspect cannot really have any pretensions to wholeness. Our insistence on aspects, our self-identification with them as if they were the whole, is to thought doubly revealing. It throws into bolder relief the native self-transcendence of every aspect; and, from the other side, it shows how the Whole cancels, in every case effectively, the attempt by the parts to claim self-completeness. Did the whole reality merely include or encompass the portions which are our lot, they could as well contain us for ever—without scruple, pain or self-reproach. Moreover, a transition in that case from an aspect to the whole would be merely arbitrary. The fact, on the other hand, is that, whatever be our precise mode of experience, an aspect is everywhere driven internally to transcend itself into a wider whole; and the suggestion is irresistible that Reality—immanent everywhere, though not in the same degree—loosens the appearances from within them, as if to work out its full nature. Our 'insistence' on an aspect heightens its self-transcendence, and makes for a deeper realization of the 'immanent' action of the whole reality. Reflections such as these throw light on some such utterances of Bradley as may seem otherwise unintelligible: '... its mere onesidedness again is but a partial emphasis, a note of insistence which contributes, we know not how, to greater energy of life.'¹ An appeal to moral life is indeed here helpful. Detachment may seem demanded by indulgence satiate.

But an alternative is an aspect itself, and is by no means the whole. Our continual tossing, in the field of ethics, between one-sided theories each claiming to be entire is, to Bradley, doubly instructive.² It exposes both the futility of acquiescing in mere aspects; and the unwisdom of ignoring any. The whole reality is immanent in the parts, making them self-transcendent; and the very flux of our experience is a partial revealer of reality.

The way has now been paved for a discussion of Bradley's basic vision. But, some characteristic emphases of his view of 'transcendence' may first be noted, primarily with a view to cancelling the suggestion that his metaphysics is only an escape from what is to us compellingly real. First, what is 'transcended' is not left out by the whole which transcends it.³ We must remember that it is its own content which is said to transcend the existence of a thing; and, further, that this transcendence means only the embedment of the thing's 'what', and so of the thing itself, in a whole of greater amplitude. Secondly, in being 'transcended', a specific experience or demand is only perfected. The first is needed to argue that the Absolute is not without content; and the second, to maintain that it is, though supra-relational, a consummation of thought's own relational form.⁴

Both are, for Bradley, important; and we have to bear them continually in mind. True, he repeatedly speaks of the Absolute as the final *harmony*. But this harmony, even like 'personality' as we commonly understand the word, is no mere boundary;⁵ it is a whole packed with content. The spatial image of a mere mould or outline is to be carefully guarded against. And in so far as our ascent to the idea of the Absolute is, in Bradley's view, the self-evolving movement of the ideality of both thought and fact to its logical close—a consummation, as it were, of the given itself— it is the *essence* of what-is which the idea of the Absolute is believed

---

[1] *Ibid* 173.
[2] Cf. *Ibid* 374–78.
[3] Provided this whole is truly a 'ground'. Cf. PL 633.
[4] AR 180.
[5] This should not, however, delude us into the belief that the Absolute is, in Bradley's view, a 'person' in the sense of excluding what is above and below personality. *Ibid* 471.

to give us, though but in outline. Nor would it be proper to suppose that, 'when the relational form is gone, the result is really poorer'.[1] If the professed goal of thought cannot be achieved except through going beyond relations, the supra-relational must be regarded as a true consummation of the relational. This is, in brief, our answer to the criticism that the restless onward movement of Bradley's dialectical thinking 'leads to its own *annihilation* in a form of mystical intuitionism.'[2]

b. *Bradley's basic vision*
We now feel enabled to cite Bradley's basic vision with a measure of understanding:

'The one reality, we may say from our human point of view, was present in each aspect in a form which does not satisfy. To work out its full nature it has sunk itself into these differences. But in each it longs for that absolute self-fruition which comes only when the self bursts its limits and blends with another finite self. This desire of each element for a perfection which implies fusion with others, is not self-contradictory. It is rather an effort to remove a present state of inconsistency, to remain in which would indeed be fixed self-contradiction.'[3]

The passage cited above suggests the following questions:
Why should the Absolute at all 'appear' if this means a fall from its status as the perfectly individual Reality? Again, how is the Reality one and immanent? Finally, why should it at all sink itself into differences if its final aim is only to transcend them?

Now, our answer to these questions could, in brief, run thus:
If they refer to the Absolute *as such*, the questions here put are admittedly unanswerable. But, in *this* sense they cannot fairly be put.[4] To view things entirely from the absolute point of view, we have to shake off our finitude; but if 'per impossibile' this could be done, we, with our attitudes as such, will have ceased to be.[5] The Ultimate as such is beyond our finite modes of willing and

---
[1] *Ibid* 180.
[2] Aliotta, *The Idealistic Reaction Against Science*, 105. Our italics.
[3] AR 161.
[4] *Ibid* 467.
[5] Cf. *Ibid* 140.

acting. It is, therefore, improper to ask why the Absolute should act or fail to act in a particular way. It is not the final Reality itself which is by Bradley said to sink itself into differences, and to work itself out through them. He makes it clear that the Absolute as such is not subject to any process: 'What I develop is in the Absolute already complete.'[1]

It is primarily of the given reality, or of existence with character taken as a whole, that Bradley here speaks; though, in so far as the metaphysical attempt to 'understand' given reality leads us to the Absolute, what the 'vision' in question suggests may also be said to hold from the viewpoint of *our idea* of the Absolute. We must of necessity talk 'from our human point of view'—that is, in the light of experience as it comes to us, and in conformity with the criterion which should, in principle, determine our actual thinking. The moment this is realized, our questions seem to become manageable. Thus, the Absolute—or the whole reality in its essential character as revealed to reflection—must be *said to appear*, because it is only by working upon appearances that we rise up to *our idea* of the final or true Reality.[2] Moreover, in so far as, being perfectly individual, our crowning idea is arrived at as the One contrasted with which the various appearances are seen to be real in varying measure, and to which they all tend, it would be a contradiction *not* to maintain that the Real reveals itself in varying degrees. Again, because our idea of the Absolute as a supra-relational and all-inclusive whole is affirmed primarily as a rebound against our gradually mounting dissatisfaction with the self-contradictory character of relational experience—an affirmation which comes as a sequel to the pursuit of consistency by thought itself—it seems only proper to say that the relational form has a necessary function to perform; and that, again from our point of view, reality sinks itself into differences with a view to asserting its final supra-relational character in a manner which is acceptable to thought. Specificity, relational form, the self-transcendence of a relational complex into ever more inclusive wholes, and finally into a supra-relational unity—these are, according to Bradley, but necessary and inter-connected emphases

---

[1] *Ibid* 523, 421.
[2] Cf. 'There is no reality at all anywhere except in appearance, and in our appearance we can discover the main nature of reality.' *Ibid* 487.

in our theoretical attempt to understand the given, not the stages of any process in actual reality. This is brought out, first, in an abstract way—that is, in his dialectic of the relational form; and secondly, in his concrete demonstration as to how the various appearances have, all of them, their varying degrees of reality, the apex being provided by the supra-relational Absolute. In other words, the full nature of reality—or its all-inclusive and supra-relational character—would, even as a general idea, remain hidden from us did it not appear to us differentiated, and so relational and self-transcendent.

Finally, the 'immanent' reality of which Bradley speaks is no mysterious entity like a soul inhabiting its body; it is only the internal or essential nature of things as revealed to reflection.[1] Consider any region of given reality. It is, first, an indissoluble unity of 'that' and 'what'. Secondly, it resists severance from what seems merely beside it; or, to put it differently, it strives for individuality. This dual character permeates whatever is there. It is the essential character of reality; and, as thus seen to partake of a common feature everywhere, reality may be said to be 'one'.

The self-transcendence of appearances, as revealed to thought, is a movement in the direction of fuller reality in so far as it tends to attenuate the contradictions which beset them. Did they not seem to move thus, and to enlarge their bounds, we would be left with standing contradictions—mere conjunctions of qualities which, though inexplicable in themselves, are not yet allowed to be resolved into any wider unity. The truth on the other hand is that, as we have seen, the very specificity of things and portions makes for self-transcendence. Attention to these two features, and to what they in the end suggest, enables us to realize, in idea and in general, the final character of Reality—Reality as all-inclusive and supra-relational.

c. *Reality and the appearances*

A summary may now be attempted of Bradley's view of the general relation of Appearance to Reality. The object's being in some measure individual is its character as reality; and the incompleteness of its unity is, on the other hand, its character as

---

[1] We can certainly decide to avoid reflection; but then, Bradley would say, we are not doing metaphysics.

appearance. In other words, what is found in fact is always reality in a measure—neither empty appearance nor absolute reality. Due, however, to our initial commitment, our search for the final Reality continues; and through the principle of self-completion beyond self—warranted, we may say, by both theory and fact—we arrive at our idea of the Absolute.

To view the matter primarily from our side, every appearance falls within, qualifies, and is necessary for the unity of the whole.[1] Taken apart from the whole, 'the several appearances are in contradiction with one another and each within itself'. But, it is precisely because of their being (in themselves) 'irremediably self-discrepant' that they are appearances of the Real',[2] the defect providing for their character as appearance, and its own grounding in imperfect inclusiveness serving as a pointer to the final Reality. The various aspects of experience all point to a unity which comprehends and perfects them. Yet, 'we never have, or are, a state which is the perfect unity of all aspects'.[3] Appearances manifest reality, but not equally.[4] Yet, though as compared to one another they are 'higher' or 'lower' in rank, they cannot be reduced to one another. 'There is not one mode of experience to which the others belong as its adjectives, or into which they can be resolved.' In relation to the Absolute they are alike essential and necessary.[5]

It is, of course, impossible to explain how all the specific appearances are included and made good in the Absolute. How are the minds of men, all irreducibly unique, and minds both good and bad, held as one in the same Absolute?[6] Now, if he is confronted with such questions, Bradley would only say that uniqueness is everywhere relative; that no mind is entirely self-complete; and that—encouraged by the possibility that a collision of differences *can* be made good in a wider reality, and impelled by the demand of thought that differences *must* all be held as one—we are, on the whole, justified in asserting that the Absolute *is* a harmony of all that is.

[1] AR 404.
[2] *Ibid* 374.
[3] *Ibid* 415.
[4] This double truth is, in Bradley's view, the centre of philosophy—a refutation of both 'empty transcendence' and 'shallow pantheism'. *Ibid* 488.
[5] *Ibid* 405.
[6] Cf. Ewing, *Idealism*, 409.

The difficulty we may here experience in agreeing with Bradley is, in our view, tempered if two precautions are taken. First, it should not be forgotten that, as already pointed out, he himself confesses inability to explain the details of the way in which appearances emerge and are resolved; and that his argument is, on the whole, but general and negative or persuasive in character. Secondly, we have to avoid confusing *our* own viewpoint with that of the Absolute.¹ *In* the Absolute, or from its viewpoint so far as it is given to us in idea, there is no contradiction. But, if we turn back to what is strictly our viewpoint, there *is* contradiction everywhere, because this viewpoint is finite. My experience, viewed as such, is self-contradictory, and though certainly actual, it is, as mine, merely a finite fact. In the Absolute, on the other hand, this experience—which (to me) seems merely mine—is in no way opposed to the experience of 'others'; and the entire Experience is one of a thoroughgoing harmony. Bradley would insist that the difficulty of understanding how contradictions could be resolved in the unity of the Absolute is aggravated by our tendency to impose on it our own finite and relational point of view.

But, does he himself succeed in giving us, even in general, a satisfactory account of appearances as they are *in* the Absolute? Our answer is negative. Let us, however, consider some of his own utterances in this context:

'We have a rearrangement not merely of things but of their internal elements. We have an all-pervasive transfusion with a re-blending of all material ... *things as such* ... *have lost their individual natures*.'²

'The fact that more is included than these several isolated differences does not prove that these differences are not there at all.'³

'... pain ... will exist, but will have ceased to be pain when considered on the whole.'⁴

---

¹ The latter, as *we* understand it. The Absolute's own viewpoint is not, in detail, given to us. On the other hand, it cannot self-consistently be held that we have *no* idea of it at all.

² AR 469. The words italicized by us contrast finely with Bradley's view, expressed elsewhere, that, though neutralized by complement and addition, the private character of an appearance remains. *Ibid* 453.

³ *Ibid* 161.

⁴ *Ibid* 175.

THE ABSOLUTE AND ITS APPEARANCES

'Every flame of passion, chaste or carnal, would still burn in the Absolute unquenched and unabridged, a note absorbed in the harmony of its higher bliss.'[1]

Now, the contrast between the first and the fourth extracts seems to be complete. That a thing as such loses its *individual* nature, and yet continues 'unabridged' in the Absolute—is this not a clear self-contradiction? We may admit that what the differences lose in the Absolute is only their isolated character or the manner in which they appear *to us*, as painful or contradictory, not their very existence or essential content. Reality, after all, cannot be less than its appearances.[2] We may also concede that, in so far as the Absolute not merely includes, but consummates the appearances —and again in so far as the relational is made good in a non-relational harmony—differences in the Absolute exist as members of a supra-relational unity. Yet, the difficulty persists as to how, in spite of this softening of their assertive individuality, they are *in no way* abridged. True, in the Absolute an appearance must suffer a re-blending of its inner elements, of existence and idea, which are in its own being but poorly conjoined. But, that in spite of this pervasive transfusion even a carnal flame of passion persists 'unquenched' in the Absolute harmony—this is to us unintelligible. The difficulty is heightened by the suggestion that there is, in the Absolute, something more than the 'isolated appearances', and that yet, on the other hand, 'outside of the field of jarring elements there neither is nor can be anything.'[3]

4. MEETING CRITICISMS

It would, however, be wrong to accept, without questioning, all the objections which are commonly made to Bradley's conception of the Absolute and of its relation to appearances.

Cohen's criticism is that the Absolute is not a determinate subject of discourse at all. Now, Bradley's answer would here simply be that what is not held up before the mind as a clearly understood object may yet be felt to operate as a positive, immanent criterion. Upon Cohen's own view, the idea of perfect individuality

[1] *Ibid* 152.
[2] *Ibid* 119.
[3] *Ibid* 374.

is not only the essential impulse behind the enterprise of knowing, but the criterion which is implied in the very realization of the incompleteness of our present knowledge.[1] But if this is so, the idea in question is not merely the ideal limit of knowing, but is internal to the latter. Even otherwise, the protest that the Absolute is 'an ideal limit rather than an actual existence'[2] hardly makes any point against Bradley. For, first, he himself refuses to regard the final reality as a (finite) existence;[3] and secondly, there is no reason why what is insensible cannot yet be regarded as being actual. What is more, the Absolute—or our idea of it—is determinate because of the necessity of the way in which we are led up to it. Our experience itself, provided we seek to 'understand' it in the way of Bradley, may be said to *imply* the notion of the Absolute; which means that if the critic expects the latter to stand for something which is determinate in the sense of being merely opposed to —or outside of—other things, he errs at once in ignoring the very way in which the idea emerges.

Bradley concludes that, though 'we cannot construct absolute life in its details', our final idea, 'so far as it goes, is real knowledge of the Absolute, positive and built on experience, and inevitable when we try to think consistently'.[4] Now, the second half of this 'conclusion' is characteristic of Bradley; and yet it is precisely this which the critics of Bradley generally tend to ignore. They forget that Bradley does not proceed from the Absolute downwards, but from what is given to, and is compelling for us, in thought and experience.

Consider, for instance, some of the objections raised by Ruggerio, Aliotta and Campbell. Ruggerio contends that the Absolute of Bradley is theoretically useless; that, being itself indeterminate, it is incapable of giving rise to our world of diversity and character; and that, finally, if we deny this incapacity, and seek to derive the world from within the Absolute, we at once get enmeshed in clear contradictions:

'The Absolute is motionless, yet movement is an appearance of the Absolute; the Absolute has no history, yet it contains in

[1] Cohen, *Reason and Nature*, 156; also 145-46.
[2] *Ibid* 158.
[3] AR 479.
[4] *Ibid* 142.

itself infinite histories; experience is imperfect, yet it is an appearance of the perfect. At times one feels as if Bradley is wilfully blind.'[1]

Now, the critic's insistence is on our helplessness from the other side, that is, from the viewpoint of the Absolute. But, to such inability Bradley himself pleads guilty. He not only admits, but insists that we cannot put or answer questions or view things from the Absolute's *own* point of view. There is necessarily some loss of truth when we seek to apply *our* attitudes, all incurably finite, to the Absolute itself. We may add (with Campbell) that the criticism, that Bradley's Absolute cannot explain the ultimate nature of things, becomes valid only if it is assumed that an ultimate explanation of things *is* possible.[2]

What we have a right to criticize is only the way in which Bradley proceeds *from our thought and experience* to the Absolute as their essential direction. But, when we move thus, we find that the self-transcendence of things and experiences, revealed to thought, blends well with the intellect's own demand for wholeness, giving point to our idea of the Absolute. The final reality, as Bradley understands it, may well appear incapable of producing the world-many. But, merely because of this we cannot refuse to accept what is *from our side* (in Bradley's view) unshakeable.

According to Aliotta, however, even 'from our side' the Absolute of Bradley is not a tenable idea. He protests thus. The supra-relational Absolute is said to be affirmed by thought as a rebound, as it were, against the self-contradictory character of its own relational form. But contradictions are nowhere to be *found*. They are Bradley's creation; and this because he introduces distinctions which do not correspond to any real division in the given, besides ignoring 'intuitive content' and 'the wealth of mind and nature', as also the continuous presence of the subject which alone can 'bridge over the gulf between one term and another . . .' Aliotta adds that if our attempt ideally to reconstruct experienced duration and change does not really succeed, what is proved is not that these appearances are 'empty', but only that 'there is an individual

---

[1] Ruggerio, *Modern Philosophy*, Translated by A. H. Hannay and R. G. Collingwood, London, Allen & Unwin, 1921, 274.
[2] Campbell, *Scepticism and Construction: Bradley's Sceptical Principle as the Basis of Constructive Philosophy*, London, Allen & Unwin, 1931, 74.

physiognomy of the world which cannot be reduced to mere systems of relations'.[1]

Now, at least in part, objections such as these suffer clearly from inadequate attention to Bradley's real view. No 'appearance' is, in his view, 'empty' in the sense of being wholly devoid of 'reality'. And does he not himself say repeatedly that the real is individual, and that the relational form of thought is unable to give us true individuality? Nor does Bradley fail to admit that contradictions are not given facts, and that they *arise*.[2] He would, however, insist that they must arise, once we set out to 'understand' things in the way he does. This may be explained. Even if we accept the self as one unbroken fact, ignoring the question as to whether or not it is metaphysically intelligible, the ground of contradiction remains very much there. The self to which two diversities are presented may be the same and continuous; but, at least in metaphysics, this mere fact cannot be allowed to prevent the *intellect* from opposing the unity of apprehension to the admitted diversity of its content. But, once this legitimate freedom is granted to thought, the bases of Bradley's dialectics, as also of his conclusions, would forthwith seem secure. Again if, as Aliotta himself contends, 'there must necessarily be a limit to the resolution of terms into relations,'[3] a part of the theoretical ground of Bradley's attempt to bring out the self-contradictory character of the relational form is at once admitted as valid.

Finally, is it proper to say that Bradley ignores concrete content? Our answer is in the negative. A basic idea of his is that quality is relational or distinctive. But, is it not primarily its concreteness which makes every detail of reality distinctive? It is true that Bradley rarely leaves the path of critical *thought*; but, on the other hand, does he anywhere forget that thought is less than reality? And in what better way could this inadequacy of thought be affirmed than by regarding reality as being all-inclusive and supra-relational? As for its activity of making distinctions, is thought merely to conform to what is perceived as distinct, or to advance as demanded by its own inherent need to understand?

[1] Aliotta, *The Idealistic Reaction against Science*, 109, 107-09.
[2] Contradictions 'appear where the subject is narrowed artificially, and where diversity in the identity is taken as excluded'. AR 505.
[3] Aliotta, *The Idealistic Reaction against Science*, 108.

THE ABSOLUTE AND ITS APPEARANCES

Here, however, another difficulty may be pressed. If the Absolute is supra-relational, are we entitled to say anything about it? This indeed is Campbell's main protest.[1] Nothing, he contends, can provide us with a real clue to the Absolute—not even feeling; for, a harmonious experience where relations have not yet emerged is obviously different from the one in which the relational form is included and made good. Again, sentience that we know is everywhere conditioned. We cannot, therefore, speak of the *Absolute* as Experience. Nor can we ever attain to a system *all* the accents of which are complementary without reserve. Should we not, then, conclude that the Absolute is wholly unknowable?[2]

Now, Bradley himself admits that an absolute system can never be secured by the intellect, and that 'fully to realize the existence of the Absolute is for finite beings impossible.'[3] We, on our part, have found it difficult to accept the doctrine that the Absolute is One *Experience*. But, on the other hand, in pronouncing Reality 'to be disparate from each and every thought-product', as Campbell wants us to,[4] can we self-consistently disown the general idea of an absolute reality, and of its character because of which it is not similar to any product of thought? And, if it is really to mark off Reality from thought, what could this idea be except that of One all-inclusive, *supra-relational* harmony?

As to Campbell's contention that, because of its *pre*-relational and self-discrepant character, feeling cannot provide any clue to our idea of the Absolute, our answer may begin by posing a question. In what legitimate sense can we at all speak of a clue to the Absolute? Whatever it be in detail, we cannot expect the 'clue' to *appear* as actually including the relational form and as making good its characteristic defect. A final transmutation of the relational form as a whole is possible only in the Absolute which, as such, cannot anywhere be *found*. Campbell's objection really amounts to saying that, if its claim to serve as a clue to the Absolute is to be accepted as valid, feeling must appear as a whole which in fact includes and transmutes all relations. But, then, what is really demanded is not a mere clue, but the Fact to which it is

---

[1] Campbell, *Scepticism and Construction*, 51, 66.
[2] *Ibid* 17–19.
[3] AR 140.
[4] Campbell, *Scepticism and Construction*, 19.

supposed to be a clue; and this Fact, we may repeat, is not as such available in the region of actual existence. If, however, what is here demanded of feeling only is that it should somehow *include* relational matter,[1] the requirement is, in one sense, clearly met; for, as Bradley insists, even a complex, psychical state may be felt as one—vaguely, yet actually:

> '... at every moment this vague state (of feeling) is experienced actually ... we cannot deny that complex wholes are felt as single experiences. For, on the one side, these states are not simple, nor again, on the other side, are they plural merely; nor again is their unity explicit and held in relation with, and against, their plurality.'[2]

We cannot—nay, we should not—expect to get any 'clue', if by this we mean *finding* the Absolute, so to speak, bodily and entire. But if, on the other hand, what is demanded is only a clue to the possibility of immediate qualification, feeling may well be regarded as the pointer that we seek.

Again, if, as a fact, feeling breaks up continually into the relational form; if what is relational may easily lapse into the manner of mere feeling; and if, as Bradley insists, all our (mediate) knowledge starts from and returns recurringly to the immediacy of the 'This-Mine', there is surely warrant enough for saying that feeling *is* a clue to the Absolute in the sense of being the substantial ground, but again as distinguished from being the true consummation, of the relational.

To conclude, it is true that, as Campbell insists, the Absolute is a *qualitative* transcendence of thought. But does this truth here come to us as an intuitive realization, or as a necessary deliverance of thought itself, an assertion of what the intellect seeks, but cannot itself secure? If it comes as the latter, that minimal description of the Ultimate which is implied directly in thought's affirmation of its ideal cannot be avoided. Bradley's endeavour throughout shows this double awareness, of what thought seeks, and of what it cannot itself achieve. And, if it be contended that this self-divided attitude of thought towards the Absolute is not quite convincing, his ready reply would be that the alternative views—that Reality

---

[1] If not relations as such.
[2] AR 462.

is known through and through, or that It is wholly unknowable—are immediately more questionable.

5. BRADLEY'S METAPHYSICAL FORMULA

We come now to a question which must be answered affirmatively if our argument as to the Absolute's reality is to gain more weight. Thought insists that there *must* be a harmony which is both all-inclusive and beyond relations. The evidence of feeling gives point to the supposal that relations *may* in fact be transcended. But, what is the warrant for believing that this actually *is* so, and that the Absolute is really there? Or, is there a Fact corresponding to our idea of the Absolute? Now, Bradley answers by putting forth his chief speculative formula: 'What *may* be, and *must* be is, though we cannot in detail specify *how* it is.'[1] Some of his own formulations of the principle may here be cited:

'For what *may* be, if it also *must* be, assuredly *is*.'

'For what is possible, and what a general principle compels us to say *must be*, that certainly is.'

'For that which is both possible and necessary we are *bound to think* real.'[2]

The above are all extracts from Bradley's treatment of error and evil. They are intended to express the same truth variously. Now, if we view these formulations in the light of one another, the following general remarks may be safely made. First, 'may be' here stands for 'possibility'. Secondly, that which 'must be' is 'necessary'; it is what we assert due to compulsion by a general principle. Thirdly, that which is actual because it is both possible and necessary, is (to thought) real **undeniably**.

Now, in so far as limitations of space do not here permit a discussion of the various theories of necessity and possibility, we may confine ourselves to a brief account of Bradley's own view of the matter. Being but phases of the hypothetical, the possible and the necessary are, in his view, both alike opposed to the assertorical and the categorical. But the possible is a species of the genus

---

[1] Stout's article, 'Bradley on Truth and Falsity', *Mind*, Vol. XXXIV, No. 133, January, 1925, 51.
[2] AR 177, 173–76. Our italics.

'necessary'; for, when a thing is said to be possible, though all the conditions which make it necessary are supposed, only some of them are assumed to exist. Again, for logic, possibility as such does not exist; it is the result of ideal construction. But, in so far as the basis of such construction is a reality which is 'assumed to exist',[1] it would hardly be tenable to believe that possibility, as Bradley understands it, is a deliverance of purely abstract thought.[2] What is possible is revealed by thought working, in part, on the evidence of actual reality.

A word now about necessity or 'must be':

According to Bradley, it is only when we are compelled by a general principle that we say that something 'must be'. Where he defends his idea of the Absolute against objections built around error and evil, Bradley talks of 'a wide theory based on general grounds', and of 'a general assurance that reality has a certain nature'.[3] So, he may be taken to hold that the principle which compels us to say that something 'must be' is wide, general and theoretical. Now, in so far as the formula under review is for *metaphysical* truth—and again in so far as, according to Bradley, the metaphysically valid is that which thought cannot but readily accept—the general principle referred to above may be taken to be the principle of contradiction. In brief, what *must be* is not a mere suggestion of the given, but an affirmation of theory working in conformity with the demand for non-contradiction.[4] This is partly borne out by such remarks of Bradley as the following one: '... the Absolute *must be* a harmonious system. We have first perceived this *in general* ...'[5]

Coming, finally, to that which '*is*', we find that it here stands for two aspects held as one. It stands, first, for the actual, as distinguished from the hypothetical. This is manifest in Bradley's argument that if the Absolute must be a harmonious system, and that if it is possible for errors to correct themselves, and, as such,

[1] PL 203.
[2] Our point is borne out by the following remark of Bradley about the 'possibility of pain, ceasing as such, to exist in the Absolute':
'We have shown that this possibility can to some extent be verified in experience.' AR 176.
[3] *Ibid* 163–64.
[4] We find it difficult to accept Wollheim's suggestion that what tells us that a thing *must be* is, in Bradley's essential view, *experience*.
[5] AR 173. Second italics ours.

to disappear in a higher experience, 'we *must* affirm that they *are* thus absorbed and made good'.[1] Secondly, 'what *is*' here stands for what 'we are bound to *think* real'; or, upon Bradley's view, for the metaphysically real. On the whole, therefore, 'certainly is', in the principle under review, affirms a metaphysical reality which is actual, and which, being metaphysical, is yet not open to any kind of perception. The entire formula is but the affirmation of a Reality which has a warrant in both theory and fact, but is itself identical with neither.

When, however, we come to consider the principle *as a whole*, a difficulty at once arises: is it proper to say that a thing *may be* even if we cannot specify *how* it can be? Bradley's answer is: yes, it is; if only the 'how' is in part or in general known to us.[2]

His task, in this context, is not merely to advance arguments, but to cite some such instances as may lend point to the possibility of the inclusion of appearances, all of them self-contradictory, in the harmony of the Absolute. He is quite alive to the difficulty of clearly explaining, in detail or even in general, how an appearance is included and perfected in the final reality. It is only in an experience which *transcends* the relational form that contradictions can be finally dispelled. But, this is precisely the form which all explanation must of necessity assume. Therefore, 'even apart from detail' we cannot satisfactorily understand 'how the relational form is in general absorbed'.[3]

But, Bradley would hasten to add that an 'imperfect view' of the way in which contradictions may be overcome can certainly be had. How this can be done in theory is by now known to us. Further assurance is provided by the region of fact. To illustrate, my condition may well be *on the whole* pleasant, 'while I still have an actual local pain'. Again, 'a contest of the good and bad wills' and the actuality of evil are in fact essential for moral development which absorbs and transmutes them; and 'just as in a machine the resistance and pressure of the parts subserve an end beyond any of them, if regarded by itself—so at a much higher level it may be with the Absolute'.[4] Considerations such as these

[1] *Ibid*. Second italics ours.
[2] 'And given a knowledge of "how" in general, a mere ignorance of "how" in detail is permissible and harmless.' *Ibid* 494.
[3] *Ibid* 173.
[4] *Ibid* 179.

certainly make it intelligible or possible to say that in ultimate Reality evil and error are included and made good without any impoverishment of their content: 'The reality owns the discordance and the discrepancy of false appearance; but it possesses also much else in which this jarring character is swallowed up and is dissolved in fuller harmony.'[1]

It may, of course, be contended that, even after the above way of arguing is admitted, the insistent quality of evil and error remains wholly unaccounted for. But, we ask, can it, on the other hand, be positively maintained that they fall wholly outside of, or remain unchanged in the Absolute?[2] What would be the warrant for saying so? It is true that the transition from our world of things to the Absolute is difficult to explain in detail. But, *is* anything really self-existent? Again, can theory accept anything finite as the ultimate reality? And, to speak generally, when we know neither the detailed nature of the Absolute, nor all the forms of error, are we really entitled to assert dogmatically that such appearances are for ever recalcitrant to assimilation in the final unity?

Bradley's view is simply this. It is an irresistible demand of thought that appearances *must* be included and harmonized in a final whole. The dissipation of discord in a wider region of reality and experience is, moreover, a genuine *possibility*. The principle here involved is intelligible; and verification by fact is, at least in part, available.[3] As opposed to this, we have seen, there is hardly any warrant for saying that an appearance may be wholly defiant of inclusion in a wider whole. So Bradley concludes:

'... we have a general assurance that reality has a certain nature, and, on the other side, against that assurance we have to set nothing, nothing other than our ignorance. But an assurance, against which there is nothing to be set, must surely be accepted.'[4]

It is, therefore, in Bradley's view, tenable to say that the Absolute *is* there, even though we do not, in detail, know how or what it is.

---

[1] *Ibid* 170.
[2] *Ibid* 172–73.
[3] *Ibid* 176.
[4] *Ibid* 164. Also see *Ibid* 455–56.

The idea is positive,[1] in so far as there are many features of actual experience which, because of the fact they are all in one sense 'felt', may be said to provide the bases for our abstract idea 'of a unity which transcends and yet contains every manifold appearance.'

'... the same unity, felt below distinctions, shows itself later in a kind of hostility against them. We find it in the efforts made both by theory and practice, each to complete itself and so to pass into the other. And again, the relational form ... implies a substantial totality ... above them ... Further, the ideas of goodness, and of the beautiful, suggest in different ways the same result. They more or less involve the experience of a whole beyond relations though full of diversity.'[2]

That the 'unity' in question cannot be explained in detail is quite another matter.

6. CONCLUSION

It would perhaps serve to reinforce Bradley's view if the matter is discussed in a free, general way:

Is it at all possible to make the transition from our idea of the Absolute to the Absolute as a reality or fact? Now, we readily answer, the protest is itself suspect. It wrongly assumes that thought and reality are quite removed from each other. We have seen how it is a feature of the given itself which is furthered by thought. And, to speak from the other side, no idea can be severed entirely from 'reality' unless the word is understood in an unduly restricted sense. Bradley rightly insists that reality must be regarded as the totality of its special regions. After all, the contents of fancy and imagination are to the poet and the dreamer given as compellingly, or with as insistent a claim on attention, as sensible things are to the average individual. And if we leave out these worlds from the scope of reality, can we fix the precise measure of sensible solidity which must be possessed by a thing before it can

---

[1] Positive and incontrovertible. Other truths which are—again, in Bradley's view—intellectually incorrigible are: the coherence theory, the doctrine of degrees, and 'reality is experience'. All other truths are limited by the conditions under which they are asserted.
[2] AR 141.

be called real?[1] On the other hand, if we realize the comprehensiveness of reality, it is easily seen that 'to hold a thought is, more or less vaguely, to refer it to Reality'.[2] Neither in fact nor in judgment is the disjunction of 'what' from reality, in any case, absolute; and the transition from thought to reality is natural and legitimate:

> 'Since Reality *is* qualified by thought, it *must* possess whatever feature thought's essence involves. And the principle ... that, given one side of a connected whole, you can go from this to the other side—is surely irrefragable.'[3]

Now, if this is so, our idea of the Absolute is, like every other idea, originally self-transcendent. It refers from the beginning to its corresponding reality—not, of course, visibly, but in the sense that, being self-incomplete, it ideally affirms the Reality in which it is included and made good.

Above all, it is only in a restricted sense of verification that the fact of the Absolute may be said to be 'unverifiable';[4] and the doubt is surely legitimate as to why verification should consist necessarily in producing a fact open to perception. Here, in metaphysics, the criterion is the satisfaction of our theoretical demand; and if it satisfies this demand, the Absolute surely is.[5]

To conclude, though it is admittedly imperfect, Bradley's idea of the Absolute cannot be easily dismissed. It meets the insistent demand of theory; works out (in his view) the necessary and immanent direction of all that there is; gives us a principle of grading things and experiences; and, in the realm of knowledge, it tempers our pride in specific achievements. What militates, till the end, against these clear intimations from the given and against the native insistence of theory is perhaps our old vicious bias—that the real is necessarily the sensible. A direct, intuitive experience of the Ultimate—such as religion and mysticism claim ability to provide—may be infinitely richer than our mere idea of it; but

---

[1] Cf. *Ibid* 61.
[2] *Ibid* 350. According to Bradley, even in the attitudes of doubt and disbelief, the severance of ideas from reality is never in fact complete.
[3] *Ibid* 350.
[4] ETR 249.
[5] Cf. CE 671.

the reasoned conclusion that the Absolute is real, as the consummation of our essential demands, is of no mean value to those who have chosen to tread the path of mere theory, may be through choice or because of some limitation of their nature.

VII

CONCLUDING REMARKS

Our task in this chapter is partly to see how Bradley's thought stands in relation to the metaphysical situation today, and partly to examine some objections to which his metaphysics seems naturally open. Some important directions in the present-day attempt to vindicate metaphysics are roughly as follows:

Metaphysics tries to give us an over-all map of reality. Its 'integrator words' are applicable to the entire range of human experience. This concern for comprehensiveness is theoretically compelling; for, truth demands adequacy of thought to reality as a whole, rather than the mere correspondence of idea to observable fact. Descriptions of science are, on the other hand, patently inadequate to the wholeness of given reality; and, what is worse, the defect is here not seen to detract from the accepted ideal of truth. The sciences work by ignoring the 'metempirical'. This is improper; for, as a matter of both theory and fact, the metempirical is the ground of all our experience. Our concern, in metaphysics, with this basic reality is by no means unimportant. 'What goes beyond experience and yet is involved in experience cannot be the infra-rational, the irrational or the absurd'.[1] Metaphysics is important in so far as it impels us to reflect on the fundamentals of experience.

1. BRADLEY AND METAPHYSICS TODAY

Now, the relevance of Bradley's work to metaphysics today becomes manifest when we reflect as to how, with regard to the different points outlined above, his attitude seems (in part) theoretically more tenable than that of many present-day metaphysicians.

(a) Take, first, the emphasis on wholeness. The basic question

[1] Daly, 'Metaphysics and the Limits of Language', in *Prospect for Metaphysics*, 203.

here is: does the metempirical merely include, or does it also explain the empirical? The modern metaphysician is clearly alive to the need that the metempirical should do both. Thus, Ramsey talks of metaphysics not merely as a pre-eminent 'venture after unity', but as 'a scheme of maximum *interpretative* power';[1] and Daly stresses the duty of 'making a sense of' the recognition of 'the existence of the metempirical within experience'. And this is only proper; for, in a true philosophical synthesis, content is not merely held, but explained.

Yet, though the recognition of the need to understand or to interpret is certainly there, the emphasis today seems confined to the greater inclusiveness of metaphysical terms, such as Self and Being; or, alternatively, to the recognition that the metempirical, though clearly real as revealed in a 'disclosure situation', provides a resolute Other to the common way in which we observe things. Thus, Daly insists that metaphysical language can be adequate to reality as a whole,[2] and Ramsey emphasizes the superior inclusiveness of the 'integrator words' of metaphysics. Of these, the word 'I' is regarded as 'a paradigm for metaphysics' in so far as, though not descriptive in itself, it can be united with any number of descriptive words.[3] Again, with a view to keeping it genuinely 'metempirical', Hawkins protests against the modern tendency to hand over 'being' to the logician, and emphasizes 'that the logic of being is not the same as ontology';[4] and Trethowan and Daly pit themselves against Ayer's contention that the Cartesian 'cogito ergo sum' does not establish the reality of the self as something *other* than its perceptions.[5] Finally, the 'inadequacy' of the empirical categories is today indicated by pointing out that they neither consider, nor are applicable to Self and Being, though in their own working they depend necessarily 'on these basic realities.'

Now, it is not difficult to see that when all has been said for it,

---

[1] Ian Ramsey, 'Possibility and Purpose of Metaphysical Theology' in *Prospect for Metaphysics*, 160. Our italics.
[2] Daly, *op. cit.* 202.
[3] Ramsey, *op. cit.* 167.
[4] Hawkins, 'Towards the Restoration of Metaphysics', in *Prospect for Metaphysics*, 113–14.
[5] Trethowan, 'Prof. Ayer on Certainty', in *Prospect for Metaphysics*, 148–49; and Daly, *op. cit.* 181–85.

the present-day attempt to revive metaphysics is, to a large extent, a half-way measure, a merely negative 'struggle to prevent man himself from being depersonalized by the methods of impersonal investigation and anonymous verification he has devised for science'.[1] We may admit, as desired, that Self and Being transcend all observational technique, but how does this prove, or even suggest, that with their help we can interpret, and not merely describe all that is there? Nor does the mere fact that it contains, or is attached to all our perceptions, make 'I' an *interpretative* principle. In other words, the metempirical so far seems to be a mere element in or around experience; it does not quite impress us as the true metaphysical ground of the empirical, because it is, *by thought*, seen neither to explain, nor to be demanded by the empirical.

Metaphysicians today rightly insist that—in so far as it is not merely involved in, but extends beyond our common experience— the metempirical 'cannot be the infra-rational, the irrational or the absurd'. But this way of speaking is merely negative; it does not positively argue for the superior worth of that which is (allegedly) not confined to, or exhausted by ordinary experience. Nor will it do merely to point to the fact that the metempirical just goes along necessarily with the empirical. A mere fact, however persistent, is to reason merely actual, and not as such rational. We must be able to say, with some show of reason, *why* the metempirical is there; or else, it is indisputably irrational. In other words, we should be made to *understand*, at least in general, how the metempirical is the higher reality.

It is precisely here that the relevance of Bradley's metaphysics makes itself felt. His emphasis on wholeness is obvious—both in his explicit definition of metaphysics and in his detailed argument as to how the various facets of our experience all point beyond themselves to an all-inclusive whole. Nor can we ignore his effective attacks on the correspondence theory of truth, and his reasoned defence of the coherence theory. What is, however, of singular importance to us today is his attempt to *argue* that the metempirical is a demand of thought itself.

(b) But, before we actually proceed to comment on this particular aspect of Bradley's work, it would help us, by preventing

[1] *Ibid* 191.

confusion, to note that what modern metaphysicians speak of as 'metempirical' *he* calls 'non-relational'; and that he talks of Immediate Experience and the Absolute, rather than of Self and Being. This difference of idiom itself seems to give him a theoretical advantage over the metaphysicians of today. For, if—as Ramsey, Daly and Trethowan all agree in believing—the self is experienced, or 'disclosed' or 'involved' in experience, we cannot categorically say that it is *beyond* experience. In fact, what they really mean only is that the self is experienced, but not as an object. But if this is so, Bradley's conception of the 'metempirical' as 'non-relational' appears truer to the purpose.

Nor does it require much effort to see that, theoretically, it is less questionable to speak of the metempirical as immediate experience than as Knowing *and* Being. True, 'knowing' is 'not a kind of capacity', and 'being is not a kind of a thing'.[1] But are we to think of Being and Knowing as *two* transcendental entities? It would be rash to say 'yes'; for, if we speak of them as two things, their plurality and thinghood, or their particularity, will at once give the lie to their transcendence. This is perhaps, in part, the reason why Heidegger warns us: '... being is not an essent and not an essent component of the essent.'[2] And then, even knowing somehow *is*; surely, it is not entirely without Being, though how Being, in its turn, necessarily involves knowing is not so obvious. This is why Heidegger regards Being as fundamental. This, again, is why Bradley appears unconvincing when, in support of his thesis that Reality is Experience, he argues that Being can never be removed from sentience. But, though it is not equally easy for thought to traverse the complex either way, 'Being–Knowing' would be a less questionable way of describing the metempirical in experience than 'Being *and* Knowing'. It is not without reason that the self, as an identity of being–knowing, is today regarded as the ideal metaphysical 'integrator'.[3]

Now, Bradley's Immediate Experience is precisely this Being–Knowing as one. If Being is other than beings, surely we cannot identify it with the (individual) self. It is easy to distinguish the

[1] Daly, *op. cit.* 197.
[2] Heidegger, *An Introduction to Metaphysics*, Translated by Ralph Manheim, Yale University Press, 1959, 88.
[3] Ramsey, *op. cit.* 163.

self from its individual perceptions, but we cannot, without ceasing to think, *cancel* its own particularity, or its opposition to the not-self. The self as an object of meaningful discourse is clearly one among the many, and is one of the beings. Conversely, Being which is truly transcendental is not *a* self. Bradley realizes this. In 'immediate experience', as he understands it, the distinction of self and not-self has not yet emerged. It may therefore be said to stand for true Being, and for Being–Knowing as one.

(c) But, is Bradley really able *to explain* our entire (relational) experience in terms of Feeling or even with the help of the Absolute? The question has to be answered with care. Why feeling breaks up into the relational form is, in Bradley's account, perhaps not very satisfactorily explained. Why should the Absolute as such at all appear?—is another question which, on his own admission, he is unable to answer. In either case, the difficulty is obvious; for, the relational manner of holding diversities 'apart' differs clearly from the pre-relational and supra-relational levels of experience.

But, and now we proceed to the crux of the matter, even if the deduction of the empirical from the metempirical be deemed to be impossible, our purpose of arguing the latter as the ground of the former *is* partly served if we are able to show, first, that the empirical (or relational) rests throughout on the metempirical; and secondly that—besides being the invariable concomitant of all experience—the metempirical caters for a demand of thought, without yet being quite within the grasp of our common ways of thinking.

To turn to Bradley's view, the metempirical, considered as 'feeling', is the continual ground of thinking and knowing; and, as the supra-relational Absolute, it is demanded and affirmed by thought's own attempt to 'understand' given reality. As for the reality of immediate experience, we have seen how, in Bradley's view, it rests partly on the evidence of fact, and partly on argument. On the one hand, he takes pains to point out that knowing as relational depends, for its unity, continually on the direct or non-relational presentation of content to self, or on feeling; and, on the other hand, he *argues* why thought can neither cancel nor reconstitute the given unity of experience as it comes to us non-relationally. The dependence is brought out in his treatment of immediate experience; and the inability is argued mainly in his analysis of thought's relational form. It is the second consideration which here deserves notice. To say *that* 'knowing', in its basic sense, always transcends our attempts to study specific kinds of knowing is one thing; to demonstrate *why* this has got to be so by exposing the limits of thought's native manner is something quite different.

Bradley's emphasis is throughout on the need to understand, and it is this which explains the distinctive quality of his way of working. The modern metaphysician emphasizes the inadequacy of observational techniques by pointing out that Knowing and Being are as such unobservable. Bradley, on the other hand, tries to examine not only the categories which are implicit in all technique, but the relational form itself which is common to all our categories. Thought's essential way of working is found (in the end) unintelligible; the individual condemnation of categories as self-contradictory may be said merely to follow. Bradley's criticism is, therefore, basic—akin, one might say, to what Heidegger calls 'authentic thinking that goes back to the roots'.[1]

What makes Bradley's work specially important to us today is his reasoned and sustained emphasis that thought is compelled rationally to posit its own transcendence in a supra-relational whole. This is, indeed, the immanent end of his entire dialectical treatment of the relational form. The 'metempirical' here is no absolute Other which is just there, and which merely envelops or transcends what is familiar: it is affirmed theoretically—and from within reason's own bosom. Our reference here is to Bradley's supra-relational Absolute, and to the way he rises up to it.

We are, in his view, led up to it irresistibly, unless, of course, we choose to stop at what is still self-inconsistent, and agree 'to put up with mere confusion'. Nor is the Absolute is a mere 'yet-to-be'. To affirm it theoretically is not to bring it into being: it is only to realize how it satisfies thought, besides other aspects of our being. As given, the 'metempirical' is, to Bradley, feeling; and, as theoretically affirmed, it is the idea of the Absolute.

Bradley insists that the Absolute is Experience. As such it is not metempirical. But it is Experience as supra-relational: in this sense, to be sure, it transcends our experience. Yet, even of such

[1] Heidegger, *Introduction to Metaphysics*, 122.

a Reality. we have held, it is wrong to say that it is in no way experienced. The vital sense in which the Absolute is metempirical for Bradley rather is that all our common modes of experience seek completion in this all-inclusive whole which transcends their special natures and makes good their native defects.

The details of Bradley's argument may be questioned, but the way he sets about it seems to us essential for an effective vindication of metaphysics. Modern metaphysicians prefer to go by the 'self' and to cultivate a due appreciation of mystery. Now, the self may be accepted as revealed in 'intuition', understood circumspectly.[1] But, we repeat, the crucial difficulty remains. Can we say justifiably that something which accompanies or includes all experience is, merely because of this necessity of fact, also a *superior* kind of reality? And can reason really bow to anything unless it is seen to be free from self-inconsistency?

Bradley shares with modern metaphysicians the view that in metaphysics everything has (in general) to be considered. But, whereas it may be desirable to consider everything, it seems unconvincing to take our stand on anything which is not theoretically irresistible. To talk of 'mysteries', and to insist on the need to cultivate 'a due appreciation' of them is merely to invite attention to some facts which are perhaps commonly ignored; it does nothing to *argue* why reason should acknowledge them as the superior revealers of truth and reality.

It indeed seems impossible to restore metaphysics as a scheme of maximum *interpretative* power unless we heed the basic canons of understanding, and insist that the final Reality must answer, in the main, some criterion of thought, though it may not itself be intelligible in detail.

This brings us to another distinctive feature of Bradley's metaphysics—the thoroughness with which he applies his criterion of reality. It has been pointed out that the theistic metaphysician also 'postulates intelligibility ... in the minimal sense that being shall not be self-contradictory, or absurd'. But if, as Daly admits,[2] this assumption is used as a theoretical criterion to demolish the arguments for *denying* God, why should not the question of self-consistency be raised also with regard to ideas and arguments

---

[1] Ramsey, Editor's Introduction to *Prospect for Metaphysics*, 11.
[2] Daly, *op. cit.* 204.

implicit in the *affirmation* of God's existence? To deny something because it is self-inconsistent, and to accept something else simply because it is there as a fact is theoretical half-heartedness. Bradley, on the other hand, applies his criterion of worth to all the major forms of human experience, as also to every important category of thought.

Metaphysics is, to him, in a sense quite necessary. Judging and rational doubting are a part of our normal experience; and, unless our task be merely to ascertain the practical usefulness of things, such attitudes necessarily involve the use of a criterion of reality. So, if metaphysics tries to find out whether things and experiences are ultimately real, and if not, why not, the attempt is a legitimate furtherance of what we normally do. If it be said, as it often is, that metaphysics gives us no understanding of reality or objective facts, Bradley would reply by pointing out that the contention is based on two assumptions which are alike questionable. First, there is hardly any warrant for supposing that 'objective fact' is, as it appears, ultimately real. Secondly, it is improper to *identify* understanding with improved acquaintance with the sensible character of fact. We surely make an important attempt to understand experience when we try to think out whether our common ways of regarding things are themselves systematic or not; and Bradley's examination of the various categories reveals at least one thing about 'objects'—that, as commonly understood, they all fail to satisfy thought finally.

To the charge that metaphysics tells us very little about the 'met-empirical', the modern metaphysician replies by citing Aquinas: 'The least knowledge that can be had about the highest things is more desirable than the most exact knowledge about lesser things.'[1] Bradley would like to emphasize the importance of our knowledge of the Absolute just as much as its incompleteness. The idea of the Ultimate as an all-inclusive harmony is important, first, because (in a way) it does justice to the sides of both theory and fact; secondly, because it dissipates the idea of a wholly inscrutable Reality;[2] and, finally, because it makes for the realization—so necessary for the growth of knowledge—that our acceptance of lesser bits and groups of experience is mere convenience.

[1] *Ibid* 205.
[2] Cf. AR 488–89.

But, both would agree in admitting that knowing is here not a matter of 'all or nothing'; that it has an 'open texture';[1] and, finally, that metaphysics does not profess to achieve 'the "impossible transparency" which Camus thought reason required'.[2] It is wrong to identify the rational with the *completely* understood.

2. CONCLUSION: SOME PROTESTS CONSIDERED

Are we then to believe that no major aspect of Bradley's thought is in any way questionable? No; it would here be improper to answer affirmatively. One important doctrine of his has seemed to us questionable; and a final decision as to the validity of his speculative formula, without which the Absolute must remain a mere idea, cannot be taken without a fuller study of the nature of necessity and possibility. Yet, on the other hand, we must take care to mark what cannot in fairness be said against his metaphysics.

Let it not be objected that his ascent to the Ultimate holds no charm at all for a man of religion. Bradley himself admits that his way to the Real is neither perfect nor the only possible one: 'The absolute knowledge that we have claimed is no more than an outline. . . . We do not know what other modes of experience may exist, or, in comparison with ours, how many they may be.'[3] We have also to remember that his professed aim is at mounting to gradually higher and wider levels of *thought*, and not at a progressive expansion and transmutation of being in and through the various levels of consciousness. Nor should we labour the protest that the net effect of even the most sympathetic reading of AR is not that of *a self-evolving Reality*—of which, we admit, Bradley talks quite freely—but only that of the competence of thought to rise dialectically to the idea of the Absolute. It is true that *such* a Reality is, to him, the ideal of theory itself; and that if this reality is experience—and also, as he chooses to put it, only 'an expansion of the common essence which we feel burningly' in the immediacy of 'this–mine'[4]—a broader consistency itself perhaps demands that

---

[1] Daly, *op. cit.* 195.
[2] *Ibid* 204.
[3] AR 485–86.
[4] *Ibid* 229.

we should somehow get imbued with, or be 'opened up' to the vitality of the Real, so that, in fact and in substance, the world may appear as a self-differentiation of, and not as a mere speculative pointer to the Absolute. But, as a metaphysician committed to the way of thought, as against men of religion and spiritual realization, Bradley does not claim to possess any direct insight into the Absolute. Whenever, in response to the demands of theory itself, he finds himself compelled to speak from the viewpoint of ultimate Reality, his utterance, we have seen, is in every case qualified.

The viewpoint from which he starts, and which he tries continually to hold on to, is that of strict thinking. And it is here, and in our attitude to it, that we must seek for the reason of that air of unreality which may be said to dog us throughout our study of his thought. The explanation is, in our view, simple. We find it difficult to work in unremitting conformity with the demands of thinking alone, and the tendency is strong to allow thought's native idiom to be swamped by the character of the context in which it proceeds, or of the object which it considers. In case we are able to think as (in Bradley's view) the metaphysician ought to, the legitimacy of his way would seem difficult to question. Its abstractness is confessed, and may therefore not be used as a charge against him. But, our liking for the concrete and the sensuous cannot be easily set aside, and hence our recurring tendency (glibly) to accuse Bradley of following the path of mere theory which he explicitly does.

The point we are seeking to make may be verified indirectly, by considering the following obvious protests:

(a) Bradley's conception of experience is unduly abstract. We are told that where it is relational, experience holds diversities apart; and that where it does not do so, it is non-relational, or is feeling. Obviously, an ideal horizontality is common to both the forms of experience as he understands them, and throughout his work one has the feeling that in traversing diversities—or in confessing failure to hold them 'apart' yet 'together'—he regards experience as a mere surface, as it were, articulate or blurred. What is dealt with is throughout a mere slice carved out of the depth and roundness of experience.[1] Grounded perhaps in the

[1] Cf. Marcel, *Being and Having*, 229.

belief that a spatial schema is involved in all highly reflective thinking, Bradley's very imagery makes it plain that he conceives of understanding as the merely extensional traversing of diversities. This is why, if we want to understand his more abstruse passages, we have to get used to such images as: 'distended', 'alongside of', 'hold them apart', 'collide and repel', 'held together distantly', 'between' and 'apart'.[1] It is perhaps only through this uniform flattening of experience into stretches and mere points that non-contradiction becomes, in Bradley's hands, a mark of metaphysical reality.

(b) But this is, to be sure, an artificial procedure. We have only to think of our experience as we live. Stripped of its concrete filling, a diversity is a mere dot, not an accent of experience. And, understood as non-relational, 'feeling' tells us nothing as to the flux of experience—its inflow and outflow. Illustration is here easy. Confession of guilt is no mere communication. It is a felt expulsion from within. Again, in moments of agony our inmost depths may seem to well up. The reverse movement is sometimes typical of moral and aesthetic life. In one of its modes, experience is here self-saturation, neither a traversing of diversities, nor merely, or even chiefly, non-relational. Moral experience is, in a sense, vertical: it elevates our being by sinking into it. The experienced vitality of an ideal is not merely felt, but inhaled. And, in both religious and aesthetic life, there are moments when one merely sucks in suggestions from the given. This is the essence of the mystic's 'via negativa', and of the poet's 'wise passiveness'. Nor can we ignore the occasional negativity in the flux of experience. A moment of despair is a recoil from meaning. Here the essence is neither the fusion of content nor the stretch of experience, but its negative direction. And, to speak generally, is it even plausible to describe serenity and self-possession as being relational or non-relational? Even 'feeling' would miss the essence of the matter—the 'stilling of the self, the lulling of tumult to sleep'.

(c) Now, we may feel impelled to complain that these felt directions of living experience, its inflow and its outflow, are wholly ignored when Bradley fixes his criterion of reality; and that perhaps it is by abstracting the accents of experience from their

[1] These images contrast finely with Heidegger's 'self-blossoming emergence', 'opening up', and the 'inward-jutting-beyond itself'.

involvement with the self that he is able to identify knowing with 'distinguishing'. The distinct is, according to him, essentially the distinguished. But, may it not be that this is a mere assumption which, by facilitating his special interpretation of quality as a diversity developed through the analysis of a whole into terms and relations, provides an unduly convenient ground for his entire dialectic of quality and relation?

(d) Clarity may sometimes be due to a perception which is not relational, but merely intense. That is, experienced diversities may be distinct, not *from* one another, but merely because of their vivid impact on personality; and the entire experience may yet be knowing. Polanyi's 'dwelling in' and Heidegger's 'to be able to stand in the truth' are no mere images. When, with 'distinguishing' suspended, the entire landscape seems lit up to the poet's or the mystic's eye, everything is clear—as intensely felt, vividly seen. Is this *no* knowing? Are we to assume that one does not 'know' an intense experience at all so long as it possesses him, and that to know it he has necessarily to come out of it, and to survey it in the manner of a detached spectator?

It would perhaps be improper to say 'yes'. There is, it appears, hardly any warrant for assuming that where experience is non-relational, understanding just cannot be. The fact rather is that in quite a few cases the only way to realize the precise pulsations of an experience is just to be it. Sudden, intense joy *is* springy, ebullient. In the good life, the occasional ebb of strength is inwardly reinforced, and the experience seems to heave as it serves to steady. Even a question, as it comes, is not merely put, but is evolved. In all such cases, analysis would miss the shift and stress of experience, and so would its description as merely non-relational.

The basic question is: how are we to understand the native feel of an intense emotional experience? Perhaps, not relationally; for the object to be understood is here non-relational. The other manner of experience is feeling. But here, in Bradley's view, we have no understanding. Does then the directness of experience provide a resolute other to understanding? Not necessarily; the impression that it does may be due only to the mistaken belief that all understanding is necessarily discursive.

(e) Finally, may it not be that the dialectical workings of

Bradley's thought are purely self-referent, and therefore incapable of giving us any knowledge of reality? And, then, what is there to justify their claim to acceptance? That the dialectical process expresses a movement of fundamental validity may, after all, be a mere assumption.

These are some important protests which Bradley's thought very commonly excites. Our view, however, is that they do nothing to damage the essentials of his metaphysics. But, let us explain:

(i) It is wrong to suggest that Bradley is totally indifferent to the inflow and outflow of our normal experience. Consider, for instance, his description of desire in ES:

> 'That the self in desire should have gone beyond itself, and yet not be beside itself ... that the self should be divided against itself in desire ... that it should ... free itself so from all other attractions, and spend its whole being in that one direction; that the realized desire is the utterance of the self ... even as the self went out in the act ...'[1]

(ii) And even if it be admitted that he has missed the directions of experience referred to above, what does an emphasis on them really serve to suggest? Only, that they should be considered. Now, they are all (at least) cases of experience as non-relational; and, in a general way, Bradley considers such experience at fair length. Perhaps, the emphasis in question is intended to draw our attention to the intensity of such experiences. It has indeed been suggested that 'experiences can be compared in *depth*, and the more deeply they affect us, the more *genuine* they may be said to be'.[2] But, what this may be allowed to mean only is that the deeper an experience the more unshakeable it is. The reference is here merely to a kind of psychological compulsion, not at all to any consideration of value. Clarity and depth may mark not only the sudden onset of grace, but an act of total disillusionment; and if the criterion employed is merely that of intensity of impact on the self, it is hardly possible to rank the one as being higher than the other. Here, it can certainly be said that the one is more directly conducive to a harmonious pursuit of values than the other; but an assertion such as this implies an acceptance of Bradley's view.

---

[1] ES 35.
[2] Polanyi, *Personal Knowledge*, 202.

CONCLUDING REMARKS

For the comparison envisaged is clearly an act of the intellect; and the principle, individuality.

(iii) Should the objector persist in saying that Bradley, in general, ignores the content of experience, our ready reply would be that this is not so, and that content *is* 'included' by him—in the only way it can be in a theoretical inquiry. Bradley does consider our religious and moral experiences, and even our experience of beauty, if only in brief.[1] Moreover, as we have seen, he not only refers to Man's highest experiences, but emphasizes the inability of thought, nay of temporal existence itself, to embody their distinctive quality. And does he not openly regard religious *experience* as (in a way) superior to philosophy?

> 'Religion is rather the attempt to express the complete reality of goodness through every aspect of our being. And, so far as this goes, it is at once something more, and therefore something higher, than philosophy.'[2]

(iv) Our going, so far, has been relatively easy. But the protest built around the law of contradiction has to be dealt with carefully. Bradley indeed talks repeatedly of the attempt to ascribe differences to the selfsame point resulting in their 'collision' and 'flying apart'.[3] But, first, though an image is here admittedly employed, the meaning is only the impossibility of *holding* that a thing can have two qualities, or be subject to two states, without itself having internal differences. Secondly, to speak strictly, even a dot is not entirely devoid of character. It is here said to defy being swamped by others; but, if it is really to do so, it must remain distinctive—with some content of its own. Perhaps a truer way of expressing ourselves here would be to say that the law of contradiction is a law not of mere thought, much less of images or facts alone, but of the basic manner in which thought and reality interact. The facts of difference and plurality not only provide an objective warrant for thought's activity of 'distinguishing', but are themselves acknowledged as 'real' by thought because of its own inherent need to distinguish. And, to speak generally, if the law in question is so basic to both thought and reality, how is

[1] AR 410–12.
[2] *Ibid* 401.
[3] PL 147.

Bradley unjustified in using it as a criterion to determine the worth of things and experiences? Nor is it easy to question the ground of his dialectic. To recognize a quality as such, and yet not to perceive it as distinct from others, is in our view clearly impossible. And where we have diversities which are merely felt, their clearness is not affirmed nor even consciously owned.

As for the charge that Bradley's dialectic is too abstract to be helpful, our view is that it can be easily met. The dialectical process *begins* by acting upon a datum, and to understand the given is its continual *aim*. If the intervening stages of the process show a relative indifference to actual existence, it does not justify us in condemning the entire process as abstract, in the sense of being wholly irrelevant to given reality. Even generally, thought nowhere shows an unremitting correspondence with every detail of fact. Rationally to condemn the relative deviations of the dialectical process from given reality, one will have to argue; but would it be consistent to protest against a process which thought itself presses? This is, in fact, the key to appreciate the basic validity of the dialectical movement of thought. The process has an internal necessity—a necessity grounded in our very constitution as rational creatures. We cannot for long be unmindful of the need to think deeply and consistently, and of the superior validity of what is more inclusive and self-consistent.

Secondly, it is important to see how the process neither slavishly follows, nor works in complete disregard of the idiom of fact; or how, in short, it is both 'a priori' and empirical. The start of the process, we have seen, is clearly empirical: the datum is given. But, from then onwards, the entire process is governed by thought's own law of working. It is not that the single idea from which we start just unpacks itself into newer ones: the idea does not itself give, but is made to deliver—by thought operating autonomously, so that its conclusions come to have a clear 'a priori' validity. According to Bradley, validity of this kind only means that, though thought refers in general to given reality, the way it develops this reference is, in the main, determined by its own essential demands: 'the point in dispute is not whether the product is 'a posteriori', but whether, being 'a posteriori', it is not 'a priori' also and as well.'[1] Finally, it seems unfair to suggest that the

[1] PL 409, 408–09.

dialectical process serves no purpose whatever. Is it no progress on the road to truth that from what is originally given as a brute fact, which the mind merely finds but cannot appropriate, we rise up to an idea which is finally acceptable to the mind, because consistent with its demand for reality?

(v) We turn, in the end, to the protest against Bradley's attitude to understanding. It is often pointed out that we come to understand not only by reasoning, but 'by experience, or by religious belief'.[1] The contention, however, cannot be accepted categorically. It is tenable only if it says that experiences which are not relational can also provide us with some intense awareness. But, and this is to us a point of basic importance, is this awareness as such understanding? Bradley's answer, here, is readily negative. So long as a man merely experiences an intense emotion, and makes no attempt whatever to distinguish its details, his state is without doubt conscious, but it is not one of 'understanding'. Bradley protests emphatically—and, in our view, reasonably—against the attempt to turn mere feeling into some kind of understanding:

'. . . to be satisfied, my intellect must understand, and it cannot understand by taking a congeries, if I may say so, in the lump . . . It has not . . . any . . . faculty of sensuous intuition. On the contrary my intellect is discursive, and to understand it must go from one point to another, and in the end also must go by a movement which it feels satisfies its nature.'[2]

To emphasize the uniqueness of an experience is merely to insist on something that *is* there. It is no direct comment as to value or disvalue. And if we at all care to compare and judge the value of our attitudes and experiences, is Bradley's criterion of worth any less helpful or compulsive than others?

---

[1] Zuurdeeg, *An Analytical Philosophy of Religion*, London, Allen & Unwin, 1959, 161.
[2] AR 509.

INDEX

Absolute
    abstract, no abstraction, 30, 49
    all-inclusive harmony, 28, 31–2, 34, 233, 235, 239, 240, 249–50, 261
    as demanded by both fact, thought, 28, 31–2, 34–5, 65–6, 80, 194, 207, 209, 211, 218, 230, 232, 235–6, 243, 249, 253
    as experienced, 229–30
    as fact, 216, 236, 245–6, 247, 251
    as 'first principle', 23
    as idea, 16, 20, 31, 47, 49, 79, 80, 230, 238–9, 242, 252
    as immediate, individual, 63, 230
    as limit to doubting, 26
    as metempirical, 258–60
    as spiritual, 233
    as supra-relational, 23, 34, 63, 66, 230, 233, 236, 241, 245
    not wholly knowable, 210, 245 (Bradley quoted)
    not wholly unknowable, 198–9, 210, 245, 247, 261
    positive, though incomplete, as idea, 22–3, 32, 50, 208, 210, 217, 242, 245, 251, 252
Aliotta, 159 n., 236 n., 244 n., 242–3
Analysis, 41–3, 47, 50–1, 88
Analytical philosophy, 73
Appearance(s)
    as self-inconsistent and self-transcendent, 36, 67
    its two meanings, 66–7, 71
    necessary, why, 79, 237
    not as such given, 67, 75
    not defiant of Absolute, 250–1
    not disjoined from reality and value, 35, 75–80, 244
    not explained away, 69–74, 77
A priori
    and fact, 182–4
    Bradley's view of, 268
    his criterion, a priori, 75
    synthetic a priori, 182–4
Aquinas, 261
Aristotle, 21
Asymmetrical Relation(s)
    as change Vs. feeling, 95–6
    Vs. the Absolute, 211–6
Aurobindo, 190 n.
Ayer, 30, 177, 183–4, 190, 255
    as against Bradley, 194–7
    on contradiction, 178–81

Being, 74, 255, 257, 259
Being-in-time, 201
Bergmann, 191
Bergson, 16
Binswanger, 19 n.
Blanshard, 30 n., 50 n., 114, 155 n., 159 n., 161, 175 n., 180 n., 183, 187, 214 n.
    on Bradley's view of logical laws, 176 n.–7
    on concrete universals, 184
    on difference, 154
    on 'internality', 151, 154, 158
    on logical laws, 176
Bosanquet, 152, 153 n.
Butler, 40

Campbell, on Bradley, 243, 245, 246
Camus, 262
Carnap, 189, 191
Categories, 70–2, 255, 259, 261
Clarity as discursive, direct, 265–6
Classification, 173
Cohen, 28 n., 175 n., 176, 231 n.
    on Bradley's Absolute, 241–2
    on 'feeling', 82
    on system in science, 173–4

INDEX

Coherence, 45–6, 194
Consistency
  as aesthetic, 44
  as criterion, 28, 29
  as theoretical, 17, 21, 44
  how ultimate, 44–5
  may be sacrificed, how, 34–6
  not merely formal, 31
Contradiction (and the law of)
  arises, 244
  as a priori, 185, 187
  as criterion, 171 (Bradley quoted), 211
  as law of both thought, reality, 45, 146, 171, 177–82, 180 (Bradley quoted), 195, 267
  how overcome, 27, 31, 65–6, 92, 136, 249–50
  infects everything, 27, 31, 46, 240
  the meaning of, 39, 119, 181, 182, 267
Cook Wilson, 114, 127, 130, 140
Correspondence, 37, 113, 192, 194, 254, 268

Daly, 254 n., 255, 257 n., 260
Definition(s), 132, 153
Descartes, 43
Dialectic
  as process, 16, 27, 39
  its validity, 265–6, 268–9
  of quality and relation, 115–21, 265
Difference
  and distinction, 39, 118, 267
  as a relation, 39, 155
Disclosure (-situation), 190, 255

Einstein, 174, 175
Epistemological argument, 233–4
Essent, 257
Ewing, 154 n., 155 n., 161 n., 167 n., 168 n., 173 n., 183, 187, 190 n., 203, 222, 223 n., 227, 228 n., 239 n.

Existence
  as not merely sensible, 59
  Bradley's attitude to, 73–4, 185–7, 193–4, 196, 200
  in time, 201
Experience
  as actual reality, 218–22, 229
  concreteness of, 263–4
  directions of, 264–6
  how reality as Absolute, 217, 231–2
  inseparable from 'experienced', 219–23, 229
  its portions, self-transcendent, 233–5, 238–9, 243
  its real nature, 218–21
  not merely sensuous, 190–1
  of unity, Vs. unity of experience, 105–7
  uniqueness of, 269

Faith, 17
Feeling
  and atomic fact, 95–7
  and change, 96
  and contradiction, 92–4
  and metaphysics, 83, 89, 91–4, 109–10
  and (or Vs.) relational experience, thought, 84, 86–91, 97, 99–100, 102–4, 110
  as actual, 86, 97, 124
  as clue to Absolute, 105–7, 245–6
  as criterion, 86, 103–4
  as determined, 93
  as different from pain, pleasure, 83
  as experience, 89, 109
  as including diversity, 100
  as including self, world, 85
  as immediate, non-relational, 57–8, 83–5, 89, 97–8, 99, 116, 120
  as metempirical, 257–9
  as this-mine, 87, 90, 91, 93
  demanded by theory, 98

INDEX

Feeling—*continued.*
  more basic than consciousness, self-consciousness, 100–1, 108–9
  not ultimately real, 82–3, 91, 105, 109
  self-transcendent, 16, 90–4, 109
    Ward's objection, 94–5
  ultimate, how, 85–6, 99–100, 101–4
  Vs. Self, 107–8
  Ward's objections to Bradley's view of, 97–109
Feigl, 161, 165
First principles: 22–4
  the same as ultimate truths, 24

Galileo, 165
Given(ness), 49, 88, 98, 113, 119, 167, 229, 252

Haldar, 41 n.
Harmony *and* inclusiveness (system), 42, 46, 50, 65, 157, 182
Hartland-Swann, 73
Hawkins, 255
Hegel(-ian), 21, 73, 97
Heidegger, 19 n., 50, 74, 181, 187, 257, 259, 264 n., 265
Höffding, 18 n.
Holmes, 19 n., 77 n.
Hume, 37, 39, 43, 161, 165, 182, 187, 191

Ideality, 16, 55, 57
Identity
  as absolute, 39, 40
  as 'first principle', 22
  as relational, 23, 39–40, 114
Immediate Experience, 82–111, 257, 258, 259, (Also see 'feeling')
Individuality
  and thought, theory, 24, 206
  as a criterion, 194, 202, 208, 241–2, 267
  as a general demand, 17, 20, 23, 233
  as perfect, 47, 60, 66, 91, 105, 110, 114, 210, 230
  the meaning of, 56
Indwelling, 192, 265
Infinite regress, argument from, 118–20
  Cook Wilson's objections, met, 130–40
  Passmore's objections, 140–5
  Russell's, 126–9
Inherence, 61, 96, 216
Integrator-words, 229, 254–5, 257
Intellect
  as discursive, abstract, 40, 157
  how finite, 54
  the autonomy of, 20–1, 29
Intuition(ive, -ed), 15–18, 33, 174, 194–5, 211, 243, 246, 252, 260

James, 191
Jevons, 185
Judgment
  aims at individuality, 204, 206
  kinds of predication in, 61–3
  specific and incomplete, 199–200
  subject in, 60–4

Kant, 21, 231
Knowing
  as 'basic', 259
  as intellectual, not psychological, 37, 38, 51
  as leading to Absolute, 46
  not always intellectual, 48, 265
  'open texture' of, 262

Language
  ancillary, 72
  its symbols, usage, 177–81

INDEX

Lazerowitz, 53, 196, 221
   his criticism of Appearance–Reality distinction, 68–80
Lewis, 161 n.
Leibniz, 21
Locke, 191
Logical constants, 183
Logical laws
   and actual reality, 175–82
   not merely formal, 176 (Bradley quoted)

Mach, 173–4, 191
Maharshi Raman, 190 n.
Marcel, 18, 19 n., 50, 74, 187, 263 n.
Meaning, 37, 161, 188
Metaphysically real, valid, 16, 34, 40, 45, 73, 249
Metaphysics
   abstract, intellectual, interpretative, 17, 19–21, 24, 29, 30, 33, 37, 43–4, 50, 74, 82, 106, 119, 125, 139, 215, 255, 260, 262–3
   and morality, religion, 33, 34–5
   and special sciences, 33, 47–8, 186, 254
   as an attempt to grade appearances, 77
   as an attempt to hold the many as one, 78, 123, 147
   as deductive, 182, 186
   as 'prosaic' alteration of language, 69
   as 'special', 49
   Bradley's defence of his own view of, 19, 48–51, 107–8, 261
   concerned with whole reality, 21, 29–30, 34–5, 46, 47, 254
   defined, by Bradley, 36, 46
   details here secondary, not ignored, 21, 42, 47, 50
   governing principle of, 44
   necessity of, 50–1
   reflection on mysteries, 19

   sceptical study of first principles, 22–8, 254
Metempirical, 254–7, 259, 261
Metz, 24 n.
Monism(ist), 15, 63, 212, 213, 216
Montague, 18 n.
Moore, 57 n.
Muirhead, 22 n.
Mystery(ies), 19, 74, 260
Mystic(-al, ism), 17, 18, 32, 33, 236, 252, 265

Nagel, 154, 156, 158, 159
Necessity
   a priori, rational, 42, 113, 138, 158, 160, 161, 168, 174, 247–8, 268
   and fact, 175, 177, 182
   as mere convention, 183
   of system, coherence, 49, 113, 193
Negation, 26
Number, argument against 'internality' from, 159–60

Ontology (izing), 182, 184–7
Osborne, 190 n.

Pasch, 43 n., 191
Passmore, 27 n., 140–1, 143–4, 182, 187–8, 189 n.
Pears, 21 n.
Pearson, 173
Phenomenalism, 79
Philosophy, 18, 49, 140, 267
Pluralism, 78, 185
Poincare, 174
Polanyi, 25, 27 n., 29 n., 173–4, 191–2, 265, 266 n.
Popper, 176
Positivist(-ic), 30, 165, 174, 177, 182–3, 185, 187, 189–90
Possibility, 222, 224, 247–8
Propinquity, 212

274

INDEX

Quality
  its two meanings, 116
  without relation, 116–18
  with relation, 118–19
Quine, 191

Ramsey, 19, 80 n., 190, 255, 257 n., 260 n.
Rationality, order in science, 173–5
Reality
  and judgment, thought, 46–7, 60–4, 113, 153–4
  as Absolute, Vs. Absolute (total) reality, 53, 55, 58–60, 251
  as character, 35, 54–5, 64, 198
  as metaphysical, 52–4, 76
  as one, immanent, 16, 233–5, 238
  as relational, 56, 58, 181–2
  as self-evolving, 262–3
  as supra-relational, 55, 78
  as system, 174
  as that-what togetherness, 39, 43, 56–8, 64, 65, 76, 237
  basic assumption as to truth and, 17, 28, 30, 31, 54 (Bradley quoted), 64, 74
  degrees of, 53, 55, 76–7, 197–202
  general features of, 42–3
  the need to see different senses of, 52–64, 217
  unifying them, 64–6
Reichenbach, 43, 174 n., 175
Relation(s)
  adjectival, 25 n., 124
  and atomic fact, 122, 125–6
  as 'appearance' or ultimately unreal, 121–2, 125 (Russell's objections met, 121–9)
  both internal and external, 169
  conjunctive, 127 (Bradley quoted)
  how real, 122–3, 126
  internal(-ity), 16, 39, 113, 135, 151–68, 169
  intransitive, 125
  irreducible to terms, 120, 123, 128 (Bradley quoted), 131–4, 144–5, 160, 244
  merely external, 64, 150, 152, 155, 160, 169
  merely internal, 168–9
  not as such given, 125
  not merely different from terms, 139–40
  Self-contradictory, self-transcendent, 31, 70, 115, 138, 145, 148–9, 214–16
  the general idea of, 127, 135, 140, 214–15
  with quality, 119–21
  without quality, 119
Relational context, fact, perception, 39, 61, 64, 124, 141, 150, 156, 159–60, 215, 237
Relational form, 57, 82, 112–13, 115, 122, 124, 148–50, 169, 237
Relational matter, 246
Ruggerio, 242, 243 n.
Russell, 43, 45, 63, 73 n., 95, 96, 114, 121–8, 143, 186 n., 187, 191, 196, 212, 214–5
Ryle, 31 n., 48 n.

Śaṁkara, 189 n.
Samples, the difficulty of finding, 188–90
Santayana, 73 n.
Scepticism
  as delivering metaphysical criterion, 33–4
  as philosophical, 15, 24–7, 33
  as ultimate, 32
  impossibility of radical, 26
  results of Bradley's, 33
  Vs. common sense scepticism, 27–8
Schlick, 114, 161–3, 165–6, 168, 174, 188
  his protest against 'internality' of causation, met, 161–8

INDEX

Self
  basis of metaphysics, how, 107–8
  Bradley's dismissal of, 76, 107
Self-completion beyond self, 83–4, 92, 239
Sense-observation, 185, 193
Sequence, regularity of, 161, 162, 166
Solipsism, 225–6
Sorley, 22 n.
Spatial schema, 39, 112, 135, 145–7, 264
Specificity, 27, 64, 67, 90, 113, 114, 156, 206, 214, 237
Standards, the various, 202–3
Stout, 45, 146 n., 186 n., 247 n.

Taylor, 32 n.
Things-in-themselves, 79, 182
This (-that, -mine), 62, 87, 90–3, 109, 262
Thought (theory)
  as 'internal' to concrete reality, 172–3, 203
  as related to reality as Absolute, 203, 207–8
  as self-transcendent, 49, 170
  its demand(s), 44, 92, 114, 146, 155–6
  its inadequacy, 37, 49, 109, 147–9, 203–6, 244
  its manner
    -abstract, 49, 58, 109
    -'propio motu', 16, 41
    -relational, 31, 58, 114, 118, 167, 170
  its setting, 20
  seeming contradiction in its relation to reality, 207–8, 217–18

Transcendence, 80, 232, 235
Trethowan, 255
Truth
  as ideal, 55, 199, 205
  as relative, 35–6
  as system, 200
  as ultimate, incorrigible, 36, 251 n.

Understanding, 37–8, 42–3, 46–7, 51, 112–14, 118, 157–8, 164–8, 183, 261, 265, 269
Understood negations, 63
Universal(s), 37, 114, 137, 184
  arguments against 'internality' from, 158–60

Verification, 30, 48, 161–2, 166, 168, 171, 250, 252
  Bradley's views on, 190, 192–4
  its status today, 50, 187–92
  objective, 201–2, 256
  of different kinds, 190–2
  weak, strong, 195

Ward, 18 n., 22 n., 34 n., 94, 95 n., 97–9, 101–3, 105–8, 226 n.
Wholeness, 19, 30, 36, 51, 229, 254–6
Waismann, 16 n.
Wittgenstein, 177
Wollheim, 15 n., 37 n., 185, 212, 218 n., 223–5, 226 n., 227, 248 n.
Wordsworth, 191 n.

Zuurdeeg, 269 n.

Printed in Poland
by Amazon Fulfillment
Poland Sp. z o.o., Wrocław